A YOUTH'S HISTORY OF THE GREAT CIVIL WAR IN THE UNITED STATES FROM 1861 TO 1865

by

Rushmore G. Horton

With Illustrations

THE CONFEDERATE
REPRINT COMPANY

☆ ☆ ☆ ☆

WWW.CONFEDERATEREPRINT.COM

A Youth's History of the Great Civil War
in the United States From 1861 to 1865
by Rushmore G. Horton

Originally Published in 1866
by Van Evrie, Horton & Company
New York

Reprint Edition © 2015
The Confederate Reprint Company
Post Office Box 2027
Toccoa, Georgia 30577
www.confederatereprint.com

Cover and Interior by
Magnolia Graphic Design
www.magnoliagraphicdesign.com

ISBN-13: 978-0692453155
ISBN-10: 0692453156

TO THE READER

    This book has been written in the cause of Truth. It has not been the object of the writer to defend any particular party or faction, but solely to vindicate democratic and republican institutions.

    There have, in all ages, been really but two parties in politics. One, that did not believe in the people, but wanted a *strong* government to control or *rule* them. The other, that believed in the people, was for retaining power in their hands to control or *rule* the government. The former is the Monarchical or Strong Government party. Its members were called Tories in the Revolution of 1776. The latter is the Democratic party.

    I shall show in this history how these parties originated in this country, and who led them – that Alexander Hamilton was the leader of the Tory or Monarchical party, and Thomas Jefferson of the Democratic party.

    I shall show how this Tory party has always been trying to subvert our Government, because it was formed on the democratic principle.

    I shall show that finally, after being defeated in every other effort, this Tory party assumed the name of Republican, and taking advantage of a popular delusion about Negroes, used it to get into power and accomplish its long cherished purposes.

    I shall show that Abraham Lincoln was the direct successor of old John Adams and his infamous Alien and Sedition laws, only that Mr. Lincoln went much further, and acted much worse than John Adams ever dared to do.

I shall show that the war was not waged "to preserve the Union, or to maintain republican institutions," but really to destroy both, and that every dollar spent, and every life lost, have been taken by the Abolitionists *on false pretences.*

This book will show that the Abolition or so-called Republican party has simply carried out the British free Negro policy on this Continent, a pet measure of all the kings and despots of Europe.

In order to reach this end, Mr. Lincoln was compelled to assume the Dictatorship, and overthrow the government as it was formed, which he did by issuing a military Edict or Decree changing the fundamental law of the land, and declaring that he would maintain this change by all the military and naval power of the United States.

It will also be seen that the war has changed the entire character and system of our Government, overthrown the ancient rights of the States, and forced upon the country a so-called Amendment to the Constitution, in the time of war, and against the free and unbiased action of the people.

This book also contains a careful and impartial narrative of all the principal events of the war, from the battle of Bull Run down to the assassination of Abraham Lincoln, and the capture of Jefferson Davis.

The writer believes it will be found accurate in all respects, and in most cases the place and date of citation are given, so that no one can have a chance to deny their accuracy.

The book is given to the Northern people, under the confident belief that they did not intend to destroy their government by the war, and that they only need to understand the aims and objects of the Tory, Monarchical or Abolition party, to forever hold it responsible for all the sufferings of the country.

To the soldiers of the Northern armies, who were deluded by the Abolitionists into believing that they were fighting to preserve republican institutions, the political *facts* of this volume are respectfully commended.

The Southern people who fought so long and so gallantly to roll back the tide of Abolitionism that has engulfed them, will, the writer trusts, find in this volume encouragement to believe that Wrong can only be temporarily successful, and that it only needs faith in the power of the press to yet overthrow the Abolition revolutionists.

Finally, to all classes, and especially to the young, this little volume is commended, in the confident hope and belief that out of the gloom of the present the grand old Union of Washington and Jefferson will yet arise, and, wiping away the tears and blood of the past, live for ages to cheer mankind with its blessing.

CONTENTS
☆ ☆ ☆ ☆

CHAPTER ONE
The Causes of the War 19

The Estrangement Between the North and the South – When It Began – The Cause of It – Different Ideas of Government – Hamilton and Jefferson, the Former a Monarchist, the Latter a Democrat – Their Opposing Ideas – Washington Administration – The Triumph of the Federalists in the Election of John Adams – The Alien and Sedition Laws – The Despotism of the Federalists – The Virginia and Kentucky Resolutions – The Triumph of Democracy over Monarchical Federalism in 1800

CHAPTER TWO
The Causes of the War, Continued 27

Further Proofs that the Troubles Come From Different Views of Government – Quotations From Mr. Jefferson – Disunion in New England – A New Issue Sought for the Negro Question Seized Upon – The Negro in Africa – His Inferior Position There – The Negro Not Regarded as the White Man's Equal – The Laws of Massachusetts – The Crime of Mulattoism

CHAPTER THREE
The Causes of the War, Continued. 33

The Missouri Question – Mr. Jefferson's Warning – The British Spy Henry – Mr. Madison Lays the Henry Papers Before Congress – The Design of the British Government to Break Down Democracy in America – Testimony of Mr. Aaron Leggett – Toryism and Federalism the Same – The Federalists in the War of 1812 – The New England Clergy Declare the Declaration of Independence "A Wicked Thing"

CHAPTER FOUR
The Causes of the War, Continued. 39

The Admission of Missouri – Other Issues – The Rise of Abolitionism – The First Abolition Paper, by Benj. Lundy – The Riots in New York – The Danger in the Question – The North Not Acquainted With Negroes – The Negro a Distinct Race – Mr. Jefferson's Suggestion – The Case Illustrated – How the Government Was Formed – William Lloyd Garrison For Its Overthrow – Wendell Phillips Also – John C. Calhoun and Jefferson Davis For Its Preservation – Extracts From Speeches Of

CHAPTER FIVE
The Causes of the War, Continued 45

A Change in the Abolition Movement – The Supporters of William H. Seward on the Scene – Mr. Seward's Position – The Organization of the Seward or Black Republican Party – Its Perversion of True Principles – A Change of the Abolition Base

CHAPTER SIX
The Election of Lincoln 49

The Growth of the Black Republican Party – The Two Factions Composing It – Its Objects – Its Endorsement of the Helper Book – Old John Brown's Kansas Raid – His Virginia Expedition – His Murder of the Doyle Family – The Republican's Endorse His Bloody Career – The Nomination of Lincoln – The Alarm of the Southern People – The Cunning of Lincoln and Seward

CHAPTER SEVEN
Secession 55

The Election of Mr. Lincoln – The Chicago Platform – What Giddings Said It Meant – The Southern States Resolve to Secede – What is Secession? – Opinions of Josiah Quincy, Judge Rawle, Mr. Jefferson, &c., Upon Coercion – John Quincy Adams, S. P. Chase, Lincoln, Seward, Edward Everett, Greeley &c., &c., Deny the Right of It – The Question of the Forts – The South Did Not Make War on the North – The War a Trick

CHAPTER EIGHT
The Policy and Object of Secession 63

Opinion in the Southern States – What General Lee Says – What the

South Wanted – To Prevent Negro Equality, Amalgamation, &c. – Its Effect in Mexico and the West India Islands – The Horrors of a Mongrel Nation – The North Did Not Understand What the South Meant – The Union Issue – Abolition Verses on the Flag

CHAPTER NINE
The Beginning of Secession 69

The Secession of South Carolina – President Buchanan's Course – What He Said to Congress – Mr. Madison's Opinion of Coercion – Andrew Johnson on Coercion – The South Wanted Equality in the Union – Jefferson Davis' Last Speech in the Senate, Extract From – The Secession of the Other States

CHAPTER TEN
Efforts of the Democracy to Save the Union 73

The Crittenden Compromise – Earnest Appeal of Mr. Crittenden – Contemptuous Course of the Republicans – They Refuse to Submit it to the Vote of the People – Senator Douglas' Plan – He Charges the Republicans with the Sole Responsibility of the Disagreement – The Peace Convention – The Abolition Efforts to Prevent Any Settlement There – Senator Chandler, of Michigan, Wants "Blood Letting" – The Democracy Fail to Secure Peace

CHAPTER ELEVEN
The Formation of the New Confederacy 77

The Southern Delegates Meet at Montgomery – Jefferson Davis Elected Provisional President and Alexander H. Stephens Vice-President – The Confederate Constitution – President Davis' Address – The Questions at Issue – The Forts – To Whom Did They Belong – The Right of a State to Defend its Citizens – The Helper Book Programme

CHAPTER TWELVE
Mr. Lincoln's Journey to Washington and Inauguration 83

The Policy of Mr. Lincoln – He Commences His Journey to Washington – His Jokes and Low Stories – He Gives No Indication of His Policy – His Escape Through Baltimore in Disguise – His Inauguration – An Armed Guard Attends Him – His Contempt For the Supreme Court – The Selection of the Endorsers of the Helper Book For His Cabinet – Ex-Governor Morehead's Visit to Mr. Lincoln – The Character of Mr. Lincoln – His Origin

CHAPTER THIRTEEN
"The First Gun of Sumter" 89

Confederate Commissioners in Washington – Deception of Seward and Lincoln – The Fort Sumter Trick – Who Began the War? – The Fleet Sent to Charleston – General Beauregard Takes Fort Sumter – Joy of the Abolitionists – The Flag Mania – The Efforts of the Administration to Get Up an Excitement – The Success of Stage Tricks in Getting Up a War

CHAPTER FOURTEEN
Mr. Lincoln's First Call For Troops 97

What Excuse He Gave For It – Its Illegality – The Joy of the Abolitionists – The Northern Governors All Respond Favorably – Those of North Carolina, Kentucky, Missouri, and Virginia Refuse – Virginia Now Secedes – Her Announcement to the World

CHAPTER FIFTEEN
The Rush of Troops to Washington 101

The Massachusetts Troops on Their Way Through New York, Singing "Old John Brown," &c. – Their Reception in Baltimore – The Destruction of the Railroad Bridges – Mr. Lincoln Issues a Proclamation Blockading the Southern Ports – The South Preparing for War – General Lee Appointed to the Command of the Virginian Troops – Harper's Ferry Evacuated – Mr. Lincoln Suspends the Habeas Corpus – The Monarchical Party Fairly Inaugurated

CHAPTER SIXTEEN
The First Great Battle 107

The Battle of Bethel – The Great Battle of Bull Run – The Bravery of Stonewall Jackson – The Defeat of McDowell – The Stampede For Washington – The Frantic Confusion – The Effect in the North – General Scott Denounced – General McClellan Appointed to the Command – The Meeting of Congress July 4th – What Congress Declared the War to Be For – Promises of Mr. Lincoln and Congress

CHAPTER SEVENTEEN
The Campaign in the West 115

Citizens of St. Louis Shot Down – Governor Jackson and the State Militia – The Skirmish at Boonsville – The Battle of Carthage and of

Wilson's Creek – Death of General Lyon – Generals M'Culloch and Price – Price Captures Lexington – General Fremont Appointed to the Command – His Ridiculous Parade – General Price Retreats to Neosho – The State Secedes – Terrible Condition of Missouri – Fremont's Scheme of a German Empire in the West – His Extravagance and Incompetency – Mr. Lincoln Removes Him

CHAPTER EIGHTEEN
Campaign in Western Virginia and Battle of Leesburg 125

The Battle of Rich Mountain – General Floyd's Campaign – Rosecrans' Success – Death of General Garnett – The Destruction of Guyandotte – General McClellan Drilling the Army of the Potomac – The Battle of Leesburg – Death of Colonel Baker – Arrest of General Stone – An Incident – Two Brothers on Opposite Sides

CHAPTER NINETEEN
Campaign in Kentucky 131

Kentucky's Neutrality – Lincoln Broke It – The Arrest of Governor Morehead – Other Arrests Contemplated – Escape of Breckinridge and Others – Peaceful Citizens Driven From Their Homes – General Polk at Columbus – The Battle of Belmont – Defeat of General Grant – The Secession Convention in Kentucky – The Arrest of Mason and Slidell – The Back Down of Lincoln and Seward

CHAPTER TWENTY
Closing Events of 1861, and the Beginning of 1862 139

The Expedition to Hatteras Inlet – The Capture of Port Royal – Billy Wilson's Regiment at Santa Rosa Island – The Confederates in Kentucky – The Battle of Mill Spring – Death of General Zollicoffer – General Grant Takes Fort Henry – The Battle of Fort Donelson – Its Surrender – The Evacuation of Nashville – The Exploits of General John H. Morgan

CHAPTER TWENTY-ONE
The Battles of Shiloh and Pittsburg Landing 145

Movements in the West – The Capture of Island No. 10 – The Battle of Shiloh – Defeat of General Grant on the First Day He is Reinforced by General Buell – The Second Day's Battle – Death of General Albert Sidney Johnston – The Confederates Fall Back But Are Not Pursued – General Pope's Swagger

CHAPTER TWENTY-TWO
The Fall of New Orleans – "Butler the Beast" 151

Flag-officer Farragut's Bombardment of Forts Jackson and St. Phillip – He at Last Runs By Them – The City Evacuated by General Lovell – Mayor Monroe Refuses to Haul Down the State Flag – General Ben. Butler Takes Possession of the City – He Plunders the Private Citizens – He Digs up the Dead – Imprisons Women – Hangs Wm B. Mumford – Receives the Title of "Beast Butler"

CHAPTER TWENTY-THREE
Stonewall Jackson in the Shenandoah Valley 157

Jackson's Habits – What His Negro Servant Said – His Personal Appearance – His Conversation – How He Fired a Cannon – Battle of Kearnstown – General Jackson Forced to Retreat – General Shields Wounded – His Return to Washington and Resignation – What He Heard Sumner Say About the War – The Removal of All Generals Not Favorable to the Abolitionists

CHAPTER TWENTY-FOUR
Embarcation of the Army of the Potomac 161

Mr. Lincoln's Plans – General McClellan Opposed to Them – Mr. Lincoln Does Not Support McClellan – The Army of the Potomac Reaches the Peninsula – General McDowell's Corps Fails to Reinforce McClellan – Yorktown Evacuated by the Confederates – Battle of Williamsburg – General Hooker Badly Wounded – The Death of Colonel Lomax of Miss. – His Body Recovered by His Negro Servant – The Negroes Aiding the Confederate Armies

CHAPTER TWENTY-FIVE
Doings of Stonewall Jackson in the Shenandoah Valley 167

General McClellan's Position Growing Critical – General McDowell Ordered to Join Him – Stonewall Jackson Makes a Counter Movement – General Milroy Defeated – General Banks Defeated – His Remarkable Run Down the Valley – Fremont – The Battles of Cross Keys and Port Republic – Stonewall Jackson Makes His Reputation

CHAPTER TWENTY-SIX
Battle of Fair Oaks and Gaines' Mills 171

The Attack of General D. H. Hill – General Joseph E. Johnston Wounded – The Result a Confederate Victory – General Lee Ap-

Contents   13

pointed to the Command – He Deceives McClellan By Pretending to Reinforce Jackson in the Valley – Jackson Really Marching to Aid in the Defence of Richmond – Attack on General Fitz John Porter's Corps – A Repulse – The Battle of Gaines' Mills – Final Charge of the Texas Brigade – Results of the Battle – McClellan Compelled to Retreat to the James River

CHAPTER TWENTY-SEVEN
McClellan's Retreat 179

Movement to the James River – Lee Vigorously Pressing the Federal Army – The Engagements at Savage's Station and Frazier's Farm – Amusing Conversation of an Old Darkey – His Idea of the War – Can't Fool Him – The Battle of Malvern Hill – Terrible Slaughter – An Incident – Death of Major Peyton

CHAPTER TWENTY-EIGHT
The Inauguration of a Reign of Plunder and Arson 185

Mr. Lincoln Calls for 500,000 More Soldiers – The Order for Plunder From Washington – General John Pope Given a Command – How He Inaugurated His Campaign – General McClellan Denounces Marauding – His Idea of the War – General Halleck's Brutal Threat – What Governor Stone of Iowa Said – The Mask of Conservatism Still Retained by Lincoln and Seward

CHAPTER TWENTY-NINE
The Second Battle of Manassas – Bull Run 191

General Jackson's Attack upon General Banks, at Cedar Mountain – Death of General C. H. Winder – General Banks Whipped Again – Rapid March of General Jackson – The Flight of Pope – He Rallies His Troops – Attacks Jackson – General Lee Comes Upon Pope – Put to Flight Again – His Army Routed – Terrible Losses – End of Pope

CHAPTER THIRTY
Lee in Maryland – Battle of Antietam 197

March of Lee Into Maryland – Jackson Takes Harper's Ferry – Great Excitement in Washington – General McClellan Given Command of the Army – Battle of Boonsboro – The Battle of Antietam – Great Slaughter – A Drawn Battle – Lee Recrosses the Potomac – McClellan is Repulsed – Is Removed From Command – General Burnside Put in His Place – The Great Mistake of McClellan – Mr. Lincoln on the Battle-field of Antietam – An Incident

CHAPTER THIRTY-ONE
Bloody Doings in the West 203

Battle of Richmond. Kentucky – Confederate Raids Through Kentucky – General Kirby Smith Occupies Lexington – General Bragg at Mumfordsville – The Abolitionists Defeated – Bragg Evacuates Kentucky – Unhappy Condition of Kentucky and Missouri – Battle of Corinth – Horrible Murder of Ten Men by the Monster McNeil, of Lexington, Missouri

CHAPTER THIRTY-TWO
General Burnside's Bloody Campaign 209

"On to Richmond" Again – General Burnside Changes Base – He Crosses the River at Fredericksburg – The Terrible Slaughter of His Troops – Awful Scenes in Fredericksburg – Condition of Burnside's Army – Burnside in a Rage at His Failure – He Removes Several Generals – Is Relieved of Command – General Hooker Put in His Place

CHAPTER THIRTY-THREE
Mr. Lincoln's Campaign in the North 215

Mr. Lincoln's Suppression of Democratic Newspapers – The Mobbing of Democratic Newspapers – What a Mob Got in Catskill, N.Y. – Arbitrary Arrests – Women Arrested – Secret Circulars in New York City – Arrest of the Rev. Mr. Stuart in Alexandria, Virginia – Seizure of the Rev. J.D. Benedict – The Police of New York – Superintendent Kennedy as Provost Marshal – Cell No. 4 – Boys Arrested and Sent to Fort Lafayette – The Arrest of the Messrs. Flanders – The Malone Gazette, Edited by the Wife of the Imprisoned Editor – Horrible Condition of Fort Lafayette – Arrests for No Causes and For Trivial Excuses – Effects of Mr. Lincoln's Policy

CHAPTER THIRTY-FOUR
The Battle of Murfreesboro – Doings in the West 223

General Bragg Attacks Rosecrans – The Confederates Successful on the First Day – Loss Heavy – The Next Day, Bragg Retreats to Tullahoma – Confederate Success at Galveston – The Siege of Vicksburg – Attack on Port Hudson – A Religious Darkey in a Fight – Amusing Account of His Heroism – Uncle Pompey Quoting Scripture

CHAPTER THIRTY-FIVE
General Hooker's Campaign 227

Another "On to Richmond" – General Hooker Crosses the Rappahannock – The Battle of Chancellorsville – The Flank Movement of Stonewall Jackson – The Flight of Hooker's Troops – The Death of Jackson – Hooker Compelled to Retreat – Falls Back Towards Washington – General Meade Appointed to Succeed Him – General Lee Marches Northward – Goes Into Pennsylvania – Panic of the People – The Battle of Gettysburg – General Lee Repulsed – He Falls Back and Crosses the Potomac in Safety

CHAPTER THIRTY-SIX

The Siege of Vicksburg 233

General Sherman's Repulse – General Grant Succeeds Him – He Tries to Turn the Mississippi – Tries a Flank Movement – Admiral Porter Runs by the Batteries – Porter Attacks Grand Gulf and is Repulsed – Grant Reaches Port Gibson – Defeat of the Confederates – General Joe Johnston Tries to Oppose Him – Capture of Jackson – General Pemberton Hemmed In – The Siege of Vicksburg – Terrible Repulse of Grant's Assaulting Column – The Confederates Forced to Surrender – Great Loss to the South – Port Hudson Also Surrendered – The Mississippi River Open – Outrages on Private Property – Negroes driven from Plantations – Terrible Outrage on a Family – They are Robbed of Everything – Death of the Lady and Her Child

CHAPTER THIRTY-SEVEN

The Naval Defeat Off Charleston – Gillmore's Repulse 241

Grand Attempt to Take Charleston – Admiral Dupont Defeated – General Gillmore Lays Siege – His "Swamp Angel" – He Throws Shot and Shell into the City – Bombardment of Sumter – Admiral Dahlgren Tries to Take It – Is Terribly Repulsed

CHAPTER THIRTY-EIGHT

Gen. Morgan's Raid Into the West Chickamauga 245

General Morgan Moves Into Ohio and Indiana – He is Captured – Put Into Ohio Penitentiary – Digs His Way Out With Penknives – The Battle of Chickamauga – General Rosecrans Badly Defeated – He is Removed From Command – General Grant Assumes Command – Battle of Missionary Ridge – Bragg is Defeated – Skirmish Between Lee and Meade in Virginia – Naval Confederate Victory at Sabine Post – General Price Driven Out of Missouri – Congress Makes Grant Lieutenant-General

CHAPTER THIRTY-NINE
The Confederate Navy and Privateers 249

The Commission of Privateers – The Sinking of the Cumberland By the Virginia – Her Fight with the Monitor – The Sumter – Florida – Alabama – Georgia – Fight of the Alabama and Kearsarge – The Confederate Rams – Their Seizure – The Reason of It – The Abolition Policy Popular With the Monarchists

CHAPTER FORTY
Events in the North in 1861 255

"Emancipation Proclamation" – Its Effect – Arming Negroes – Flags to Negro Regiments – Letters From Soldiers – Dissatisfaction in the Army – Connecticut Election – General Burnside in the West – Arrest of the Hon. C.L. Vallandigham – Kentucky Election – Mobbing Democratic Newspapers – Killing of Mr. Bollmeyer – Chicago Times Suppressed – Mr. Lincoln Backs Down – "The Sons of Liberty" – The New York Riots – Hanging of Negroes – The Draft Stopped – Alleged Cruelty to Federal Prisoners – Confederate Prisoners – The Object of the Abolitionists

CHAPTER FORTY-ONE
The Opening Events of 1864 265

General Sherman's Expedition Towards Mobile – Its Failure – The Defeat at Olustee, Florida – General Banks' Red River Expedition – General Forrest in Kentucky – John S. Mosby – Kilpatrick's Raid on Richmond – Death of Ulric Dahlgren – The Object of the Raid – The Papers Found on Dahlgren – The Evidence of Their Authenticity – How Abolitionism Brutifies Mankind

CHAPTER FORTY-TWO
General Grant's "On to Richmond" 271

General Grant Starts for Richmond – The Battles of the Wilderness and Spottsylvania Court House – Terrible Slaughter – Movement to the North Anna River – Battle of Cold Harbor – March to the James River – Attempt to take Petersburg – The Result of Grant's "Hammering" – The Explosion of the Mine – Grant Suspends Offensive Operations – Hunter's Raid on Lynchburg – General Early Crosses into Maryland – Defeat of General Lew. Wallace at Monocacy – Sheridan Sent to the Shenandoah Valley – He Defeats Early – Utter Devastation of the Valley

CHAPTER FORTY-THREE
General Sherman's "On to Atlanta" 281

The Movement from Ringgold – The Battles of Resaca and Kenesaw – Death of General Polk – The Complaints Against General Johnston – His Removal From Command – General Hood Appointed in His Place – The Battles before Atlanta – General Hood Evacuates the City – Sherman's Cruelties – His Depopulation and Destruction of Atlanta – General Hood Tries a Flank Movement – Starts For Chattanooga and Nashville – The Battles of Franklin Hood – Defeated Before Nashville and Retreats

CHAPTER FORTY-FOUR
The Presidential Election and Other Events of 1864 287

The Conspiracy Successful – The Government Centralized – Mr. Lincoln's Administration – Its Shameless Extravagance and Corruption – Congressional Report Thereon – The Party of "Moral Ideas" – Mr. Lincoln Re-Nominated by the Abolitionists – General McClellan Nominated by the Democrats – No Fair Elections Allowed – General Butler Sent to New York – His "Campaign" There – Mr. Lincoln "Re-Elected" – Attack on Mobile – Butler's Expedition to Fort Fisher

CHAPTER FORTY-FIVE
General Sherman's March to Savannah and Goldsboro 293

Sherman's Start From Atlanta – His Destruction of the City – General Foster at Port Royal – Capture of Fort McAllister – Sherman's Devastations – Evacuation of Savannah – Sherman Resumes His March – Burning of Columbia – Horrible Scenes – Who is Responsible? – General Hampton's Letter – Sherman's Foragers and His Threats – General Hampton's Reply – Sherman's Swath of Fire

CHAPTER FORTY-SIX
Events of 1865 – General Lee's Surrender 301

General Terry's Capture of Fort Fisher – Fall of Wilmington and Charleston – Efforts For Peace – Meeting at Fortress Monroe – Its Failure – General Lee's Weakness – His Attack on Fort Steadman – Evacuation of Richmond – The Confederate Government Moves to Danville – Mistake as to Supplies – Lee's Troops Wanting Food – Sheridan's Attack – Surrender of Lee's Army – Affecting Scenes – Surrender of General Johnston – The Terms Rejected – Mobile Captured – Surrender of Kirby Smith – The Last Fight at Brazos, Texas – Victory of the Confederates

CHAPTER FORTY-SEVEN
The Assassination of Mr. Lincoln 307

> The War Ended – What Now? – Mr. Lincoln's Broken Pledges – He Goes to Richmond – His Interview With Judge Campbell – His Agreement to Allow the Virginia Legislature to Meet – Breaks His Promise – He is Shot by John Wilkes Booth – Mr. Seward Also Attacked – Fearful Excitement – Mr. Lincoln's Funeral – Booth, his Capture – His Body Mutilated – Trial of His Confederates – The Court Illegal – Singular Fact in Relation to Mr. Lincoln's Death

CHAPTER FORTY-EIGHT
The Capture of Jefferson Davis 315

> Mr. Davis Moves Southward – He Joins His Family – Captured by Colonel Pritchard – Falsehood as to His Dress – He is Taken to Savannah, and Thence to Fortress Monroe – Put in Solitary Confinement – Is Shackled – Still Denied a Trial – The Union Yet to be Restored – Trust in God

CHAPTER ONE
The Causes of the War

Many histories of the Great Civil War through which we have just passed have already been written, but they are not such as convey to the youth of our land a full and true account of the causes which led to it, who were the real authors of it, and what were its objects and purposes. To understand fully the causes which produced it, we must go back a good ways in the history of our country.

Whatever produced a feeling of enmity and estrangement between the Southern and Northern States must be looked upon as one of the causes leading to the war. This feeling of hostility between the two sections began to show itself at a very early period, soon after the formation of the Union, almost a hundred years ago. We may say it began, in the first place, in the different political opinions held by the leading men of the North and the South.

This difference was indeed very great. It may be understood by briefly reviewing the different sentiments entertained by Alexander Hamilton and Thomas Jefferson. Hamilton was the idol of what may be termed the New England or Monarchical party, and Jefferson was equally the idol of the Southern or Democratic party. There were many individuals in the North who followed Jefferson, as there were some in the South who adopted the principles of Hamilton, but the prevailing sentiment of the North was with Hamilton, as that of the South was with Jefferson.

Hamilton was a monarchist. That is, he wanted to establish in this country a government that should be, in everything but its name, a *kingdom* instead of a *republic*. There is abundant proof of this fact.

Luther Martin, one of the most distinguished statesmen in the convention that made our Constitution, speaking of the Hamilton party in that body said: "There was one party, whose object and wish was to abolish and annihilate all the State governments, and bring forward one general government, over all this extended continent, of a monarchical nature."

In many places in the letters and writings of Jefferson we find that great statesman and pure patriot alluding, with just condemnation, to these monarchical doctrines of Hamilton. He and Hamilton were in Washington's Cabinet together; and thirty years afterwards, while calmly reviewing the opinions of Hamilton, he says: "Hamilton was not only a monarchist, but for a monarchy bottomed on corruption."

In another place he says: "Hamilton declared openly that there was no stability, no security, in any kind of government but a monarchy." Again he assures us that even while Hamilton was in Washington's Cabinet as Secretary of the Treasury, he declared: "For my part, I avow myself a *monarchist*. I have no objection to a trial of this thing called a republic, but," etc., etc.

At the date of August 13th, 1791, Mr. Hamilton had a conversation with Mr. Jefferson, in which he said: "I own it is my opinion, though I do not publish it in Dan or Beersheba, that the present government is not that which will answer, and that it will be found expedient to go into the British form." That is, to become a monarchy. This language was uttered by Hamilton three years after our present Constitution had been adopted. He was then, as we have said, Secretary of the Treasury under President Washington.

Washington hearing, from various sources, that his Secretary had avowed such shameless sentiments, wrote him a letter, July 29th, 1792, asking for an explanation of these rumors. About a month after Hamilton received this letter, that is, on August 16th, he wrote a complaining kind of letter to Mr. Adams on the subject, in which he said: "All the persons I meet are prosperous and happy, and yet most of them, including the friends of the Government [i.e., of Washington's Administration] appear to be much alarmed at a supposed system of policy tending to subvert the Republican Government of the country."

But, not only the friends of Washington's Administration were alarmed, but the alarm was shared by Washington himself. It was under the pressure of this very alarm for the honor of some members of his Cabinet that Washington said: "Those who lean to a monarchical government, have either not consulted the public mind, or they live in a region which is much more productive of monarchical ideas than is the case with the Southern States."

Washington, like Jefferson, was a Virginian, and had no sympathy with the monarchical principles of Hamilton and his followers. Washington well intimates that these treasonous principles had no friends "in the Southern States." The statesmen of the South, with scarcely an exception, were for a republican form of government, while the friends of the monarchical principle were mostly confined to the Eastern States.

So you see that as early as 1790 there was a great difference growing up between the leading statesmen of the North and South, on the subject of government. Indeed we may go back three years further, and find these very parties existing in the convention that formed the Constitution. There we find what we may call the *Jeffersonian* and the *Hamiltonian* parties pitted against each other. The one, in favor of a government of the people, with powers cautiously limited and clearly defined in the Constitution. The other, in favor of what they called "a strong government," with similar powers to a monarchy, without its name. We may say that the Jeffersonian idea was that the people are the masters of the government; while the Hamiltonian idea was that the government is the master of the people. The conflict between these opposing ideas caused all the debates in the Constitutional Convention. But finally the Jeffersonian, or the anti-monarchical party, triumphed in the production of a democratic Constitution. The great disappointment which this result gave to Mr. Hamilton, may be seen in a letter which he wrote to Mr.

Morris, Feb. 27th, 1802, where he says:

> Mine is an odd destiny. Perhaps no man in the United States has sacrificed or done more for the present Constitution than myself, and contrary to all my anticipations of its fate, as you know from the beginning, I am still laboring to prop the frail and worthless fabric; yet I have the murmurs of its friends no less than the curses of its foes, for my reward. What can I do better than withdraw from the scene? Every day proves to me more and more that this American world was not made for me.

In the above extract we find Mr. Hamilton characterizing the Constitution of his country as "a frail and worthless fabric," and bitterly threatening to abandon his country forever. This was after the Constitution had been in operation fourteen years. His experience had certainly been a very hard one for a man of his political principles. He was an avowed monarchist. But his countrymen had, notwithstanding his earnest labors to the contrary, established a democratic Constitution. Failing in getting his principles incorporated into the Constitution, he next tried, as a leading member of Washington's Cabinet, to give a monarchical interpretation to a democratic Constitution. This conduct on his part produced a murmur among the people, and caused the letter of inquiry from Washington above referred to. His disheartened and peevish letter to Mr. Morris, from which I have given an extract above, was written two years after the election of Mr. Jefferson to the Presidency, which event certainly seemed to give a finishing blow to the Hamiltonian ideas of government in the United States. His party had made a desperate effort to subvert the Constitution under the presidency of John Adams, which was terminated by the election of Jefferson in 1800.

General Washington served his country as President eight years, when John Adams was elected to succeed him in that high office. During Washington's term the Hamiltonians, who called themselves "Federalists," and who embraced a great majority of the men of wealth and high social position in the Northern States, were not permitted to make any visible headway in subverting the Constitution. The overshadowing popularity of Washington kept down everything like the ambition of cliques and sections. But no sooner was his Presidency at an end, than the "Federalists," the enemies of the democratic principle of government, showed the cloven foot of monarchism again, and nearly every safeguard which the Constitution throws around the liberty of the people was disregarded and overthrown. Then it was that the antagonism between the political principles of the leading statesmen of the North and the South assumed a tolerably well defined shape in the division of parties. Adams was originally a democrat, and had performed most valuable service to his country in the Revolution which won the independence of the American colonies. In a letter to General Washington, dated Philadelphia, May 8th, 1791, Mr. Jefferson thus feelingly alludes to Mr. Adams' apostacy: "I am afraid the indiscretion of a printer has committed me with my friend Mr. Adams, for whom I have a cordial esteem, increased by long habits of concurrence in opinion in the days of his republicanism, and even since his apostacy to hereditary monarchy and nobility; though we differ, we differ as friends." Again Jefferson says: "Mr. Adams had originally been a republican [democrat]. The glare of royalty and nobility, during his mission to England, had made him believe their fascination to be a necessary ingredient in government. He was taken up by the monarchical Federalists in his absence, and on his return to the United States, he was by them made to believe that the general disposition of our citizens was favorable to monarchy."

Under Mr. Adams' Administration, the most foolish and oppressive acts were passed by the Federalist majority of Congress – among them the infamous "Alien and Sedition laws," which gave the President power to banish all aliens from the United States, or to lock them up in prison during his pleasure – also to cause the arrest and imprisonment of any person who should write or speak anything against the President or Congress. In a word, these acts endowed the President with despotic powers, putting the liberty of every Democrat in the United States in jeopardy, and producing a reign of cruelty and terror which lasted to the end of Mr. Adams' Administration.

As a specimen of the despotism of that Administration, we will mention the case of Hon. Mathew Lyon, a Democrat and estimable citizen, who for "ridiculing the ridiculous or idle parade" of the President, was seized and thrust into a cold dungeon six feet square, where he was left freezing and starving for a whole winter, and his liberation then authorized only on condition of his paying a fine of one thousand dollars. The Federalists everywhere ran riot in cruelty and mob violence. One of the most distinguished patriots of the United States, General Sumter, was brutally knocked down and beaten, by one of the officers and spies of the Administration, at the theatre in Philadelphia, because he neglected to take off his hat when it was announced that the President was coming in. General Sumter was at this time an old man, as ripe with honors won in the service of his country, as with years. But neither age, nor virtue, nor patriotism afforded any shield from the malice of the supporters of the king-aping President.

As a specimen of the monarchical spirit of those times, we will give the following brief extract of a public address made to the President, dated Boston, May 1st, 1798:

> We, the subscribers, inhabitants, and citizens of Boston, in the State of Massachusetts, deeply impressed with the alarming situation of our country, beg leave to express to you, the chief magistrate and *supreme ruler* over the United States, our fullest approbation of all the measures, external and internal, you have been pleased to adopt, under direction of *divine authority.*

It is proper to mention that the only "alarming situation of our country" at that time was the natural and growing indignation of the people at the despotism of the party in power. The historian of these events, John Wood, says:

> During the scenes of tyranny which were daily exhibited, the Federal papers throughout the Union were filled with an address to the President, complimenting him upon his mildness and justice, the impartiality of his administration, his attachment to liberty, and his benevolence to foreigners....
>
> These factions admired John Adams, because John Adams admired the British constitution and cursed the French republic. They bestowed unbounded panegyrics upon Alexander Hamilton for the same reason. They thought the administration

and the government ought to be confounded and identified; that the administration was the government, and the government the administration, and that the people ought to bow in tame submission to its whims and caprices.

It does not need one to come from the dead to tell you that during the last five years we had a resurrection of the same party, which had lain in its grave ever since it was driven from power in 1800, by the election of Mr. Jefferson to the Presidency. Its defeat and overthrow then was owing to the patriotism and decision of the united South under the lead of Jefferson and Madison. In opposition to all these unconstitutional and despotic acts of the Federalists, these patriots drew up the celebrated Kentucky and Virginia Resolutions of 1798, which were adopted by the Legislatures of Kentucky and Virginia, and accepted by the whole South, with as much unanimity as they were condemned by the North. These resolutions are too long to quote here, but their substance may be given in a few words. They pointedly condemn all the revolutionary and despotic acts of the Adams Administration as subversive of the free government of the United States, and clearly set forth all the powers of the Federal Government as resulting from a compact, or agreement, between independent and sovereign States, each State possessing "an equal right" to decide "for itself as well of infractions as of the mode and manner of redress." As one of these sets of resolutions was drawn by the very hand which wrote the Declaration of Independence, and the other by that which wrote the Constitution of our country, they were received by all the friends of free government as the utterance of the highest wisdom and patriotism. The monarchy-aping Federalists raised a wild outcry of alarm, but the friends of democracy at once adopted the resolutions as their written creed. On the platform of these resolutions Jefferson was elected President, and the Federalists hurled ignominiously from power.

No language can equal the violence and indecency of the vanquished Federalists. For defeating their plans of revolution, Jefferson was denounced as an "infidel," a "jacobin," a "traitor," a "scoundrel." These offensive epithets were hurled at the head of the patriotic author of our Declaration of Independence from pulpits, from the legislative halls of the Northern States, and from the columns of every Federal newspaper in the land, just as similar indecent jeers are now heaped upon the true followers of the great and good Jefferson, by those who are trying to overthrow the democratic government made by our fathers.

The hatred of Jefferson, as of all the leading statesmen of the South, which rankled in the bosoms of the discomfited Federalists, knew no bounds. It did not die with that generation. The parents taught their children to hate, not only the name of Jefferson, but the whole Southern people.

CHAPTER TWO
The Causes of the War, Continued
☆   ☆   ☆   ☆

In continuation of the proofs that the enmity between the North and South, which resulted in the war, was laid, at a very early period, in the conflict of fundamental principles of government, we will summon again the testimony of Jefferson himself. In a letter, dated April 24th, 1796, addressed to the historian, Mazzel, and published in the Paris *Moniteur,* January 25th, 1798, Mr. Jefferson says:

> Our political situation is prodigiously changed since you left us. Instead of that noble love of liberty, and that republican government, which carried us through the dangers of the war, an Anglo-monarchic-aristocratic party has arisen. Their avowed object is, to impose upon us the *substance,* as they have already given us the form, of the British Government. Nevertheless, the principal body of our citizens remain faithful to the republican principles. I should give you a fever if I should name the apostates who have embraced these heresies, men who were Solomons in council and Sampsons in conflict, but whose hair has been cut off by the Delilah of England. They would wrest from us that liberty which we have obtained by so much labor and peril; but we shall preserve it.

In another letter of a later date, Jefferson says:

> The Alien and Sedition laws are working hard. For my own part I consider these laws merely as an experiment on the American mind, to see how far it will bear an avowed violation

of the Constitution. If this goes down we shall immediately see attempted another act of Congress declaring that the President shall continue in office during life, reserving to another occasion the transfer of the succession to his heirs, and the establishment of a Senate for life.

This severe language of Mr. Jefferson is fully borne out in a letter from John Langdon to Samuel Ringold, dated at Portsmouth, N.H., October 10th, 1800, in which he says:

> In a conversation between Mr. Adams, Mr. Taylor, and myself, Mr. Adams certainly expressed a hope or expectation that his friend Giles would see the day when he would be convinced that the people of America would not be happy without an hereditary chief magistrate and senate, or at least for life.

Now let us return and quote farther from the letter of Jefferson:

> A weighty minority of these [Federalist] leaders considering the voluntary conversion of our Government into a monarchy as too distant, if not too desperate, wish to break off from our Union its eastern fragment, as being in fact the hotbed of American monarchism, with a view to the commencement of their favorite government, from whence other States may gangrene by degrees, and the whole thus by degrees be brought to the desired point.

This assertion of Mr. Jefferson is fully sustained by no less eminent an author than Mathew Cary, who, in his celebrated work, entitled *The Olive Branch,* gives a great many facts in relation to a conspiracy in New England to break up the Republic as early as 1796. He says:

> A Northern Confederacy has been the object for a number of years. They have repeatedly advocated in public prints a separation of the States, on account of pretended discordant views and interests of the different sections. This project of separation was formed shortly after the adoption of the Federal Constitution. Whether it was ventured before the public earlier than 1796, I know not, but of its promulgation that year there is most

indubitable evidence. To sow discord, jealousy and hostility between different sections of the Union was the first grand step in their career, in order to accomplish the favorite object of a separation of the States. For eighteen years, therefore, [i.e., from 1796 to 1814] the most unceasing endeavors have been used to poison the minds of the people of the Eastern States towards, and to alienate them from, their fellow-citizens of the Southern States. Nothing can exceed the violence of these caricatures, some of which would have suited the ferocious inhabitants of New Zealand rather than a civilized and polished nation.

Here you have proofs that the war upon the South was really begun by New England as early as 1796. In that year an elaborate series of papers was published in Hartford, in the State of Connecticut, under the signature of *"Pelham."* These papers, Mr. Carey tells us, were the joint production of men of the first talents in New England. The following extract from the first number of this *Pelham* series of essays fully justifies all that either Mr. Jefferson or Mr. Carey has said of the malcontents of New England:

> The Northern States can subsist as a nation without any connection with the Southern. It cannot be contested that if the Southern States were possessed of the same *political ideas,* our Union would be more close, but when it becomes a serious question whether we shall give up our Government or part with the States south of the Potomac, no man north of that river, whose heart is not *thoroughly democratic,* can hesitate what decision to make.

This, you must bear in mind, was written in 1796. It proves that the republican, or democratic principle of government, which was so tenaciously adhered to by the people of the South, was the cause of all the cunning hatred and abuse heaped upon them by the Federal monarchy-loving leaders of New England. They deliberately proposed to destroy the Union then, because the South *was so "thoroughly democratic."* Incompatibility of *"political ideas"* was given as a sufficient reason for maligning the character of a whole people, and for desiring to break up the Union which had been established by the Constitution only eight years before.

As early as the above date, then, we must fix upon as the starting point of a political and social war upon the South on the part of the Federalists in the Eastern States, which went on gathering and increasing in intensity of estrangement and hatred, until it ripened, at last, into the late terrible strife. There is a good maxim which tells us that "continual dropping will wear a stone." If all the vile and all the false things which have been published in Northern papers and books for the last seventy years, or from 1796 to 1866, ostensibly against the South, but really to make democracy odious, were gathered into one work, it would make a hundred volumes, each as big as a folio Bible. Is it not a wonder that the fatal conflict did not come before? The political peace, the moral peace, the social peace of this Union was broken by the old Federal party more than seventy years ago. But the complete triumph of the Democratic party over that pernicious faction saved the country from an open rupture for the long period of sixty years.

The hatred of the South, however, engendered by the old monarchist party of New England, could never be worked out of the anti-democratic portion of the Northern people. If the ground on which their hatred rested was worn away by time, or rendered no longer a decent excuse for opposition, their leaders were sure to hunt up some new issue on which to hang another chance of securing the end they had in view. Thus, when there no longer remained a chance or a hope of revolutionizing or changing the Government of the United States into a form more congenial to the monarchical views of Hamilton and Adams, another excuse was sought for by which the cherished objects they had in view might be accomplished. After they could no longer make headway against the democracy of Jefferson, the old Hamilton party hunted round for some new issue on which they could rally and keep alive their waning partisan strength. They hit upon the Negro. Not that they had in their own hearts any peculiar love for him, or any objection to Negro subordination as it existed in this country. A great many of the leading men of their party had become rich out of the "slave trade" – that is, in bringing Negroes to these shores and selling them to the Southern States. Negro subordination had existed also in every Northern State; but the climate was so cold that the Negro was found to be unprofitable as a laborer, and so he was declared "free." But no State did this for the reasons now given. Abolitionism or Negro equality, as now understood, did not exist among the Federal leaders. The Negroes were quite universally looked upon as an inferior and helpless race, incapable of sustaining themselves as civilized beings, and as every way better off under the institution of servitude, as it existed in this country, than they were in their own native Africa. There they are all slaves to uncivilized heathen masters. They live upon snakes and worms, and lead a life that is only just above that of the brute creation. Their lives also are entirely at the disposal of their barbarian masters. Sometimes as many as three or four thousand of them are taken out one after another, and butchered like so many pigs, as a sacrifice to the Negro divinities. The most wretched Negro in the Southern States was a great deal better off, every way, than he was in his own native country. All well-informed people knew this to be true. Therefore the great majority of good and intelligent men believed the institution of servitude in the Southern States to be a real blessing. A comparison made between the Negro with a master and the Negro without one, almost always resulted in favor of the former, as the happier of the two. Very few good people, therefore, had any objection to the condition of the Negro in this country. It was conceded by all candid observers that there was nowhere on earth to be found another population of Negroes so happy and so contented as those of the South. Washington, Jefferson, Madison, and nearly all the greatest and best men who fought against England for our liberties, and who were the means of establishing the Government of the United States, were "slaveholders." They were not only great statesmen, but they were celebrated for their moral and Christian character. And they were "slaveholders." I have said that they considered the Negro as belonging to an inferior race, not entitled to associate with White people, except as a servant. This had been the opinion of all Christian nations for more than two thousand years. Indeed it was the opinion of all wise men who lived in the world many thousands of years ago, even before the birth of our Saviour. If any taught otherwise, they were looked upon as ignorant dreamers, fanatics, and as men of no standing in society. No respectable White man or woman would have associated with a person who admitted a Negro to be his equal. This was the state of opinion, not only in our country, but throughout the civilized world. Even Massachusetts, no longer ago than 1836, passed a law to imprison any justice of the peace, or clergyman, who should be guilty of marrying a White person to a Negro. The laws of every State in the Union wisely denied Negroes an equality with White people. I say this was a just and necessary provision in order to prevent what is called mulattoism or mongrelism, that is, a mixture of the White and Black races, which history and experience have proved to be one of the greatest curses that can befall society. Every nation on the face of the earth where such a mixture has taken place to any considerable extent, has declined in its civilization, and gradually sunk down in ruin, as if wasted by a slow poison. And that is just what it was God's, punishment upon men for violating His laws.

CHAPTER THREE
Causes of the War, Continued

I have said that when the political descendants of the old Federalists pitched upon the Negro question they were governed by no love for the Negro, but solely by their old hatred of democratic principles. The very Northern States which, in 1787, voted against the immediate abolition of the "slave-trade," a few years after led off the mad crusade against the States in which so-called slavery existed by law, and under the protecting shield of the Constitution of the United States. This agitation was, virtually, a declaration of war against the Southern States. It was, indeed, the beginning of hostilities. Of hostilities, unprovoked on the part of the South, and having no foundation even in any portion of Northern opinion, except in that which was the hereditary foe of a democratic form of government. This revival of the unfriendly and revolutionary spirit of old Federalism began in opposition to the admission of the State of Missouri into the Union as a "slave" State. This was in 1820. Ex-President Jefferson at once saw that the Negro question was only the excuse, while the real motive was to reinstate the lost fortunes of the old democracy-despising Federalism. In a letter to General Lafayette, Mr. Jefferson said: "On the eclipse of Federalism with us, although not its extinction, its leaders got up the Missouri question under the false front of lessening the measure of slavery, but with the real *view of producing a geographical division of parties* which might ensure them the next president. The people of the North went blindfold into the snare."

This was a very cunning dodge on the part of the Federalists. By their avowed leaning to monarchism, and their hatred of the democratic form of government which had been adopted by the majority of the people, they had made their principles and their very name despised. It was therefore necessary for them to take a new name, and to bring out some new issues in order to get back into power. But, whether under a new name, or with professedly new objects, the real object was the same. It was to overthrow democracy, and to carry out its long-cherished desire of revolutionizing our government in fact, if not in form.

I have shown that the sagacious and far-seeing mind of Jefferson fully understood the plans of the Federalists when they hit upon the Negro question as a means of party agitation. I have already quoted what he wrote to General Lafayette, who left his own country, France, and came to assist our forefathers in their noble struggle for independence. In another letter Mr. Jefferson wrote as follows:

> The question is a mere party trick. The leaders of Federalism, defeated in their schemes of obtaining power by rallying partisans to the principles of monarchism – a principle of personal, not of local division – have changed their tack, and thrown out another barrel to the whale. They are taking advantage of the virtuous feelings of the people to effect a division of parties by a geographical line; they expect that this will insure them, on local principles, the majority they could never obtain on principles of Federalism.

While the old Federalists had ceased to openly avow their design to break up our Government, they cunningly sought the same object by arraying one half of the Union against the other on this subject of the status of the Negro. So far as history informs us, this infamous trick was first suggested to the Federalists by a British spy of the name of John Henry, who was sent to this country in 1809 to lay plans to destroy the Union. Henry was commissioned to assist in this work by the British Governor of Canada, whose name was Craig.

The following is an extract from Governor Craig's letter of instructions to Henry:

The Causes of the War, Continued 35

Quebec, February, 1809.
I request you to proceed with the earliest conveyance to Boston. * * * The known intelligence and ability of several of its leading men, must give it a considerable influence over the other States, and will probably lead them in the part they are to take. * * * It has been supposed that if the Federalists of the Eastern States should be successful, and obtain the decided influence which may enable them to direct public opinion, it is not improbable that, rather than submit, they will exert that influence to bring about *a separation from the general Union.* * * * I enclose a credential, but you must not use it unless you are satisfied it will lead to more confidential communications.

The fact of this conspiracy between the agents of the British Government in Canada, and the leading Federalists of New England, came to the knowledge of Mr. Madison, who was President of the United States, and he laid all the proofs before Congress. In his message to Congress on the subject, President Madison said:

I lay before Congress copies of certain documents, which remain in the department of State. They prove that, at a recent period, on the part of the British Government, through its public minister here, a secret agent of that government was employed, in certain States, more especially at the seat of government in Massachusetts, in fomenting disaffection to the constituted authorities of the country; and intrigued with the disaffected, for the purpose of bringing about resistance to the laws, and eventually, in concert with a British force, of destroying the Union, and forming the eastern part thereof into a political connexion with Great Britain.

The laying of these documents before Congress created a great fluttering among the Federalists. They contained the indisputable proofs of their guilty intentions to overthrow the Union, if they could not otherwise subvert the democratic form of government established by the people.

I have said that the plan of subverting our Government, or overthrowing the Union, by agitating the Negro question, was probably first suggested by this British spy and conspirator,

Henry. He wrote back to the authorities who had employed him in Canada, that although he found the leaders of the Federalists of New England ripe for any measure which could sever the Union, yet that he found the sentiment of Union so strong among the masses of the people that he doubted if it could be immediately dissolved. He suggested that the best way to further this scheme of disunion would be to get up some sectional domestic question on which the prejudices and passions of the people could be permanently divided. This, he was sure would, in time, accomplish disunion. The sectional question at which he hinted was "slavery." He did not miscalculate. It did its work. It accomplished disunion.

As I shall show you before we get through with these pages, the great design that the British Government had, was to break down the glorious government which Washington had fought to establish, and when they saw they could not do it by open warfare, they resorted to deceit and trickery. One proof of this may be found in the following circumstance.

Mr. Aaron Legget, an eminent New York merchant and a quaker abolitionist, declared that, while in Mexico, at the time of the abolition of "slavery" in the West Indies, he met Deputy Commissary General Wilson of the British army, and at that time an agent appointed by the British Government to make the final arrangements connected with the abolition of "slavery" in the West Indies, who told him that the English Government, in abolishing "slavery" in that colony, were not moved by any consideration for the Negro.

> Mr. Wilson said that the abolition of slavery in the British colonies would naturally create an enthusiastic anti-slavery sentiment in England and America, and that in America this would, in process of time, excite a hostility between the free States and the slave States, which would end in the dissolution of the American Union, and the consequent *failure of the grand experiment of democratic government;* and the ruin of democracy in America would be the *perpetuation of aristocracy in England.*"[1]

---

1. The reliability of this statement is attested in a letter written by Sidney E. Morse, Esq., of this city, to whom Mr L. related it.

There has always been a party of men in the Northern States who fully sympathized with the wishes of England in this respect. Indeed the whole progress of the Abolition movement shows that it has been a plot of British monarchists, aided by a set of men in this country, to destroy the Government as it was formed by Washington.

Sir Robert Peel said, when the $100,000,000 was paid to "free the Negroes in the West Indies, that it was the best investment ever made for the overthrow of republican institutions in America." The British aristocracy always seemed to feel and know that Negro equality would overthrow our Government.

The statement of the spy, Henry, that he found the leading Federalists of New England ripe for disunion, but not the masses of the people, ought to be noted. It goes to show that the great body of the people all over the country are patriotic, and if they go wrong, are misled by wicked and ambitious leaders. When I refer to New England, I only mean a majority of the leading men, who have miseducated the people and deceived them. Various causes have conspired to give them an opportunity to practice deception, particularly in New England, which I will more fully explain hereafter. But that section contains thousands of sound and good men, who have ever been true to the Government as it was formed. That they have generally been in a minority is all the more honor to their courage and patriotism, for it proves beyond question the sincerity of their political convictions.

The facts in the case, however, prove beyond a doubt that at the time to which we refer, the British conspirator, John Henry, was favorably received by the leading men in the Eastern States as an agent for overthrowing the Union. The Federalists treated with him for this purpose. Mr. Jefferson saw the full extent of their designs. In a letter to Governor Langdon, he says:

> For five and thirty years we have walked together through a land of tribulation; yet those have passed away, and so, I trust, will these of the present day. The Toryism with which we struggled in 1777, differed but in name from the Federalism. of 1799, with which we struggled also; and the Anglocism [i.e., English monarchism) of 1808, against which we are now strug-

gling, is but the same thing in another form. It is longing for a king, and an English king rather than any other. This is the true source of their sorrows and wailings.

In the war between the United States and England in 1812, the New England Federalists took sides with England against their own country, so far as they could without actually taking up arms against the United States. Even John Quincy Adams, a Massachusetts man himself, was compelled to confess that: "In the Eastern States, curses and anathemas were liberally hurled from the pulpit on the heads of all those who aided, directly or indirectly, in carrying on the war." I dwell on these matters to show you that there was always a party in New England which was an enemy to the Government of our country. At the time of which I have been speaking, Caleb Strong was Governor of Massachusetts. General Fessenden introduced the following resolution into the Legislature of that State: "And therefore be it resolved, that we recommend to his Excellency, Caleb Strong, to take the revenue of the State into his own hands, arm and equip the militia, and declare us independent of the Union."

At this time Fisher Ames, one of the most distinguished men of New England, said: "Our country is too big for Union, too sordid for patriotism, too democratic for liberty. Our disease is democracy; it is not the skin that festers, our very bones are carious, and their marrow blackens with gangrene." Rev. Dr. Dwight said: "The Declaration of Independence is a *wicked thing*. I thought so when it was proclaimed, and I think so still." One of the leading papers of Boston declared: "We never fought for a republic. The form of our Government was the result of necessity, not the offspring of choice." The Boston *Gazette* threatened President Madison with death, if he attempted to compel the Eastern States to fight against England at that time. I could make a large book with extracts from the leading men and the principal papers of New England of those days, showing that there was, through all that section, a wide-spread and a bitter hatred of our democratic form of government, and of the Union.

CHAPTER FOUR
The Causes of the War, Continued

The admission of Missouri into the Union and the restriction of "slavery" to a line south of thirty-six degrees and thirty minutes, quieted the agitation of the question, so far as political parties were concerned. Other issues arose, however, such as the bank, tariff, and similar questions upon which political parties divided. But as those issues were such as could be equally understood in all sections of the Union, they did not furnish material for disunion. True, South Carolina, feeling aggrieved with the tariff act of 1828, threatened to nullify the law, but the timely modification of the act prevented all trouble. It has been often represented that General Jackson secured the obedience of South Carolina by threats of force, but the truth is, it was effected by a compromise. A great cry has been made over this act of nullification on the part of South Carolina, and I do not intend here to do more than allude to it and say that when nearly every Northern State not only nullified, but carried into effect their nullification of a plain law of Congress, it does not become those thus guilty to upbraid South Carolina. The act in relation to the return of "fugitives from service," was openly and distinctly nullified by nearly every Northern State.

The great contests on the bank, tariff, and other questions, were mainly fought out between the years 1820 and 1840. During that time such patriots and statesmen as Jackson, Clay, Calhoun, Webster, Woodbury, Silas Wright, Hayne, and others, met in debate and contended for the mastery. However much these men differed, they all loved their country, and could not bear the thought of seeing it disrupted. But during the whole of this time a wonderful change was going on in the popular mind on the question of the Negro race. It seemed that no sooner had the Missouri question been disposed of, and the agitation banished from the halls of Congress, than fanatics sprang up all over proclaiming "the enormity of slavery as a sin and crime against God." In 1821 Benjamin Lundy commenced the publication of the *Genius of Universal Emancipation,* believed to be the first out and out Abolition paper in this country. In 1823 the first Abolition society was organized in England. This period in history, that is, from 1820 to 1835, was characterized by a general uprising of societies of all kinds. Large sums of money were raised to spread the new doctrine that "slavery was a crime," and that "slaveholders" were "thieves" and "murderers." At first, as may be naturally supposed, these slanders upon Washington, Jefferson, Madison, and other great and good men who had founded our Government and whose glorious memories were still fresh in the hearts of the people, provoked difficulties. Riots broke out all over the North. The natural instincts of the people, unperverted as they had been as yet by Abolition teachings, revolted at the doctrine of Negro equality. They mobbed the prominent movers in it all over the country. The house of Arthur Tappan, in New York city, was mobbed in July, 1834. About the same time the church of the Rev. Dr. Cox was attacked. A large hall was burned down in Philadelphia. All these disorders were directly owing to the revolting doctrines of the Abolitionists, which were utterly disgusting to the public opinion of that day. Still these men kept on, printing books, tracts, pamphlets, magazines, newspapers, etc., etc., and spreading them gratuitously all over the country. They had now gotten hold of that "social question" which the British spy, Henry, had suggested as the one thing necessary in order to produce disunion.

The question, too, was one admirably adapted to their purposes. The Negroes were mainly in the Southern States. The Northern people could not be expected to understand a race of which they knew but little. They must rely upon the reports of newspapers, often printed by unprincipled men or ambitious politicians, whose whole interest consisted in misrepresenting facts. But above and beyond all, there was another cause which contributed more than all others to aid the Abolitionists. The subject of the races of men had never been investigated. Mr. Jefferson had referred to this matter and said it was "a reproach to us that though for a century and a half we had had under our eyes the races of Black and of Red men, yet they had never been viewed as subjects of natural history." And he went further, and said, "I advance it as a suspicion only that the Blacks, whether originally a different race, or made distinct by time and circumstances, are inferior to the Whites in the endowments both of mind and body." Later investigations have proved beyond a doubt that the Negro and the Caucasian, or White man, are *distinct* races or *species* of men. Whether they were originally made so or not, the Creator of all only knows, but there is no doubt that they are so now, and if different, of course we cannot expect the same things of them. No one expects a goat to be a sheep. No one expects a mastiff to be a hound. If Blacks and Whites are not distinct races or species, then it would be proper and beneficial to amalgamate with Negroes, and to make them our equals in every respect.

The Abolitionists, however, assume that there is but one human race, and as that has been generally assented to, it gave them a fine field for their delusion. How natural for everybody to feel that if the Negro is a man like ourselves that he ought to have the same or equal rights. And above all, if "slavery," "bondage," etc., has repressed his energies, kept him down, and made him what he is, how much more of a duty it is to lift him up and do him justice. But all the pathetic stories of the Abolitionists proceeded from a false basis. The Negro was *not* a man like the White man. He had never been so elevated at any time in the history of his race as the four millions in the Southern States. Our form of society had civilized and Christianized the only Negroes that had ever been civilized or Christianized. This is simple historical fact, which no one dare deny. But still, as no one met the Abolitionists in this way, they had the field to themselves. It is not until late years, not until the whole people had been more or less deceived and corrupted, that the question of distinct races was explained, and the justice of legal and social distinctions between them not only avowed, but placed upon clear grounds.

Now even the youngest child can see that it would be wrong and cruel to ask or expect the Negro to feel or act as we do, simply because the great Creator of all has given him but one talent, while he has given to us ten talents. It is our duty, as the superior race, to care for these people whom God, in His Providence, has given us. We should try to understand their natures, their capacities, and their wants, and then adapt our laws so that they will be in the happiest, the healthiest and best condition it is possible for them to attain. That was what the Southern people tried to do, and though no society is perfect, yet all must admit that the Negroes were better off every way before the war than now. A million, it is estimated, have died in the effort to make them *act like White people.* Every young person can see how wicked it would be to take an ox and try to make it go as fast as a horse, and yet it is no more sinful nor cruel than to take the Negroes and demand that they shall act the same as White people. As it would kill the ox to try to make him a horse, so it kills the Negro to try and make him a White man.

I have explained this at some length because it is so important to understand it, and because it is really so simple when understood that any one can comprehend it. Every person can readily see how cruel it would be to deprive all children of their fathers and mothers, and yet it was no more cruel than to deprive, at a single blow, every Negro in the South of the care and protection of his master and mistress. Thousands of these poor creatures have died of small pox and other loathsome diseases. Hundreds have starved to death or died of exposure, and all because of the false teachings of the Abolitionists, who deceived the people, and told them that society as it existed at the South was "a sin and a crime."

The Abolitionists, however, did not stop here. They declared that the Government, as it was formed by Washington, Jefferson, and Madison, protected the Southern people in their form of society. And this was, of course, true; for it is not within the bounds of reason to suppose that those men, all of whom were "slaveholders," would have organized a government against themselves! I have already shown you how the old Federalists hated the Government; and you will now see how this same spirit was breathed forth by the Abolitionists.

William Lloyd Garrison, who has been called the father of the Abolition societies, inaugurated his Abolition movement by publicly burning the Constitution of the United States. Many years after this infamous act, he declared in a speech: "No act of ours do we regard with more conscientious approval or higher satisfaction, than when, several years ago, on the 4th of July, in the presence of a great assembly, we committed to the flames the Constitution of the United States." Again he says: "This Union is a lie! The American Union is an imposture – a covenant with death, and an agreement with hell. I am for its overthrow! Up with the flag of disunion!"

Wendell Phillips, the ablest and honestest of all the Abolition leaders, declared the object of the agitation to be the overthrow of the Constitution. He said: "The Constitution of our fathers was a mistake. Tear it to pieces and make a better one. Our aim is disunion, breaking up of the States."

A resolution passed at an annual Abolition convention reads as follows: "Resolved, that the Abolitionists of this country should make it one of the primary objects of this agitation to dissolve the American Union."

Thus boldly and wickedly did these men assail the Government of our fathers. You have no doubt heard Mr. Calhoun of South Carolina called "the father of disunion," but the history I have already given you shows that disunionism arose in the North. Mr. Calhoun, in a speech in the Senate of the United States, March 7th, 1850, delivered while he knew himself to be a dying man, said:

> No man would feel more happy than myself to believe that this Union, formed by our ancestors, should live forever. Looking back to the long course of forty years' service here, I have the consolation to believe that I have never done one act to weaken it; that I have done full justice to all sections. And if I

have ever been exposed to the imputation of a contrary motive, it is because I have been willing to defend my section from unconstitutional encroachments.

In a speech made by the same great statesman in the Senate, nearly thirty years ago, that is in 1838, he said:

> Abolition is the only question of sufficient magnitude and potency to divide this Union, and divide it it will, or drench the country in blood if not arrested. There are those who see no danger to the Union in the violation of all fundamental principles, but who are full of apprehension when danger is foretold, and who hold, not the authors of the danger, but those who forewarned it, responsible for the consequences. If my attachment for the Union were less, I might tamper with the deep disease which now afflicts the body politic, and keep silent until the patient was ready to sink under the mortal blows.

Jefferson Davis, in a speech in the United States Senate, June 27th, 1850, said: "If I have a superstition, sir, which governs my mind and holds it captive, it is a superstitious reverence for the Union. If one can inherit a sentiment, I may be said to have inherited this from my revolutionary father."

It will thus be seen that at the very time that the Abolitionists were preaching up a mad crusade against the Union, and educating a generation to hate the Government of our fathers, Southern men, the great leaders of the South, were begging and imploring that it might be preserved.

CHAPTER FIVE
The Causes of the War, Continued
☆ ☆ ☆ ☆

The Abolition movement, however, was destined to undergo a change. The Garrisonian Abolitionists, in educating a generation to believe that the subordinate position of the Negro was a sin and a crime, had created a great moral power; but after all it was more or less ineffective. The Constitution and Government of our forefathers were so interwoven in the heart of every honest and patriotic American that the denunciations that it was "a covenant with hell" only provoked disgust or excited derision, and outside of the few delirious fanatics whom they addressed, it exerted no influence. They might have preached a hundred years probably, and would never have destroyed the relation of the races, or broken up the Union in that way. But, as the Whig party dissolved after the bank and tariff questions had, it was hoped, forever been disposed of, the old Federal Hamiltonian element in that party looked around for some now issue upon which to delude the people.

About this time, that is, from 1850 to 1854, there came prominently into public view a cunning, crafty, and entirely unscrupulous politician in the State of New York, by the name of William H. Seward. He had been Governor of the State, and was at this time Senator in Congress. He was a Hamiltonian Federalist. But more than any other man he seemed to comprehend "the situation." He saw that the Abolitionists had, by their thirty years' education of the popular mind, created a great hatred in the North against the South, and he determined to use this to obtain power.

He had raised an excitement in the State of New York against the Free Masons to get power there, and why might he not do the same thing again on a larger scale? He went to work at this with great cunning and subtlety. He saw at a glance that Garrison's programme of the open denunciation of the Constitution and the Union would not answer. Mr. Garrison said, and said truly, "the Constitution protects slavery."

Mr. Seward inaugurated his plan of battle by declaring (see his *Works*, vol. iii. p. 301): "Correct your error that slavery has only *constitutional guarantees* which may not be released and *ought not to be relinquished.*" Again says Mr. Seward (vol. i. p. 71): "You answer that the Constitution recognizes property in slaves. It would be sufficient, then, to reply that the constitutional recognition *must be* void, because it is repugnant to the law of nature and of nations." Here Mr. Seward sets up *his* idea of the laws of nature and of nations against the solemn compact of our forefathers. But he went further; he declared that there was an "irrepressible conflict" between Northern and Southern society, that "slavery must be abolished," that there was "a higher law" than the Constitution, that "it was for the South to decide whether they would have slavery removed gradually, or whether they would have disunion and civil war."

Such was the wicked programme that this wily politician laid out for the ruin of this country. Garrison would have been willing to have separated from the South and let her alone in the enjoyment of her rights, but Mr. Seward aimed at nothing less than seizing upon the Government through a sectional party and consolidating in it all power as the old Federalists had desired, and thus have one despotic government over the whole country.

He accordingly organized his scattered forces in a new party. On the 26th of September, 1854, a convention was called to meet at Auburn, *the home of Wm. H. Seward,* the object of which was announced to be "to organize a *Republican* party which should represent the *friends of freedom,*" which means, of course, the friends of *Negro* freedom, for no White men were deprived of their freedom *then.* This meeting recommended that a convention of delegates from the Northern States *only,* be held on the 4th of July, 1856, to nominate candidates for President and Vice-President of *all* the United States. This convention afterwards met, and nominated Fremont and Dayton.

When the Seward Republican party was first organized, some of the Abolitionists thought it did not go far enough, but Wendell Phillips, with his sagacity, saw that its programme was a cunning one. He declared "that it was the first crack in the iceberg. It is the *first sectional* party ever organized in this country. *It is pledged against the South.*"

This new party soon swept into it all those who had been deluded by the Abolition teachings. It made loud protestations of devotion to "free speech, free press, and free men." It pretended to more and better republicanism than the democracy, for it desired to apply republicanism to Negroes. Hence it very properly got the name of *Black* Republican, for it bore no more resemblance to genuine republicanism than an old Federalist did to a Jeffersonian Democrat.

And strange to say, this Tory-British party in disguise actually seized hold of the name of Jefferson to delude the people. They even perverted the glorious Declaration of Independence from its plain meaning, and tortured it into an excuse for Negro equality. When Mr. Jefferson said "all men were created equal," he referred to his own race and to no others, for if he meant Negroes then he was himself insincere, for he should have "freed" his own on the spot, which he did not do.

In a word, there was no deception that this party did not resort to. No effort to influence the public mind was spared. The South was universally denounced, and when warned by democrats that the Southern men would not live under a government which was to be administered to destroy them, they laughed the warning to scorn. The North was strong enough, if all the States could be secured, to elect a President in spite of the South, and this they determined to do. If they could accomplish this, they could revolutionize the Government by engrafting on it the monarchical doctrines of Hamilton and the Negro equality theories of Garrison, and so both would be satisfied. This, then, was the object of the Black Republican party leaders. They desired to overthrow the Government *as it was formed*. How they succeeded this history will tell.

About this time occurred the great Kansas excitement. This was a new territory west of the State of Missouri. When it seemed probable that it would be mainly settled by Southern men, the people of New England organized "Emigrant Societies," and filled it up with Abolitionists, so as to prevent it from becoming what they called a slave State. They also raised large sums of money and purchased arms and ammunition, and sent out men there, prominent among whom was old John Brown, to get up a war if they could.

The churches of New England were very active in this business, and the Abolition clergy all over were zealous workers in inciting to bloodshed. One minister, the Rev. Henry Ward Beecher, declared that "Sharp's rifles were better than Bibles," and "that it was a crime to shoot at a slave-holder and not hit him." All over the North, but mainly in New England, this insanity was prevalent. Ministers of the Gospel distributed guns and rifles for the work of bloodshed. The North was being slowly educated for the great war that followed.

John Brown Receiving Rifles For His "Kansas Work."

CHAPTER SIX
The Election of Lincoln

I have already shown you that there has been, here in the North, ever since the formation of the Federal Government, a powerful party opposed to the Union as it was formed. But during all this long period, there was never a single statesman in the Southern States who was not devotedly in favor of the Union as it was organized by our patriotic forefathers. The South was united in its admiration of the principles of government on which the Union was founded. On this subject the North was divided. The Democratic party was attached to the Union, and was devoted to the principles on which it was established, while the Black Republican party was an enemy both to the Union and the Constitution.

These Black Republicans, for many years, used to mockingly call Democrats "Union-savers." But as I have said, there were also two factions among the Black Republicans themselves – one, that of the fanatical Abolitionists, and the other, the enemy of the democratic form of government, as you have seen in the history of the old Federalists. This latter faction was an adherent to the exploded monarchical principles of Alexander Hamilton. They wanted to destroy these States and establish one great despotic government, or empire, over all this country. Their plan was foreshadowed in a speech by Governor Banks of Massachusetts, in 1856, in which he said:

> I can conceive of a time when this Constitution shall not be in existence – when we shall have an absolute dictatorial gov-

ernment,[1] transmitted from age to age, with men at its head who are made rulers by military commission, or who claim an hereditary right to govern those over whom they are placed.

When the war broke out, this same Governor Banks became a general, and in a speech made at Arlington Heights, he pointed to the Capitol in Washington, and said: "When this war is over, that will be the Capitol of a great nation. Then there will be no longer New Yorkers, Pennsylvanians, Virginians, etc., but we shall all be simply Americans."

The meaning was that the war would result in the destruction of all the State governments, and consolidate them into one great despotic government. The same idea was expressed by Senator Cameron, at a public dinner in Washington at about the same time.

But both of these factions – that is, the Abolitionists and the disciples of Hamiltonian monarchism – were agreed in their desire of revolutionizing the Government. Nothing that the South could have done, short of an entire surrender of their institutions and their rights as States, could have satisfied them. The people of the Southern States honestly believed that their society and their lives would not be safe in the Union as administered by these men. The presidential campaign, which resulted in the election of Mr. Lincoln, had been conducted with such a spirit of violence and malignity towards the South that it might well alarm the people of that section. An infamous and murderous work, known as the *"Helper Book,"* which had been published one year before, and a hundred thousand copies of it circulated by subscription of the leading Black Republican members of Congress, was the chief campaign document of the Lincoln canvass. This horrid book plainly threatened the people of the South with assassination and death. It was full of such sentences as the following:

> Against slaveholders as a body we wage an exterminating war.

---

1. This was precisely the kind of government the Black Republican party did force upon the country in the Administration of Abraham Lincoln.

The Election of Lincoln 51

> [It counseled the North:] Do not reserve the strength of your arms until you are rendered powerless to strike.
>
> We contend that slaveholders are more criminal than common murderers.
>
> The Negroes, nine cases out of ten, would be delighted at the opportunity to out their masters' throats.
>
> Small pox is a nuisance; strychnine is a nuisance; mad dogs are a nuisance; slavery is a nuisance; and so are slaveholders; it is our business, nay, it is our imperative duty, to abate nuisances; we propose, therefore, with the exception *of strychnine, to exterminate this catalogue from beginning to end.*

A book of three hundred pages filled with such horrid threats as these, and circulated as a campaign document in the canvass that elected Mr. Lincoln, might well fill the South with alarm. I have said that all the leading Black Republican members of Congress subscribed for the free distribution of one hundred thousand copies of this work. Mr. Seward gave it his especial endorsement in a card which declared it "a work of great merit." The book had been preceded by speeches from Northern politicians scarcely less brutal in tone. Mr. Giddings, a prominent politician in Ohio, had said:

> I look forward to a day when I shall see a servile insurrection in the South. When the Black men, supplied with bayonets, shall wage a war of extermination against the Whites – when the master shall see his dwelling in flames, and his hearth polluted, and though I may not mock at their calamity and laugh when their fear cometh, yet I shall hail it as the dawn of a political millennium.

The Hon. Erastus Hopkins had said: "If peaceful means fail us, and we are driven to the last extremity, when ballots are useless, then we will make bullets effective."

For many years Northern pulpits and Northern newspapers had teemed with such bloody threats as these against the people of the South. And less than two years before the election of Mr. Lincoln, "Old John Brown," a notorious murderer from Kansas, who was a native of New England, went into Virginia with a posse of assassins, for the purpose of getting up an insurrection among the Negroes, to murder the White men, women and children. Brown's gang was armed with pikes made in New England, and with plenty of ammunition and fire-arms purchased by money secretly contributed in the North. The whole plot was discovered, and he was tried and hanged. The execution of this admitted assassin produced a fearful outbreak of threats and fury in the North. Prayer-meetings were held in nearly all the churches of New England, and indeed throughout the West, to invoke the vengeance of heaven on those who had caused the just penalties of the law to fall upon one of the most pitiless murderers ever known in this country. And yet bells were tolled to glorify the memory of this fiend.

As my readers may not have heard of Brown's terrible murder of Mr. Doyle and his two sons in Kansas, I will relate it. He went to the house about midnight with a gang of men, and told him that he and his two sons were wanted as witnesses upon an "Investigating Committee," and that they had been sent to summon them. No sooner had they got them in the yard than they *killed all three in cold blood.* The poor heart-broken wife and mother of the murdered men went almost crazy with grief, when the fiends returned to the house and threatened to shoot herself and only son. Mrs. Doyle fell on her bended knees, and implored

Old John Brown killing the Doyle family.

The Election of Lincoln

for mercy for herself and only child. After a while the villains left the poor woman and her son to the sorrowful sight of the three corpses in their door yard.

At a meeting in Massachusetts, attended by United States Senator Henry Wilson, the following resolution was unanimously passed: "Resolved, that it is the right and duty of slaves to resist their masters, and the right and duty of the people of the North to incite them to resistance, and to aid them in it."

At Rochford, Illinois, a public meeting, called by the leading citizens, unanimously "Resolved that the city bells be tolled one hour in commemoration of John Brown."

Horace Greeley said: "Let no one doubt that history will accord an honorable niche to old John Brown."

Ralph Waldo Emerson declared that the hanging of this assassin "made the gallows as glorious as the cross."

Again said Emerson: "Our Captain Brown is, happily, a representative of the American Republic. He did not believe in *moral suasion,* but in putting things through."

This terrible temper pervaded the whole North.

A book of a thousand pages might be made of extracts from sermons, prayers, speeches and newspapers, of a similar character.

Can we wonder that, under such a state of things, the Southern people should have felt it necessary to take some steps for their own safety? In the midst of this wild excitement Mr. Lincoln was nominated for the presidency by the party which had so universally endorsed old John Brown's murderous raid into Virginia. He was nominated at Chicago, in a temporary edifice built for the purpose, and, as if indicating the designs of the party, called a *"wigwam."* Over the chair of the president of the nominating convention was placed a huge wooden *knife twelve feet long,* a fitting foreshadowing of the bloody designs of the party putting him forward. At least the people of the South so interpreted it; and they demanded some pledges that the threats put forth in the Helper book should not be visited upon them.

In answer to these reasonable demands, they received only sneers, reproaches, and more threats. When they declared that "unless they could have their rights in the Union they would withdraw," they were answered, that "the North could not kick them out of the Union." The truth is, that war was resolved upon by the Black Republican leaders. I shall show you in another chapter what cunning tricks were resorted to by Mr. Lincoln and Mr. Seward to bring about what was called "an overt act" on the part of the South.

If I failed to lay this whole matter out truly before you, I should make myself a party to the monstrous falsehoods which have been put forth as *history* on this point. The whole Southern people had always been contented with the Union as it was established by our forefathers. They never talked of secession, except as a remedy for aggressions upon their constitutional rights. On the contrary, in the North, as you have seen, there has always been a busy and determined party, which has been working to overthrow the Union, because it hated the Constitution, and was at enmity with the South from an old grudge, growing out of the early conflict between the monarchical principles of Alexander Hamilton and the democratic principles of Thomas Jefferson. This old hatred on the part of the North, which had been brewing and smouldering ever since the establishment of the Government, was now recruited by the fiery and fanatical element of Abolition to such a degree that the conflict, long threatened by the Northern malcontents, and dreaded by the South, burst upon the country. Failing, as they thought, to receive any guarantees of security and rest in the Union, the Southern States determined to withdraw. All but South Carolina came to this conclusion slowly and unwillingly.

CHAPTER SEVEN
Secession

In the fall of 1860 Mr. Lincoln was elected President by a party and by men such as I have described in the last chapter. He carried every Northern State except New Jersey, and received a majority of the electoral votes, but not a majority of all the people. You know the President is elected by the *States,* not by the people – that is to say, each State gives as many votes for President as it has Representatives and Senators in Congress. Mr. Lincoln had a majority of these, but he was nearly a million and a half in the minority, counting the votes of all the people. But although Mr. Lincoln was elected by what is called State Rights, yet he went to work at once to destroy State Rights, as we shall soon see.

The Southern people were, of course, greatly alarmed when the result was known. The party coming into power had declared war against them. True the Chicago Platform was cautiously worded, but it is the spirit and temper of a political party which give the *true* meaning of its purposes. I have shown you fully what these were, from the mouths of its leading men.

And I may mention here as a singular fact that Joshua R. Giddings, of Ohio, who was known all his life as an out and out Abolitionist, declared in the Chicago Convention that its nominees could not get the support of the Abolitionists unless the resolutions pledged the party to carry out the doctrine that *"all men are created equal."* I have already mentioned that the Abolitionists meant by this phrase to include Negroes. The Chicago

Convention, therefore, according to their own interpretation of its resolutions, was pledged to change Southern society, and make the Negro the equal of the White man. How then can any Black Republican pretend that their own party platform was not an open declaration of war upon the South? Although they cunningly disguised their intentions by making a false use of a popular phrase, they did not deceive the Southern people. They instinctively knew that this party meant to overthrow their society, "peaceably, perhaps, if they were permitted to do so, but forcibly if they must." Mr. Seward himself avowed this sentiment in a speech in the United States Senate, March 11th, 1850.

The means which the Southern States resolved to resort to, in order, if possible, to save themselves from this calamity, was what has been called secession – that is, to withdraw from the Union or Confederacy. The States had all joined the Confederacy by their own act. There had been no compulsion used, and it had been held by the wisest and best men, both North and South, that the States, having only delegated the exercise of certain powers to the Federal Government, could resume them whenever they felt that their interests aud welfare demanded it. If this was not the case it was held that it made the Federal Government the judge of its own powers, and that is the definition of a despotism.

I will now give you the opinions of some of the old Federalists, as well as others, on the right of secession. Josiah Quincy, of Massachusetts, was one of the bitterest of all the Federalists, and it only goes to show that the Black Republican party is a lineal descendant of old Tory Federalism, when I tell you that this man, Josiah Quincy, lived to a great age, and became a warm supporter of Mr. Lincoln and the Abolitionists. He was a member of Congress during Mr. Jefferson's Administration, and violently opposed that great statesman. Mr. Jefferson saw the future greatness of this country, and purchased all the Louisiana Territory of France, which Mr. Quincy and the Federalists opposed. In a speech, in 1811, against the bill to admit Louisiana into the Union, Mr. Quincy said that if it passed "it would be the *right* of all, as well as the *duty* of some of the States to prepare for *separa-*

tion, amicably if they can, forcibly if they must." Some member called Mr. Quincy to order for making a treasonable utterance, but the House of Representatives sustained him.

One of the earliest as well as ablest constitutional lawyers in our country was Judge William Rawle of Pennsylvania. As a statesman and a patriot he ranked very high. General Washington appointed him District Attorney of the United States in 1791, and afterwards tendered him a seat in his Cabinet. In his work entitled *A View of the Constitution of the United States*, Judge Rawle says:

> It depends on the State itself to retain or abolish the principle of representation, because it depends on itself whether it will continue a member of the Union. To deny this right would be inconsistent with the principle on which all our political systems were founded; which is, that the people have in all cases a right to determine how they will be governed. The States, then, may wholly withdraw from the Union, but while they continue, they must retain the character of representative republics.

The same sentiment was briefly expressed by President Jefferson in these words: "States may wholly withdraw their delegated powers." And again, in a letter to Dr. Priestly, in 1804, he said:

> If the States west of the Alleghany declare themselves a separate people, we are incapable of a single effort to retain them. Our citizens can never be induced, either as militia or soldiers, to go there to cut the throats of their own brothers or sons, or to be themselves the subjects instead of the perpetrators of the parricide.

President Madison affirmed the same principle, when speaking of the States as the parties to the compact which formed the Union, he said: "The parties [i.e., the States] themselves must be the judges, in the last resort, whether the bargain made has been preserved or broken."

Such, indeed, is the meaning of the celebrated Resolutions of 1798, referred to in a previous chapter, and on which both Jefferson and Madison were elected to the Presidency.

But, whether a State had or had not the right to secede, there never had been scarcely a difference of opinion as to the right and the policy of resorting to coercion. Ex-President John Quincy Adams, in 1833, speaking of secession, said that whenever that time arrived, "it would be better for the people of these *disunited* States to part in friendship from each other rather than to be held together by constraint." In 1850, Mr. Salmon P. Chase, now Chief Justice, in a speech in the United States Senate, declared that in "the case of a State resuming her powers, he knew of no remedy to prevent it." Even Mr. Lincoln and Mr. Seward avowed this doctrine as late as April, 1861. In a despatch to Mr. Dayton, our minister to France, dated April 10th, 1861, Mr. Lincoln instructed Mr. Seward to say:

> That he [the President] was not disposed to reject a cardinal dogma of theirs [the seceders], namely, that the Federal Government could not reduce the seceding States to obedience by conquest, even although he were disposed to question the proposition. But in fact, *the President willingly accepts it as true.*

The late Mr. Edward Everett, Feb. 2d, 1861, said: "To expect to hold fifteen States in the Union by force is preposterous. * * * If our sister States must leave us, in the name of heaven let them go in peace."

Again said Mr. Everett:

> The suggestion that the Union can be maintained by numerical predominance and military prowess of one section, exerted to coerce the other into submission, is, in my judgment, as self-contradictory as it is dangerous. It comes loaded with the death-smell from fields wet with brothers' blood. If the vital principle of all republican governments is the "consent of the governed," much more does a union of co-equal sovereign States require, as its basis, the harmony of its members, and their voluntary co-operation in its organic functions.

The leading newspaper organs of the Black Republican party held to the same views. The New York *Tribune,* only three days before South Carolina seceded, said "that the Declaration of Independence justified her in doing so." On Feb. 23d, 1861, the editor of the same paper acknowledged to be the exponent of the Black Republican party, said: "If the cotton States desire to form an independent nation, they have a clear moral right to do so."

In the face of all this history, how could the South imagine that the North would construe its withdrawal to be an act of treason? Much less could it reasonably suppose that the North would wage a relentless and exterminating war for an act which our own leading statesmen and politicians have always admitted to be, in the last resort, a *right*. No fair-minded person can doubt that the Southern States honestly believed that they had a right – in the language both of Washington and Jefferson – "to resume their delegated powers." They wished and intended to do so in peace. Their act of withdrawal was, in no sense, a declaration of war upon the Federal Government. But the Federal Government made war on them to have them remain, as the history soon to be related will clearly show. They offered and entreated peaceful negociation in relation to all the property claimed by the Federal Government, located within the jurisdiction of the withdrawing States. The forts which they seized, but which they expressed a willingness to pay for, were originally built for the protection of the harbors and cities of those States. They could not have been built without the consent and co-operation of the States within whose limits they were erected.

They were, indeed, partnership property; and each of the States was an equal party in the ownership. The Federal Government, strictly speaking, was not a party in this ownership at all, but was only the general agent of the real parties, that is, the several States composing the compact of the Union. These forts were the joint property of all the States; but as they were designed each for the protection of the States where they were located, it was held that such forts necessarily went with the withdrawing States to which they belonged. If South Carolina deprived New York of its share of the ownership in the forts in Charleston harbor, South Carolina also relinquished its share of ownership in the forts in the harbor of New York.

But the seceding States expressed a desire to settle all these matters by a mutual and friendly agreement. They avowed their determination to inflict no wrong upon others, but only to resume the powers they had delegated, and govern themselves without the interference of the States which they honestly believed had broken the compact made by our forefathers. They were neither rebels by law nor by intention. They acted upon what they believed to be their right, and upon what had been the understanding of a very great number of the ablest statesmen and patriots our country has produced – and upon what was the unanimous understanding of the States when they adopted the Constitution. Not a single State would have become a member of the Union had it imagined that the Federal Government would ever attempt to hold them in it by war and bloodshed. Indeed when the States are held together by the bayonet, the government is no longer a *Union,* but a *Despotism.* It ceases to be the government our fathers made, and becomes a tyranny like that of Austria or Russia.

The South, you see then, made no war on the North by separating from us. They simply exercised what they sincerely believed to be their right, and what the ablest statesmen of the North, and the wise founders of our Government, admitted to be such. So far from imagining themselves traitors, they religiously believed themselves patriots.

Nor did the leaders of the party which opened war upon them believe them traitors. These leaders, you have seen, were old disunionists. Some of them had been talking and threatening secession themselves for more than thirty years, as their predecessors had for more than forty years before. It was not love for the Union that caused them to wage the war. It was hatred of the South in some, a foolish, fanatical love of Negroes in others, and still in others a traitorous desire to overthrow the free Government of the United States, and establish a consolidated or single government, after annihilating the sovereignty of the States.

I am speaking of the leaders. The mass of the soldiers were drawn into it, some by patriotic motives, and some without a definite motive of any kind. There was a wild and senseless excitement, which drove the whole community mad. Men did not reason – they raved. The men who attempted to reason were knocked down. This was all a necessary part of the machinery for working up the war. The cunning instigators knew well that if the people were permitted to reason, and to talk dispassionately on the matter, the war fever could not be kept up a single hour. When men know they have a bad cause, they do not permit discussion, if they can help it. So the Black Republican leaders contrived to have every man in the North mobbed who attempted to think and argue on the subject of the war. Men were hurried or driven into the army like sheep into a slaughter-pen. The least intelligent were actually made to believe that the South was making war on the North, when all the time it was the North which was waging war upon the South, as you will see when we come to trace the conflict step by step.

CHAPTER EIGHT
The Policy and Objects of Secession
☆ ☆ ☆ ☆

While very little, if any, difference of opinion existed at the South as to the *right* of secession, there were many people who doubted the *policy* of the movement. Prominent among these was the Hon. Alexander H. Stephens, of Georgia, who advised against the step. It was felt by such men that it was going to place great power in the hands of the Abolition party, who might then set themselves up as in favor of the Union, and use the very prestige and power of the Government, which Southern statesmen had mainly created, to make war upon them. They distrusted the peaceful professions of the Black Republican leaders, who were talking against coercion, and who were announcing themselves as willing "to let the South go."

Alexander H. Stephens

As it has turned out, it would seem that these men were right; for the Abolition party did raise large armies in the name of the Union, actually to overthrow it – to subvert its form of government, and to bring a doom on the Southern people which words cannot describe. However, the overwhelming impulse of the great majority of the Southern people at the time of which we are writing was to get away from the North. They did not wish to be associated any longer with a people the majority of whom could deliberately elect a man President on a platform of avowed hostility to their States. They desired to get away from people who would not keep their compacts.

Yet they wished the North no harm. The debates of the great leaders in Congress at the time of withdrawing prove that they went more in sorrow than in anger. They evinced indeed a great reluctance to go; but they felt that the North had already sundered the political bands made by our forefathers, and that there was nothing left for them but to go, or stay and acquiesce in the overthrow of their Government. They chose to go, declaring that their object was to preserve and perpetuate the sacred principles of liberty and self-government which our forefathers established.

General Robert E. Lee, in a letter written since the war, dated January 6th, 1866, says: "All the South has ever asked or desired is, that the Union founded by our forefathers should be preserved, and that the Government as it was originally organized should be administered in purity and truth." Now the Abolitionists could not say this. They desired the Government, as it was formed, overthrown. General Lee desired the Government to remain just as it was. Mr. Seward said "No, slavery must and shall be abolished." Mr. Lincoln stood on the same platform.

The great and overwhelming object the South had was to preserve to themselves the right of self-government, and thus save themselves from the horrible consequences of amalgamation and social death. They knew from their practical knowledge of the Negro that he belonged to a distinct species of man; that his brain, his bones, his shape, his nerves, in fact that every part of his body was different from the White man's. They knew that he was liable to different diseases from the White man; that he required the care and protection of the superior race. They knew that to equalize the races was simply to follow the fate of Mexico and Central America.

What a splendid country was Mexico while under the control of the White blood of the pure Spanish race! Now what is it, after the White blood has all become mixed and diluted by amalgamation with the Black race? When the Black race held its natural position of subordination to the White race, Mexico was one of the richest and most prosperous countries on the globe; but now it is one of the meanest and most contemptible. The White man's proud and glorious civilization has faded out on the dead plain of amalgamation and Negro equality. The White blood has become so muddy and polluted by admixture with the inferior race, that no lapse of time can ever redeem that population from the utter degradation and uncivilization into which it has fallen. So of all those once rich and flourishing countries to the south of the United States since the abolition of Negro subordination to the White race, they have all fallen back in civilization, and sunken down in a slough of social, political, and moral filth, and wretchedness! It makes the heart sick to contemplate them.

The West India Islands which, under Negro servitude, or when the White man was sole master, were among the richest and most flourishing spots on the globe, now, under Negro equality, are the poorest and most detested sinks of sorrow and pollution that oppress the imagination of man.

To save the most beautiful and productive portion of our country from a similar terrible fate, was the great motive which made the Southern States desire separation from the abolitionized States of the North. To save our country from the terrible scourge of Negro amalgamation and Negro equality, which the Black Republicans are now forcing upon us, was a patriotic and sacred thought in the minds of those who wished no further union with the madmen who were determined to force the shame and horror of Negro equality upon us.

God only can tell what the consequences of this amalgamation policy may be to the cause of liberty and civilization! Unless the people arise and put a stop to the further progress of the disgusting and brutalizing notions of Negro equality, we shall inevitably land at last where Mexico, the Central American States, and the West India Islands have gone already. Negro emancipation and Negro equality are driving us on that fatal shore with alarming rapidity. A mongrel nation, or a nation of mixed races, never yet remained free and prosperous.

The English, Irish, French, Spanish or Germans may amalgamate without detriment, because they are only different families of the same, or the White race; but the Negro being of a different and lower race, the offspring of such a union are *hybrids* or *mongrels,* and are always a weak, degraded, and wretched class of beings – as inferior to the White race as the mule is to the horse.

Such, then, were the points involved in the *policy* and *objects* of secession. If the Northern people could have understood the great wrong they were forcing upon the South, they never would have blamed her for seeking to save herself from the degradation of amalgamation. But they had, unfortunately, been made to believe that it was wicked to hold Negroes as inferiors of White people. They did not understand the horrible sin and crime, disease and death involved in equalizing races. Hence they thought that the South acted "without good cause."

They were made to believe that she resisted Lincoln's election from mere spite, and from a long cherished desire to break up the Union. While the real truth was, that the great mass of the people of the South loved and cherished the Union, and only withdrew from it when they felt themselves not only compelled to do so, but actually driven out by the Abolition party, who came into possession of the Government, threatening to use it to bring upon them and their children the most horrible doom that can possibly be inflicted upon any people.

In the North, where there are but few Negroes, it is difficult to understand this subject, but if our population were one half Blacks, we would very soon begin to comprehend what it meant to give the Negro the same rights as the White man. Every child can see that in such a society only two things are possible. Either one race or the other would be master, or else they would be compelled to fraternize – to mingle – and with that comes all the horrible consequences we have just depicted.

In the light of subsequent events, nearly all will now allow that the South made a mistake when they demanded unconditional separation. True, they had many reasons to lose faith in the

North, and to believe they would stand by no agreements if made. But if they had said all the time, "we stand ready to resume our places in the Union, when you of the North give us plain and distinct pledges and guarantees that you will abide by the Constitution and Union as they were formed," they would have deprived Mr. Lincoln and his party of nine-tenths of their capital. They could not then have set themselves up as "the Union party," while in fact they were the real *disunion* party, and always had been. Nor could they have made such a hue and cry about "the flag," which they had denounced as a "flaunting lie."

Perhaps you never saw the verses on the American flag which the Black Republicans circulated in 1854, just about the time they organized their party. I will give you two of them:

> All hail the flaunting lie
> The stars grow pale and dim,
> The stripes are bloody scars –
> A lie the vaunting hymn.
>
> Tear down the flaunting lie,
> Half-mast the starry flag,
> Insult no sunny sky
> With hate's polluted rag.

Now it does not look reasonable that a political party which endorsed such poetry could have been at all sincere in love for the American flag. They simply put forth the cry of "the Union," and "the flag," to get the war started. After which they believed they could use it to accomplish their *real* purposes, which were the overthrow of our form of government, and its revolution from a White man's government to that of a *mongrel* nation, in which Negroes should have the same rights as White people.

This is now plainly apparent, if it never was before; and however mistaken the South may have been as to the *means* used to avert this calamity, no one not deluded with Negro equality will deny that they were justified in taking any step which would save them and their children from such horrible consequences.

CHAPTER NINE
The Beginning of Secession

The first State which seceded, after the election of Mr. Lincoln, was South Carolina. On the 20th day of December, 1860, that State formally dissolved its connection with the Union, by a unanimous vote of a convention of the State.

This act produced great excitement and alarm among the true friends of the Union in the whole North. But by the leaders of the Black Republican party, or the party which elected Mr. Lincoln, it was received either with cold indifference, or with the too evident signs of suppressed delight.

President Buchanan promptly sent a message to Congress, recommending such measures as he hoped would stay the further progress of secession. But a very large majority of the members were Black Republicans, and they refused to take any notice of his recommendations, or to suggest any measures of their own to prevent the Union from going to pieces.

Indeed, President Buchanan, in his annual message, which had been transmitted to Congress eighteen days before South Carolina seceded, had anticipated the event, and had elaborately discussed the proper remedies as well as the powers of the Federal Government to deal with a seceding State. Referring to these events since they transpired, Mr. Buchanan says:

> To preserve the Union was my supreme object. I was well aware that our wisest statesmen had often warned their countrymen in the most solemn terms, that our institutions could not be preserved by force, and could only endure whilst concord

of feeling and a proper respect by one section for the rights of another should be maintained.

This conclusion is sustained by President Madison, who is called "the father of the Constitution," who said in the convention which made the Constitution: "Any government for the United States, formed upon the supposed practicability of using *force* against the unconstitutional proceedings of the States, would prove visionary and fallacious." So President Jackson said in his farewell address to the people of the United States: "The Constitution cannot be maintained, nor the Union preserved, in opposition to public feeling, by the mere exertion of the coercive powers confided to the General Government."

Such, I could show you had I space, has been the opinion of all the greatest and wisest statesmen of our country ever since the foundation of our Government. President Buchanan manifested a sincere desire to impress upon Congress what were the constitutional and proper means to be applied to prevent the spread of secession. All remedies which the Constitution allowed, he was anxious for Congress to apply promptly in order to save the Union. He was also anxious to impress upon Congress the wrong of attempting unconstitutional measures.

The point was clearly stated in his message in the following language:

> The question fairly stated is, has the Constitution delegated to Congress the power to coerce a State into submission which is attempting to withdraw, or has actually withdrawn from the Confederacy? If answered in the affirmative, it must be on the principle that the power has been conferred on Congress to make war against a State. After much serious reflection, I have arrived at the conclusion that no such power has been delegated to Congress, or to any other department of the Federal Government. It is manifest upon an inspection of the Constitution, that this is not among the specific and enumerated powers granted to Congress. So far from this power having been delegated to Congress, it was expressly refused by the convention which framed the Constitution.

A few days after the delivery of this annual message, President Johnson, then a member of the United States Senate, while debating with the Black Republicans, said:

> I do not believe the Federal Government has the power to coerce a State; for by the eleventh amendment to the Constitution of the United States, it is expressly provided, that you cannot even put one of the States of this Confederacy before one of the courts of the country as a party.

The Attorney-General of the United States had just before given an opinion, marked with great ability and research, to the same effect. No Black Republican member of either branch of Congress attempted to combat these conclusions. But no arguments, no appeal to the solemn sanctions of the Constitution, could arouse a spark of patriotism in the bosoms of the Abolition party. Constitutional remedies that would have prevented secession they despised. One fact there is which will rise up in judgment to condemn the Black Republican party forever. They could have preserved the Union without the loss of a drop of blood by just pledging themselves to administer the Government as it had been administered by all of Mr. Lincoln's predecessors. All the South asked was *equality in the Union* – that the Northern States should not take away their rights.

In the last speech ever made in the Senate by Jefferson Davis, on December 6th, 1860, he plead for the Union in the following earnest language:

> The Union of these States forms, in my judgment, the best government instituted among men. It is only necessary to carry it out in the spirit in which it was formed. Our fathers made a Union of friendly States. Now hostility has been substituted for fraternity. I call on men who have hearts, and who love the Union, to look the danger in the face. This Union is dear to me as a Union of fraternal States. *Long have I offered propositions for equality in the Union. Not a single Republican has voted for them.* We have in vain endeavored to secure tranquillity, and obtain respect for the rights to which we are entitled. As a necessity, *not a choice,* we have resorted to the remedy of sep-

aration. We have never asked for *concessions;* what we wanted was justice.

It was very evident, however, soon after the meeting of Congress, in December, 1860, that the Black Republican party were determined to do nothing. Their plan was to let things drift until Mr. Lincoln should come in on the 4th of March, 1861, and keep their policy, whatever it was, a profound secret. Seeing no chance for guarantees against the amalgamation policy, five other States, in January, 1861, followed the example of South Carolina, viz.: Mississippi, January 9th; Alabama, January 11th; Florida, January 11th; Georgia, January 19th; and Louisiana, January 25th. Those were all the States that seceded previous to the inauguration of Mr. Lincoln. The other States remained, hoping against hope, that some plan of adjustment would yet be agreed upon.

CHAPTER TEN
Efforts of the Democracy to Save the Union

While the Black Republican party was doing its utmost to prevent any pacific measure, or compromise, which should arrest the progress of secession, the Democratic party exerted every power to save the Union, and restore confidence and peace to the country. Among the plans brought before Congress for this patriotic purpose was a set of resolutions introduced by the venerable Senator Crittenden, of Kentucky. These resolutions are known as "The Crittenden Compromise." If passed by Congress, they would have restored instant peace and stopped secession. And their terms were a perfectly fair proposition for a final settlement of the whole difficulty.

If any section was to make a sacrifice it was the South, by the adoption of this Crittenden Compromise. It proposed, in effect, to give up to the North more than three quarters of all the territorial domain belonging to the United States, when, in point of law and justice, the South had an equal right with the North in all these territories. But the South offered to make this sacrifice of so much of her rights for the sake of peace, and for the sake of the Union.

Mr. Crittenden, in presenting his compromise, said:

> The sacrifice to be made for the preservation of the Union is comparatively worthless. Peace and harmony, and union in a great nation were never purchased at so cheap a rate as we now have it in our power to do. It is a scruple only, a scruple of as little value as a barleycorn, that stands between us and peace

and reconciliation and Union. And we stand here pausing and hesitating about that little atom which is to be sacrificed.

But in vain did this patriotic Senator from the South plead with the Black Republican party to take this little step to save the Union. Senator Hale, of New Hampshire, declared, "this controversy will not be settled here." He knew that his party were determined to have war. And this was further proved by the fact, that while every Democratic member voted for the Crittenden peace propositions, every Black Republican member voted against them.

But the Democrats, and the Southern members of Congress, did not give up the effort to save the Union even then. Mr. Clemens, of Virginia, introduced a resolution in the House of Representatives to submit the Crittenden peace resolutions to the people of the United States. This produced a great flutter and alarm among the Black Republicans. They knew that if the people were allowed to vote on the question, the resolutions would be adopted. So they promptly voted down the proposition to let the people of the United States decide the question for themselves. Here again the Democrats voted to submit the matter to the people, and every Black Republican voted against it.

But even this was not all the Democrats did to save the Union. Senator Douglas, after the Crittenden plan had been voted down, introduced another proposition of his own, which was also voted down by the war-wishing Black Republicans. Senator Douglas, on the defeat of his proposition, said:

> If you of the Republican side are not willing to accept this, nor the proposition of the Senator from Kentucky, Mr. Crittenden, pray tell us what you are willing to do? I address the inquiry to the Republicans alone, for the reason that in the Committee of Thirteen, a few days ago, every member from the South, including those from the Cotton States [Messrs. Toombs and Davis] expressed their readiness to accept the proposition of my venerable friend from Kentucky, as a *final settlement* of the controversy, if tendered and sustained by the Republican members. Hence the *sole responsibility* of our disagreement, and the *only* difficulty in the way of an amicable adjustment, is *with*

the Republican party.

When all these measures for peace and union had failed, Senator Douglas pointed to the side of the Senate Chamber where the Black Republicans had their seats, and exclaimed with great energy, "You want war." And so they did. Every act shows that they wanted war. They meant to force war upon the South. But you have not yet heard of all the Democratic party did to save the Union, and to prevent all the bloody horrors of war.

When every effort to induce the Abolition members of Congress to accept some terms of peace had failed, the noble old State of Virginia came forward with a proposition to call a convention of one or more commissioners from each State, to see if they could not hit upon some plan whereby the Union could be preserved. This proposition was received like a firebrand by the Black Republicans. But seven of the Southern States immediately sent their peace commissioners to Washington, and there was such a clamor from the people throughout the North for peace, that the Abolition leaders were obliged to consent that the Northern States should be represented in this peace conference. But they diligently set themselves to work to prevent any men who really wanted peace from being sent to the conference.

Carl Schurz, a notorious agitator and disunionist, from Wisconsin, telegraphed to the Governor of that State: "Appoint commissioners to Washington conference – myself one – to strengthen our side." By *"our side,"* he meant those who were opposed to any peace measures to save the country from war, and preserve the Union. Senator Chandler, of Michigan, wrote a letter to the Governor of his State, to the same effect, in which he profanely declared, that, "Without a little blood-letting, this Union would not, in his estimation, be worth a curse."

The "Republicans" wanted "a little blood-letting," in order to make as wide as possible the gulf between the North and the South. This Peace Conference, therefore, was a failure, because the Abolitionists were determined there should be no peace. I have already shown you that a portion of these traitors were moved to this course because of a blind and fanatical sympathy for Negroes, while others were impelled by a desire to overthrow this Union of our fathers, and to establish one great despotic government on its ruins.

All efforts of the Democrats to make peace were, therefore, in vain. They left no stone unturned to save our country from the horrors of bloodshed and war, and never gave up these efforts until they saw that nothing but "blood-letting" would satisfy the revolutionary temper of the Black Republican party. And they did not give up even then, but kept on diligently trying to stay the black tide of fanaticism and death, even after the war had begun.

CHAPTER ELEVEN
The Formation of the New Confederacy

While the Black Republican members of both Houses of Congress were thus closing up every avenue to peace, six more of the Cotton States, as I have stated in a former chapter, followed South Carolina, and passed acts of secession. On the 4th day of February, 1861, these States assembled, by their delegates, at Montgomery, Alabama, for the purpose of organizing a provisional government. A provisional government is a temporary organization, or one that is not intended to be permanent. Of this provisional government Jefferson Davis was unanimously elected President, and Alexander H. Stephens, Vice-President. They adopted a new Constitution, which was simply the old Constitution of the United States altered essentially only in such parts as had been perverted and misinterpreted by the Abolitionists. And the main point was in relation to the *status* of the Negro. In the Confederate Constitution his inferior position was distinctly recognized, so that the Abolitionists could no longer declare that the Government in-

Jefferson Davis

tended to include him in the ranks of citizenship. And this was, after all, the turning point of the whole issue between the North, as represented by Lincoln and his party, and the South. The Abolitionists desired to make the Negro a citizen. The South said, "No, this is a White man's government. It was made so by our forefathers, and we will not submit to its overthrow."

President Davis, in delivering his address on taking his seat as Provisional President, declared distinctly that the design was not to make any change in the system of government as originally established. In this speech he clearly showed that he had no desire or expectation that the separation between these States would be permanent – for he referred to the fact that, as their new Constitution was substantially the old one, freed of all chances for sectional quarrels, there was nothing to prevent all the States which wished for permanent rest and peace, from joining them.

No doubt the wish and the belief was that all the States which preferred a real Union – just such a Union as our fathers made – to one perpetually vexed and torn by a degrading conflict about Negroes, would ultimately unite their fortunes with the new organization. While the temper of the Abolitionists, or the Black Republicans, of the North was savage, fiery, and full of blood, that of the Southern leaders was calm and dignified. The record I have already presented of the conflict between the two sections is proof of this, notwithstanding the many falsehoods told to the contrary.

In the last speech Mr. Davis delivered in the Senate of the United States, he said, with a mildness and dignity of voice and manner truly ennobling:

> But we have proclaimed our independence. This is done with no hostility or desire to injure any section of the country, nor even for our pecuniary benefit, but solely from the high and solid motives of defending and protecting the rights we inherited, and transmitting them unshorn to our posterity. I know that I feel no hostility to you, Senators here, and am sure that there is not one of you, whatever may have been the sharp discussion between us, to whom I cannot now say, in the presence of my God,

I wish you well. And such is the feeling, I am sure, the people I represent have toward those you represent. I therefore feel I but express their desire when I say I hope, and they hope, for those peaceful relations with you (though we must part) that may be mutually beneficial to us in the future.

There will be peace if you so will it; and you may bring disaster upon the whole country if you thus will have it. And if you will have it thus we invoke the God of our fathers, who delivered them from the paw of the lion, to protect us from the ravages of the bear; and thus putting our trust in God, and our own firm hearts and strong arms, we will vindicate and defend the rights we claim. In the course of my long career I have met with a great variety of men here, and there have been points of collision between us. Whatever of offence I have given which has not been redressed, I am willing to say to Senators in this hour of parting, I offer you my apology for anything I may have done; and I go thus released from obligation, remembering no injury I have received, and having discharged what I deem the duty of a man, offer the only reparation in my power for any injury I have ever inflicted.

This is not the language of a conspirator or a traitor! On the contrary, is it not rather the language of one who regretfully takes a step which he feels that duty compels him to take? And with what temper he was answered from the Black Republican side of Congress, let the brutal language of Senator Chandler of Michigan, which we have quoted in a previous chapter, answer.

After the Cotton States had withdrawn and formed the new Confederacy, they expressed their wish and determination to take no step that should provoke hostilities, except what was absolutely necessary for their own safety and preservation. The forts, arsenals, etc., situated within the limits of the several retiring States, necessarily went with the States, and, in reality, belonged to the States as their own necessary defences. It is true they were built with the joint property of all the States, as I have shown in a former chapter, but then they were built for the benefit of the *several States in which they were located,* and not for the aggrandizement and power of the Federal Government. Each State held a certain jurisdiction over all the forts, arsenals, post-offices, etc., situated within its own limits.

That is, the State of South Carolina has a certain jurisdiction over Fort Sumter, situated in its harbor at Charleston, but it has no jurisdiction over Fort Warren, located in the harbor of Boston. And the State of Massachusetts has a certain jurisdiction over Fort Warren, but has none whatever over Fort Sumter, though the money of Massachusetts helped build Fort Sumter, as the money of South Carolina helped build Fort Warren. It is a part of the compact of Union between the several States that each State shall have these defences provided from the general fund; while, at the same time, each State retains a certain jurisdiction over all such United States works as are located within its boundaries.

The United States has no right to deprive any State of its jurisdiction over such works. To illustrate: when the State of New York ceded to the United States the spot on which Fort Hamilton, now called Fort Lafayette, is built, it reserved to itself a certain jurisdiction over the fort when built, and expressly provided that should the fort ever be used for any purpose other than that for which the State had ceded the spot, the whole should revert again to the State of New York. That is, if the Federal Government should ever attempt to use the fort for any other purpose than that of the defence and protection of the city and harbor of New York, for which it was built, the Federal Government would lose all title to it, and the whole become the lawful property of the State. When the Federal Government converted that fort into a Bastile, under the administration of Mr. Lincoln, it undoubtedly forfeited all title to the property, had the State of New York strictly insisted upon its rights.

These considerations show you in what light the seceding States regarded the forts situated in their harbors. You have been told by the Black Republicans that those States, when they went out, "stole all our forts," etc.; but the above facts prove that "theft" is by no means a just or proper word to apply to their action in this respect. Every State, at all times, and under all circumstances, has an undoubted right to take any steps which are immediately necessary to protect the lives and property of its people, from whatever quarter the danger may come. Any State has just as much right to protect itself from the threatened illegal violence of the Federal Government as it has to protect itself from the invasion of Russia, or any other power. Its right to exist as a State carries with it the right to protect and defend that existence. The Federal Government was formed by the States for the purpose of giving greater protection and security to themselves; and whenever it is certain that the object for which that government was formed is sacrificed, and, instead of being a protection, becomes an oppression and a danger, it is the right and the duty of every State thus threatened to do the best thing it can for its own safety.

Suppose the Southern States had elected a strictly sectional President on a programme of bloody hostility to us here in the North – on a programme of threats to steal our property, and murder our men, women, and children, if necessary, in doing it – should we not have had the undoubted right to take any step which we might think necessary for our protection? If the South believed that the barbarous and terrible threats of the Helper Book, and of the leaders of the Black Republicans, were to be visited upon them in the Lincoln Administration, can we blame them for attempting to provide against such a horrible outrage? Does any good man question their right to put forth all the powers God had given them for self-protection? Acting under this belief, were they to be regarded as traitors and rebels?

Almost everybody at the North said, before the beginning of the war, if Mr. Lincoln and his party did really intend to do what the South declared they did, then they would be justified in any course they saw fit to pursue. It is now seen that they have done just what the Southern leaders predicted they would.

CHAPTER TWELVE
Mr. Lincoln's Journey to Washington and Inauguration

While the Confederate Government was thus being peacefully organized in the South, matters in the North were in a state of doubt and uncertainty. No one knew what the policy of the new President was to be further than they could gather it from the platform and principles of the party upon which he was elected. I have explained what interpretation the South placed upon these, and every effort was made by patriotic and conservative men to induce Mr. Lincoln to make an avowal to quiet the country, and assure the Southern States that he would not use the Federal Government to destroy their domestic institutions. But all such efforts were in vain. Mr. Lincoln maintained an ominous silence up to the time of his departure from his home at Springfield, Illinois, for Washington.

But when he commenced his journey to Washington, he made such an exhibition of himself, by speeches all the way along, as to leave no doubt upon the minds of the Southern leaders that the Abolitionists had in him a convenient tool for all the villainy they had threatened to carry out. His progress to the capital of the United States was more like that of a harlequin than the President of a great country. While the country was agonized to its very heart, he amused the crowd which came out to greet him on his way with jokes, and often with low stories. He even made jests that were at once surprising and disgusting to the respectable portion of his own party. To a young man who, in New York city, offered to measure height with him, he replied, "No, I have not time now to measure with you, but if you will bring on your sister I will kiss her." The whole style and manner of the man was that of a low joker, rather than that of a statesman and patriot. When publicly questioned as to what he thought would be the result of secession, he jocosely replied, "O, I guess, nobody is hurt."

In no one of his speeches, however, did Mr. Lincoln give the slightest indication of retracting any threat which his party had made. When he reached Philadelphia, however, he made a speech which evidently showed that he was determined to carry out the idea of "Negro freedom" let what would happen. Making use again, as he often did, of Mr. Jefferson's phrase, "all men are created equal," he pointed to Independence Hall, where it was first enunciated, and declared, that "he would rather be assassinated on the spot than to give it up."

Abraham Lincoln

Now, when we remember that he used these great words as referring to Negroes, and not as Mr. Jefferson did, as applied to White men, we then see what a terrible significance there was in this speech. Mr. Lincoln meant to say, "I will be assassinated before I will give up my effort to carry out my idea that Negroes are equal to White men." It was as much as to say, "I will change, I will revolutionize this Government from a White man's government to a mongrel government, in which Negroes shall be placed upon equality with White men." At the time he made this remark, many people did not seem to see the true meaning of it, but they have since learned it by sore experience.

At Philadelphia a singular and ludicrous incident occurred. Some one started the report, that when Mr. Lincoln passed through Baltimore, he would be killed; that a conspiracy existed in that city to take his life. Instead of boldly meeting the danger, if any existed, as a brave man and a great man would have done, who had been elected President of such a country, Mr. Lincoln appears to have got greatly frightened, and instead of going directly to Washington, ran away from his family, and dodged through Baltimore in disguise. As there never was any reliable evidence furnished the public of the alleged designs upon Mr. Lincoln's life, it is generally believed that the story was concocted to excite the North against the South, and pave the way for war. Mr. Lincoln's inauguration was a singular spectacle. For the first time in our history had any President been afraid to meet the people face to face. In passing along Pennsylvania Avenue, he was hid from view in a hollow square of cavalry, three or four deep. Troops were posted all over the city, and sharp-shooters were stationed on the tops of the houses. He delivered his inaugural address surrounded by rows of glittering bayonets.

There was nothing in it to reassure the Southern mind or give it the slightest reason to hope for safety. It contained a few cheap words of affected fairness, but the heart of it was full of the temper and doctrines of the Abolition party. He insinuated right in the face of the venerable Chief-Justice Taney, that he would not be governed in his Administration by the construction of the Constitution as had been laid down by the Supreme Court in the celebrated *Dred Scott* case, viz., that Negroes were not citizens. This was, in effect, reaffirming the Helper declaration of war on the South, and so indeed her leading men regarded it.

The inaugural address of Mr. Lincoln, together with the selection of his Cabinet, now banished all hopes of peace. The worst and most violent Abolitionists were appointed by him to office. William H. Seward, who had endorsed the Helper book, declaring it a work of "great merit," was made Secretary of State. Salmon P. Chase, of Ohio, was made Secretary of the Treasury. Cassius M. Clay, another endorser of the Helper book, was sent minister to Russia. Joshua B. Giddings was sent to Canada. This man had declared that "he wished to live to see the day when bayonets would be placed in the hands of Southern Negroes."

These are merely samples of Mr. Lincoln's appointments. They observed very plainly his spirit and temper, and the States that had hesitated to secede now began to take steps in that direction.

The statesmen of Virginia had been decidedly opposed to seceding, even after several of the Cotton States had withdrawn. Senator Hunter of Virginia said: "If the Southern States can obtain guarantees which will secure their rights in the Union, it is all we ask." Governor Letcher, who was then Governor of that State, said: "If the North will respect and uphold the rights of the States, the Union will be perpetual." Ex-Governor Morehead of Kentucky, came to Washington for a personal interview with Mr. Lincoln, in hopes that he could induce him to make some public declaration to the effect that the terrible things threatened in the Helper book, and in all the principal speeches of the Abolition campaign, should not be carried out. But this patriotic visit, like many other similar visits from distinguished Southern statesmen, was in vain. Mr. Lincoln would give no assurance – no hope. Governor Morehead is a refined and accomplished gentleman, and the vulgar manner in which he was received by Mr. Lincoln, both filled him with disgust and drove from his bosom the last lingering hope that the country had anything but evil to expect from such a man.

Governor Morehead relates an incident that goes to show what sort of a man Mr. Lincoln was. He said that while conversing with him, Mr. Lincoln sat with his shoe off, holding his toes in his hand, and bending them backwards and forwards in an awkward manner. Such an exhibition of low manners was, perhaps, never before known in a President. Shortly after this Mr. Lincoln had Governor Morehead arrested, and locked up for a long time in Fort Lafayette at New York, without any cause whatever.

Mr. Lincoln had never been much in good society. While he was in Congress, his habit of telling low stories pretty effectually banished him from the company of refined people. In his debate with Senator Douglas, he made this remarkable confession himself: "I am not a gentleman, and never expect to be."

The Hon. George Lunt, of Boston, in his excellent work *The Origin of the Late War,* gives the following portrait of Mr.

Lincoln, intellectually:

> The new President was a person of scarcely more than ordinary natural powers, with a mind neither cultivated by education, nor enlarged by experience in public affairs. He was thus incapable of any wide range of thought, or, in fact, of obtaining any broad grasp of ideas. His thoughts ran in narrow channels.

And the author might have added, "in low channels."

His messages and proclamations were shocking specimens of bad sense and bad grammar. But I think that Mr. Lincoln must, after all, have possessed a good deal of what is called mother wit. Without that it seems impossible to account for his having risen from his extremely low origin to the posts he several times filled. He had the misfortune not to know who his father was; and his mother, alas, was a person to reflect no honor upon her child. Launched into this world as an outcast, and started on the road of being without parental care, and without the advantages of even a common school education, he certainly was entitled to great credit for gaining even the limited mental culture which he possessed. Running away from his wretched home at the early age of nine years, to escape the brutal treatment of the man who had married his mother, and forced to get his bread by working on a flat boat on the Mississippi River, he unfortunately contracted that fondness for low society and for vulgar jests and stories, which he ought to have known were out of place in the position he now occupied.

We cannot wonder that a gentleman of Governor Morehead's refinement should have gone out from that exhibition of toes in Mr. Lincoln's parlor with a mind fully impressed with the unwelcome conviction that the Southern people had little to hope from the honor and justice of the incoming administration.

CHAPTER THIRTEEN
"The First Gun of Sumter"

Immediately after the inauguration of Mr. Lincoln, the Confederate Government appointed Commissioners to proceed to Washington for the purpose of negotiating for a peaceable settlement of all matters connected with the forts and other United States property situated within the seceded States. Arriving in Washington, these Commissioners addressed a note to Mr. Seward, Secretary of State, explaining the purposes of their embassy, and expressing in the most respectful terms the strong desire for an amicable and just understanding between the two sections. Mr. Seward answered in language well calculated to deceive as to the belligerent intentions of the Administration, that at that moment it would be impossible to receive these Commissioners in an official capacity, but left upon their minds the impression that some amicable adjustment would ultimately be entered into.

And there these Commissioners remained deceived, from week to week, by verbal assurances, which all turned out to be cheats and delusions. For in the end, it was proved that all the time Mr. Seward and Mr. Lincoln were holding these Southern Commissioners contented in Washington, they were secretly planning and organizing one of the largest naval war fleets to attack Fort Sumter and Charleston that is known to modern history. While Mr. Seward was blandly exhorting these Commissioners that they should be patient and trustful, he was preparing to strike a fatal and deadly blow, and lay the Southern cities in ashes. He promised these Commissioners that no demonstration should be made upon Fort Sumter; and it was cunningly given out in the Administration papers that the fort was about to be evacuated by the Federal troops.

This was all a part of the general game of deception. For, even while these Commissioners were trusting that the arrangements entered into between themselves and Mr. Lincoln and Mr. Seward, to the effect that the Federal troops in Fort Sumter should have access to the markets of Charleston for provisions, and that no attempt to reinforce the garrison should be made, the most stupendous preparations to reinforce and to make war, were secretly progressing. Fortunately for the honor of the Southern Commissioners, Judge Campbell, of the Supreme Court of the United States, was the agent through whom this friendly verbal treaty had been made. And after the mask fell from the faces of Mr. Lincoln and Mr. Seward, Judge Campbell wrote to the latter, fully accusing him of his whole course of fraud and deception in the matter. To those grave charges Mr. Seward has never dared to attempt an answer to this day. Judge Campbell read to Mr. Seward a letter which he had written to President Davis, detailing the agreement entered into between Mr. Lincoln and the Southern Commissioners; and Mr. Seward, pointing to the letter, said, "Before that letter reaches its destination, Fort Sumter will be evacuated." At that very moment he was making the most gigantic preparation not to evacuate it. When some days had elapsed, and the fort was not evacuated, Judge Campbell became uneasy as to the good faith of Mr. Seward in all his promises, and wrote him a letter to that effect, to which Mr. Seward telegraphed this laconic answer: "Faith as to Sumter fully kept – wait and see." Judge Campbell and the people of Charleston had only to wait six short days, and they did "see" – the largest war fleet threatening the destruction of their city that had ever traversed the waters of this continent before.

By the law of nations the appearance of such a fleet as this, under the circumstances, was *a declaration of war*. It needs not the firing of a gun to make war. The putting of the first gun into a war ship, with the design of using it against a city, or a

State, is *a declaration of war* against that city or State. This fact was stated by the leading journals of Europe in commenting upon these events at the time they occurred. It was correctly held by them that the war was opened not by the South in firing upon Fort Sumter, but was fully begun by the Abolitionists of the North in the very act of fitting out that vast war fleet. To allow Mr. Lincoln's troops to reinforce Fort Sumter would have been to put the fate of the city of Charleston, with all its priceless treasure of life and property, at the mercy of the men in power at Washington, who had just proved that they were incapable of showing the least respect to their own most solemnly uttered promises.

The preventing of the reinforcement of the fort was held to be a necessary act of self-preservation. Under the circumstances, it was not, properly speaking, an act of *aggression,* but of *self-defense.* The first gun at Fort Sumter was not, then, in a legal point of view, the beginning of the war. It was morally begun by the Abolitionists more than thirty years ago. It was fully organized by the formation of the Black Republican party, and the election of Lincoln on the platform of the Helper Book. And it was formally opened and declared by the sailing of the great war fleet against Charleston. The "first gun" of the war was the first gun put into that war fleet. The "first gun" at Sumter was only the first gun of self-defense. This is the simple fact of the case stripped of all the nonsensical verbiage with which it has been surrounded by the Abolitionists.

General Beauregard, in order to prevent Fort Sumter from being reinforced by Abolition soldiers, opened fire upon it on the morning of the 12th day of April, 1861, at day-break. The firing was continued without intermission for twelve hours; the fort under the command of Major Anderson returning the fire constantly all that. At dark the firing from the fort almost stopped, but it was kept up by General Beauregard at intervals during the whole night. At seven o'clock in the morning, however, the fort resumed its fire; but shortly afterwards it was seen that it was on fire, and Major Anderson was compelled to run up a signal flag of distress. General Beauregard immediately sent a boat to Major

Anderson, offering to assist in putting out the fire, but before it had time to reach the fort, Major Anderson hoisted the flag of truce.

This was the whole of the famous bombardment of Fort Sumter. Not a man was killed on either side. When Major Anderson surrendered his sword, General Beauregard instantly returned it to him, and permitted him on leaving the fort to salute the United States flag with fifty guns. In doing this, however, two of his guns burst and killed four men.

It is a remarkable fact, that during the whole time of the bombardment of Fort Sumter, Mr. Lincoln's war-fleet, embracing two or three of the most powerful United States sloops-of-war, lay in sight of all that was passing, without offering to fire a gun or to render the least assistance to the fort. The real object of all that warlike display was to produce a battle – to force upon the South the necessity of "firing upon the flag," as they called it. Mr. Lincoln and Mr. Seward had calculated rightly upon the use they could make of such an event in the grand scheme of raising an immense army.

The very night on which the news of the bombardment of Fort Sumter came, Mr. Lincoln was particularly cheerful, and gave a reception at the White House, at which he displayed more than his usual vivacity. Two days after he issued his first war proclamation. It was the occasion of all others that suited him and his party. Without some such event as the bombardment of Fort Sumter, it was impossible for him to raise a respectable army to effect the grand scheme of Abolition. The news of that bombardment was therefore received with delight by the whole Abolition party. Those who had been praying for such a thing rubbed their hands for joy, exclaiming, "Now we have got 'em! now we can make an end of slavery!"

Then commenced the business of "working up the Northern mind," as they called it. Then they instantly started the "flag mania." By a concert of action the cry was everywhere shouted forth, "the flag has been fired upon!" Those who for years and years had denounced the flag of our country as "a flaunting lie," and "a polluted rag," ran out a flag from their window, or went into the streets to mob every house which had not a flag out. Men who saw and dared to smile at the bold and impudent hypocrisy of all this sort of demonstration, were knocked down by the bullies whom the Black Republicans had engaged to perambulate the streets for this purpose. In the beginning of this sort of display the whole was a piece of sheer hypocrisy on the part of the leaders of Abolitionism. But gradually the thing grew into an absolute mania, and swept over the North like a hurricane.

Many years ago, in the early history of New England, what is now known as the *witchcraft mania* stained that section of our country with innocent blood. Hundreds who had always borne a good character believed themselves bewitched. Respectable men and women testified under oath that they had seen certain old women riding broomsticks a mile high in the air. These old women were arrested and tried and hanged as witches. The most remarkable part is, that many of the accused admitted themselves to be witches, and died on the gallows confessing that they were witches and that they had ridden on broomsticks through the air.

All this monstrous delusion began, in the first place, by the imposture of a few bad people, but it went on until the thing grew to be a mania, infecting the whole community with a belief in witchcraft; and it was not until many innocent persons had suffered death that it could be stopped. Now, that was a case where a whole community became insane on the subject of witchcraft. The ministers of the Gospel were among the most deluded victims of the insanity, and were the most zealous advocates for the hanging of all who were accused of witchcraft. But the mania at last passed off, and all who had been engaged in the matter were ashamed of the part they had borne in the fatal business. Perpetual infamy attaches to the memory of those days.

Our war excitement was not less a mania than that of witchcraft. Started, in the first place, and worked by a thousand cunning tricks of bad people, and of Abolitionists who were bent upon the insane idea of making Negroes the equal of White people, it was driven on until hundreds of thousands who had really no sympathy with the abominable objects of the war, were swept into its bloody current. Hundreds of thousands of honest soldiers who, in their own hearts, firmly believed that the Negro was best off in "slavery," enlisted and risked their own lives in fighting to emancipate him.

Two-thirds of all our soldiers abhorred the idea of *Negro equality,* even while they were fighting for it. Had they been allowed to follow the bent of their own reason and their own sympathies, they would a thousand times sooner have fought to keep him in his natural place of subordination than to elevate him to an equality with themselves. It was only through a great excitement, amounting to a *mania,* and through the most stupendous deception, that they were drawn into the business of fighting for the sole benefit of *Sambo.*

As I have shown you in former chapters, the cry for the "flag," and for the "Union," was all an hypocrisy and a cheat on the part of the Black Republicans. They had been long known as enemies of the Union, and as despisers of the flag of our country.

And it was a cunning trick, precisely worthy of Mr. Seward and Mr. Lincoln, to cause the bombardment of Fort Sumter in order to "fire up the Northern heart," as they called it. The sole design of the whole thing was to "fire up the Northern heart" to fight the guilty battle of Abolitionism. The war was gotten up with as much trick and skill in management as a showman uses to get the populace to visit his menagerie. Our whole country was placarded all over with war posters of all colors and sizes. Drums were beating and bands playing at every corner of the streets. Nine-tenths of all the ministers of the Gospel were praying and preaching to the horrible din of the war-music, and the profane eloquence of slaughter.

There was little chance for any man to exercise his reason, and if he attempted such a thing he was knocked down and sometimes murdered. If an editor ventured to appeal to the Constitution, his office was either destroyed by the mob, or his paper suspended by "the order of the Government." The moment the war opened for the emancipation of the Negroes, the liberty of the White man was suspended.

The historian of these shameful and criminal events needs

no other proof that the managers of the war knew that they were perpetrating a great crime than the fact that they refused to allow any man to reason or speak in opposition to their action. The cause of truth and justice always flourishes most with all the reasoning that argument and controversy can give it. Whenever men attempt to suppress argument and free speech, we may be sure that they know their cause to be a bad one.

CHAPTER FOURTEEN
Mr. Lincoln's First Call For Troops

So far as the "firing on Fort Sumter" had gone in the way of getting up an excitement in the North, Mr. Lincoln's plans for inaugurating a great Abolition war had succeeded to his satisfaction. But there was a great legal difficulty in his way. The Constitution gave him no power to raise a volunteer army for the purpose of fighting any of the sovereign States of this Union. When in the Convention which framed the Constitution a proposition was made to give the Federal Government power to use military force against a non-complying State, it was unanimously voted down, and no such power was ever given to the Federal Government in the Constitution.

Mr. Lincoln knew this very well, and after he had made up his mind to call for 75,000 men to fight the Southern States, he was at a loss to find even the shadow of a legal excuse for such a call. But usurpers have rarely waited long without inventing some excuse for any action they wished to perform. Mr. Lincoln did not wait long to find an excuse for his extraordinary call for an army to fight the States. He was not quite shameless enough to pretend that the Constitution gave him any power to make such a call, but he hunted up an old act of Congress passed in 1795, to enable the Federal Government to assist the State of Pennsylvania in putting down what is known as the "whisky rebellion" in that State.

But unfortunately for Mr. Lincoln, that act of 1795 only provided for calling forth the militia to suppress an insurrection against a State government, and made no provision that can even be used as an excuse for calling forth an army to assist in suppressing an opposition to the Government of the United States, or in plain words, to enable the Federal Government to make war against a State government.

President Buchanan understood the import of that old act of 1795 perfectly, and he said:

> Under the act of 1795, the President is precluded from acting even upon his own personal and absolute knowledge of the existence of such an insurrection. Before he can call forth the militia for its suppression, he must first be applied to for this purpose by the appropriate State authorities, in the manner prescribed by the Constitution.

Mr. Lincoln's call for troops based on this old act, therefore, was not only illegal, but it was supremely ridiculous. We are not to suppose that he was really so ignorant as to imagine that the act justified the call for troops to operate against the governments of States, which was passed for the sole purpose of assisting States to put down insurrections against their own government. The very fact that the act does not permit the President to send troops into a State to assist in putting down an insurrection which he may know to exist, until called upon by the authorities of the State, settles the question forever as to the illegal and criminal use which Mr. Lincoln made of it.

His call for troops to resist the acts of State Legislatures and Conventions of the people of the States was, therefore, no more justified by the act of 1795, than old John Brown's invasion of the State of Virginia was justified by that act.

Mr. Lincoln's first call for 75,000 troops was received with a shout of joy by all the old enemies of the Union as our fathers made it in the North. With the most indecent haste they jumped to begin the slaughter. It was discovered that the State of Massachusetts had been quietly preparing for war, even before the election of Mr. Lincoln. Indeed the "Republican" party, during the Lincoln presidential campaign, was a military organization. The infinite number of "Wide-awake" clubs were simply so many military companies. They had military drills in their secret lodge-rooms, were all uniformed alike with a sort of military cape and cloak in their public parades, and had their general officers, captains, lieutenants, etc.

In fact, the Black Republican party, or at least that portion of it which did all the work of the presidential campaign, was a military organization. In case of Mr. Lincoln's election they were determined to have war. Some, as they declared, "to make an end of slavery." Others, to overthrow the sovereignty of the States, and carry out the old Federalist hope of making what Hamilton called "a strong government," by which was, as we have seen, meant something like a monarchy. But all sorts of Black Republicans were apparently made happy by the prospect of war.

Mr. Lincoln's proclamation also aroused the greatest excitement in the whole South. Every Abolition governor of course responded to the call for troops with great alacrity. But those governors who were alike opposed to abolition and secession promptly declared that under our Constitution and form of government, the President had no power to make war upon a State for any cause.

Governor Magoffin, of Kentucky, informed Mr. Lincoln that his State would "furnish no troops for the wicked purpose of making war upon States."

Governor Ellis, of North Carolina, though opposed to secession, telegraphed to Washington as follows: "I can be no party to this wicked violation of the laws of this country, and especially to this war which is being waged upon a free and independent people."

Governor Jackson, of Missouri, replied to Mr. Lincoln: "Your requisition, in my judgment, is illegal, unconstitutional, and revolutionary, and in its objects, inhuman and diabolical."

Governor Letcher, of Virginia, who was also opposed to secession, wrote to Mr. Lincoln that his call for troops was "not within the purview of the Constitution or the act of 1795."

Not until Mr. Lincoln's war proclamation did the State of Virginia pass an act of secession.

The act of secession passed by Virginia on the 17th day

of April, 1861, declared that:

> The people of Virginia recognize the American principle, that government is founded on the consent of the governed, and the right of the people of the several States of this Union, for just cause, to withdraw from their association under the Federal Government, with the people of the other States, and to erect new governments for their better security; and they never will consent that the Federal power, which is, in part, their power, shall be exerted for the purpose of subjugating the people of such States to the Federal authority.

There was nothing new in the principle here announced. It is precisely the same as that of our Declaration of Independence. It is precisely the same as Jefferson urged in opposition to the old monarchist party in this country. But the tide of death and destruction was then let loose. It was a grand and bloody carnival of those dark spirits who had always hated the democratic government of the United States. Those who hated the perfectly free system of government established by our fathers, and those wild fanatics who were bent on Negro equality had united bloody hands over what they meant to be the grave of the old Union and the final overthrow of the democratic principle of government.

CHAPTER FIFTEEN
The Rush of Troops to Washington

I have said that Massachusetts began to prepare for war before the election of Mr. Lincoln. Governor Andrew of that State boasted of the fact himself. So the troops of Massachusetts were the very first to jump into uniform at the call of the President. They were passing through the streets of New York, on the way to Washington, even before the President's proclamation had been generally read. They did not march through the streets of New York City, so much as they skipped, and hopped, and jumped. They came on screaming and yelling like Indians, and went through the city, singing "John Brown's soul is marching on!"

Alas, it was too true that John Brown's soul was marching on. For it was just that and nothing more. It was to "finish the work of the martyr, old John Brown," which they declared they were going to do. John Brown's own *raid* was one which appeared to be pretty much on his own hook; but now we were to witness something of a similar kind on a grander scale, and carried on by a Federal Administration, at the expense of the people of the United States.

These Massachusetts soldiers, rushing on so hot and clamorous towards the scene of bloodshed, were a sad sight for any good man or true patriot to witness. They were the representatives of the very traitors and fanatics who, only a few years before, had publicly burned the Constitution of the United States in Boston, on the Fourth of July. They came from a State which for a quarter of a century had supported a newspaper which flaunted the motto that, "The Union is an agreement with hell, and the Constitution a covenant with death." The leaders of the party in Massachusetts from which these armed Puritans came out, had cunningly instructed them to say that they were going to "fight for the Union." That was the cry they were told to keep up on the way; but in the gushing passion of their hearts they everywhere sung out their real mission, to "revenge the martyr, old John Brown!"

A majority of these wild soldiers of Massachusetts comprehended nothing higher than that. The leaders and politicians, whom they had left in safety at home, cared nothing for old John Brown, except so far as his name was useful to them in pumping up the bitter waters of a strife which was to end in the overthrow of the democratic principles of our Government.

A merchant of Boston, a man of prominence in his State, said to the writer of this history during the second year of the war: "This war will put an end to democracy, and that alone will be worth all the blood which is shed." Alas, that so many democrats should have run blindly into their trap.

As these Massachusetts soldiers went on, dancing and singing, a great excitement was aroused, and applause greeted them at almost every point along the route, until they reached the city of Baltimore. In that city the march of the first installment of the Abolition army was met with the resistance of what appeared to be the whole people. The railroad track was barricaded so effectually as to entirely prevent the passage of the cars, and every street and avenue was blocked up by thousands of people, armed with stones and clubs, to resist the advance of the soldiers. The soldiers fired indiscriminately into the dense crowd of men, women and children, which produced a scene that was frightful to look upon, in which a number of citizens and soldiers were killed.

For several weeks no more soldiers were allowed to pass through Baltimore. The railroad bridges in the vicinity of the city were all destroyed, so that all the Abolition troops were obliged to go round through Annapolis on the route to Washington.

The war so long looked for, so long prayed for, by the Abolitionists was now begun in earnest. On the 19th of April Mr. Lincoln put forth another proclamation to declare all the ports of the South blockaded.

The new Confederate Government now formally recognized the existence of war, and commenced in great earnest to prepare for the worst. Virginia, which had so long tried in vain to induce the Black Republicans of Congress and Mr. Lincoln to accept the fair terms of compromise and peace offered by the South in the Crittenden resolutions, was now already swarming with hostile Abolition soldiers. At that time Robert E. Lee was a colonel of cavalry in the United States army, but when he saw his native State invaded, he resigned his commission, and at once assumed command of the State forces of Virginia. A large force of Mr. Lincoln's troops held Harper's Ferry in Virginia, but were compelled to evacuate it in consequence of the general rising of the Virginians to defend their own homes. Before leaving, however, they set fire to all the buildings, machine shops, and other public structures. This took place on the 19th of April.

The next day Mr. Lincoln's soldiers were ordered to use the torch in another part of Virginia. All the works of the Norfolk Navy Yard were fired, producing such a conflagration that the city of Norfolk was with the greatest difficulty saved from the devouring flames. All the ships, except one, in the harbor, were fired and scuttled. The sword and the faggot were now fairly launched upon their long and terrible errand of destruction. The awful fact stared the whole South in the face, that the only hope of protection against the objects of the Black Republican party lay in its means of self-defence. A tremendous army was gathering at Washington. The Black Republican members of Congress, and the papers of that party, breathed only threats of appalling slaughter. They were going "to leave the ruts of their war-chariots so deep in the soil of the South, that eternity would not wear them out." That was the kind of language they habitually used.

At that moment the despotic designs of the Lincoln Administration were fully revealed in events passing in Maryland. That State, while it passed resolutions against the invasion of sovereign States by Federal troops, took no steps to secede. Indeed the State Legislature passed a resolution against calling a convention to discuss the propriety of seceding. But this was no protection against the despotism agreed upon in the Black Republican councils at Washington. The mayor and police of Baltimore were seized and plunged into a military prison, where they were treated with a barbarity truly revolting. They were not allowed the privileges which always in civilized countries are permitted to convicted murderers.

The constitution, laws, and courts of the State were all stricken down by a single blow. The State Legislature was dispersed at the point of the bayonet, and its members spirited away to distant dungeons. Private houses were searched by the officials of the usurpers at Washington. Private letters of ladies and gentlemen were seized and sent to Washington to be read by Mr. Seward and Mr. Lincoln as they sat upon their new throne of usurped authority. Men were thrown into dungeons on the suspicion of having "sympathies" in opposition to Black Republicans. Any debased wretch could easily procure the arrest of a gentleman or lady against whom he had a spite. And when the venerable Chief Justice of the United States issued the writ of *habeas corpus* to bring these victims out to ascertain the cause of their arrest, Mr. Lincoln telegraphed to his military tools to pay no respect to the orders of the Chief Justice of the Supreme Court of the United States!

So you see that the party had at last come fully into power which tried to establish a government of monarchical powers after our Revolution. You have also seen, in previous chapters of this history, that the same monarchist party attempted to revolutionize or overthrow the free government our fathers did establish while it was in power from 1796 to 1800, under the Administration of old John Adams. This party, so long hating, so long opposing the free democratic government of our country, found in Abraham Lincoln a willing tool of its revolutionary and despotic principles.

His official newspaper in Washington, edited by a man of the most infamous political reputation, by the name of Forney, did not scruple to confess that the plan of revolutionizing our Government had been fully determined upon, and in a leading editorial he said:

> Another principle must certainly be embodied in our re-organized form of government. The men who shape the legislation of this country, when the war is past, must remember that what we want is *power and strength. The problem will be to combine the forms of a republican government with the powers of a monarchical government.*

Here we find Mr. Lincoln's own organ confessing that they had fully entered upon the business of changing the free government of our fathers into a government possessing the *power of a monarchy!*

At the same time another leading Black Republican paper, the *North American* of Philadelphia, said: "This war has already shown the absurdity of a government of limited powers; it has shown that the power of every government ought to be and must be unlimited."

Did ever the Emperor of Austria talk in language more contemptuous of a republican form of government, or more laudatory of monarchical power? So you see that not only the acts of Mr. Lincoln, but the tone and language of the leaders of his party, were all in harmony with the idea of despotic power. Under the cunning but hypocritical cry for the Union, these traitors were aiming, not only at the eternal overthrow of the Union, but at the destruction of the free system of government established by the patriots of the Revolution.

CHAPTER SIXTEEN
The First Great Battle

Before the great battle of Manassas, or *Bull Bun,* as it is generally called, there were several smaller engagements between the Federal and Confederate soldiers. The first of these occurred at Bethel, in Virginia, on 10th of June, 1861. At that place Colonel Magruder was intrenched with a small force, when General Butler sent General Pierce, of Massachusetts, to engage them. You may be sure that General Butler did not go himself, for he made himself quite as remarkable for always keeping out of the range of bullets himself, as he did afterwards for his thefts and brutal treatment of all men or women who fell as prisoners into his hands.

This attack upon Colonel Magruder's force proved most disastrous to the assailing party. The Massachusetts troops met with a most ruinous defeat. At this engagement, Major Winthrop, a most gallant Federal officer and estimable gentleman, was killed. The Confederate Colonel Hill, of a North Carolina regiment, in his official despatch, referred to the daring bravery of Major Winthrop with terms of soldierly admiration for a brave enemy. Major Winthrop belonged to General Butler's staff, and was in all respects a most honorable contrast to his cruel and cowardly commander.

Immediately after this little battle of Bethel, a grand movement of the Federal army was made towards Richmond, which had then become the capital of the new Confederate Government. The main column of the army under General McDowell bore directly down upon the Confederate forces under General Beauregard at Manassas. In numbers and equipment, it was a splendid army, and is supposed to have been at least four times as large as the Confederate force under Beauregard, which it was marching against. The Abolitionists and all their sympathizers and supporters were flushed with the wildest ideas of a sudden and complete overthrow of the "rebellion," as it was called.

How *sovereign States,* which are in no sense *subjects* of any government, can *rebel,* I have never heard anybody attempt to explain. It is easy to see how the Federal Government, which exists only by the limited and defined powers delegated to it by the real and only "sovereigns," the States, or the people thereof, can rebel against its makers and owners, but that the makers, that is, the States, can rebel against its creature, that is, the Federal Government, is as foolish as to say that the Creator of the world can rebel against the creatures He has made. The word *rebel* is not applicable to sovereign bodies. States may be guilty of breaking the compact which they have made with each other, but that is simply a *breach of compact*, and not a *rebellion,* because they are equal sovereign communities. Least of all can the States rebel against the Federal Government, because that is not a party to the compact at all – but only an *agent* delegated by the compact.

But those who rushed in to swell the ranks of the tremendous Abolition army did not reason so far as this. All that the Black Republicans cared about was the overwhelming and the destruction of the Southern States. They did not stop to ask whether their cause was just – whether the Constitution of our country gave to one section the right to raise such a tremendous army to destroy the other. Oh, no, such a thought never entered into their considerations. They had a splendid army, which they felt sure would march, almost without interruption, to the capture of Richmond, and thence on through the South to the Gulf of Mexico, if it pleased.

But when it reached Bull Run, a few miles from Manassas, it was suddenly confronted, on the 18th day of July, with the advance brigades of General Beauregard's army at Manassas. The engagement which took place resulted in the decided repulse of General McDowell; so much so, that it convinced him that Manassas could not be reached by his army on that line, and a new, or what is called a flank movement was at once resolved upon. So three days after this defeat at Bull Run, General Scott gave his orders to General McDowell for a grand advance of the whole Army of the Potomac on Manassas.

So confident were the authorities at Washington of perfect success, that no secret was made in any circles of the grand movement. Congress adjourned to witness, as one of the members said, "the fun of the battle." All the roads between Washington and Manassas were literally jammed with noisy and jolly spectators going to witness the fight. Besides members of Congress, and high officials of the Administration, there were ministers of the Gospel, gay women, and merchants and editors from Philadelphia, New York, and Boston, all rushing, crushing, and joking along, as though they were going out to a horse-racing, instead of to the awful slaughter of their fellow men. It was a grand and jolly picnic, with plenty of rum, whisky, brandy, and champagne along to be drunk at the general merrymaking and jollification which was to be held after the tremendous and triumphant slaughter of human beings. The idea of the defeat of this grand army seems never for an instant to have entered into the heads of these confident Abolitionists.

General McDowell ordered his army to be in motion at two o'clock on the morning of the 21st of July. By nine o'clock the work of death commenced. The slaughter was terrible on both sides. The surging masses, now rushing forward and now falling back on each side, showed that the fight was intensely desperate. The terrible and ceaseless roar of the cannon, together with the clouds of smoke and dust which obscured the heavens, clothed the whole scene with a woe as terrible as the judgment day of the ungodly. It was Sunday. A strange time and a strange occasion to be used as a gala day by so many distinguished officials, ministers of the Gospel, and other professed Christian people!

At mid-day it seemed that the Confederate forces were surely being crushed by the vastly superior numbers that were constantly massed and hurled against their shattered and mangled columns. There was a moment when the Confederate commanders evidently thought they had lost the day, but their troops fell back sullenly, as if they preferred to die on the field of battle rather than yield to the foot of the invader. General Bee, whose command seems to have been entirely overwhelmed by vastly superior numbers, rode up to General Jackson and in despairing accents said: "General, they are beating us back."

"Sir," coolly replied the invincible Jackson, "we'll give them the bayonet."

At these determined words, General Bee appealed to his overwhelmed and disheartened soldiers to stand their ground and meet death rather than yield to the foe, and pointing to General Jackson, he said: "See! there is Jackson standing like a stone wall!" It was from this circumstance that General Jackson obtained the name of *"Stonewall,"* a name which he will wear as long as the fame of his heroism survives; and that will be as long as the memory of man lasts.

The example set by General Jackson and his men, of *standing like a stone wall,* under the most terrible and deadly fire, together with his cool and determined words, "Sir, we'll give them the bayonet," acted like magic upon the discouraged and yielding men under General Bee's command. Again the Confederates, it could be seen, were gaining ground inch by inch, and at three o'clock, reinforcements having arrived under General Joseph E. Johnston, decided the fate of the day.

General Bee fell mortally wounded at the head of his command while gallantly leading it through an open field.

The defeat of the Northern troops was complete. It was more than a defeat; it was a *rout.* An army that an hour before was displaying the greatest confidence and heroism in battle was flying in the wildest confusion and dismay. Panic-stricken soldiers, and still more frightened members of Congress, merchants, ministers, gay ladies, heads of departments, teamsters, and loafers of every description, were all rushing, scrambling, dashing and tumbling along together in frantic confusion. The very horses seemed to partake of the general fright. Wounded soldiers imploringly caught hold of the carriages of members of Congress and others with grasps of despair, and were actually beaten off with heavy blows upon their fingers. Confederate cannon were roaring behind them. Shot and shell hissing over their heads; while Stuart's cavalry was hotly dogging the rear of the flying legion.

Thus the defeated army not only ran back to Washington, but great numbers actually ran through Washington, and kept up the flight until the plains of Maryland and the hills of Pennsylvania were reached as asylums of safety. Hundreds of soldiers exchanged clothes with the Negroes, in order the more easily to effect their escape.

All the champagne and other expensive wines and liquors, taken out for the Congressional picnic, fell into the hands of the Confederates. So might Washington have easily fallen into their hands, too, had they kept up the pursuit. For there was nothing to prevent the capture of Washington after this deplorable rout at Manassas. And why the Confederates did not follow up their great victory, and render it complete by the capture of Washington, remains the great mystery of the war. Rumor says that it was the wish of General Beauregard, and also of General Jackson and General Johnston, to push right on and take the capital, but that they were withheld by the orders of President Davis.

It is said, by those who may be supposed to be well posted, that this refusal on the part of President Davis to allow the Confederate army to advance upon Washington, caused ill feeling between him and Generals Beauregard, Jackson and Johnston. So far did General Jackson carry his feeling of disappointment and mortification at what he denounced as "a fatal policy," that he actually tendered his resignation, but was induced to reconsider that determination by the entreaty of friends, aided by his religious conviction of the justice of their cause.

The effect of the humiliating defeat at Manassas was fearful indeed. Disappointment and mortification, however, are not the words to express the state of the Black Republican sentiment and feeling at the North. *Rage* is the word. Every man in the streets who did not join in swearing eternal vengeance against the South, was "spotted" as a "rebel sympathizer." Bands of noisy bullies paraded the streets, insulting and threatening every man whose conversation was not as violent as the rest. It was almost dangerous for a man to wear the manners of a gentleman. Everybody was expected to rave. Black Republican sentiment was especially severe on General Scott. It was declared that he was too old to manage such a campaign. Some went so far as to accuse him of being at heart a "rebel," and of "wanting the South to succeed." There was, of course, not the slightest justice in such a charge.

General Scott was not capable of comprehending the real design for which the war was waged, nor of measuring the political magnitude of the bloody events upon which the country was entering. He viewed the whole matter only with the eye of a soldier, which is not of the eye either of statesmanship or justice. But there was truth in the complaint that General Scott was too old. General McDowell also came in for his full share of abuse. He was denounced as "incompetent;" and the command of the Army of the Potomac was conferred upon General George B. McClellan, who had just won laurels in a small battle at Rich Mountain, in Western Virginia, and who was probably the ablest general connected with the Black Republican army. General McClellan at once set himself to the work of repairing the broken and utterly demoralized Army of the Potomac. It was a long and laborious task, as this history will show.

Gen. George B. McClellan

Mr. Lincoln, in order to give a flourish of patriotism to his war, had called Congress to meet together in special session on the national anniversary of the Fourth of July. The result of the battle of Manassas had shown that the South was not to be subjugated in "sixty days," as many shallow people had predicted. The army, or what was left of it, was mostly three months' men, who had volunteered to defend the capital. It was now necessary to raise a large army for longer terms of enlistment. But under the general belief existing that the Black Republican party intended to carry out their Negro equality principles, it was difficult to induce men to enlist.

Some assurances on this point were absolutely necessary, or else it was doubtful whether the Northern masses could be got into the war. Accordingly Congress, immediately after the battle of Manassas, passed the following resolution defining the objects of the war:

> Resolved, That this war is not waged on our part in any spirit of oppression, or for any purpose of conquest, or for interfering with the *rights or established institutions of those States,* but to defend and maintain the supremacy of the Constitution, and to preserve the Union with all the dignity and rights of the several States unimpaired – and that as soon as these objects are accomplished the war ought to cease.

Upon the solemn promise embraced in this resolution, an army of 500,000 men was called for, and an expenditure of $500,000,000 authorized by Congress to carry on the war. That this pledge was shamefully broken after the men had been got into the army, will surprise no one when it is remembered by what a mean trick Mr. Seward and Mr. Lincoln had inaugurated the war itself.

To show still further how shamefully Mr. Lincoln deceived the people, we will quote from a letter written by Simon Cameron, Secretary of War, in August, 1861, to General Butler, at Fortress Monroe, wherein he says: "It is the desire of the President that all existing rights in all the States be fully respected and maintained. The war now prosecuted on the part of the Federal Government is a war for the Union, for the preservation of all the constitutional rights of the States and the citizens of the States in the Union." All intelligent people knew that this was false, and that the war was prosecuted for no such purpose. Yet it served the object for which it was intended. It deceived thousands and tens of thousands of ardent young men, and thus got them into the army. After the object of the war was changed, they were shot down for mutiny if they refused to fight to free Negroes!

CHAPTER SEVENTEEN
Campaign in the West

While the events I have described, were going on in Virginia, the campaign in the West was moving on vigorously, though in a smaller way. At St. Louis many citizens were shot down in the street. In some instances women and children were thus murdered by the Black Republican soldiery. The State had taken no steps towards secession. But as the laws of the State and the property and lives of its citizens were already the prey of soldiers in Federal uniform, it is certainly true that the Federal Administration began the work of subjugating the State in earnest before any signs of secession were apparent in the people or authorities of the State.

Governor Jackson called out the Missouri militia, who were encamped under the laws of the State at a place called Camp Jackson, near the city of St. Louis. These State troops were compelled to surrender to a superior force of Abolition soldiers under Captain Lyon, who was afterwards made a general by Mr. Lincoln, and was killed not long after at the battle of Springfield. Immediately after this surrender, Governor Jackson called for 50,000 volunteers for State defence. He appointed Stirling Price Major General of the State forces of Missouri, and also appointed eight or nine brigadier generals.

On the 20th of June, 1861, General Lyon, at the head of 7,000 well armed and well drilled Federal troops, started for the capture of Booneville. At that place was stationed Colonel Marmaduke, with about 800 State troops, poorly armed with the poorer sort of rifles and shot guns, with no cannon, and very little ammunition. Understanding the superior force and equipment of the enemy, and well knowing that it would be impossible for eight hundred men poorly armed to stand against 8,000 men well armed, Colonel Marmaduke ordered a retreat. But this the men refused to do, declaring that they would not leave without giving the foe, as they called it, "a peppering." So they stood their ground, with no commander but their captain and lieutenant. A fight ensued which lasted nearly two hours, in which three Missourians were killed and twenty wounded, while the Federal loss was, in killed and wounded, over one hundred. But "the barefoot rebel militia," as they were called, were forced to fly, after that gallant little resistance.

There were several unimportant fights following immediately this skirmish at Booneville. A man who called himself Colonel Cook, a brother of the infamous B.F. Cook, who was hanged with old John Brown in Virginia, had raised a force of Abolitionists, under the name of "Home Guards," to the number of about one thousand. Upon this force, Colonel O'Kane, with a small body of State soldiers, fell one morning at daybreak, and almost annihilated them, as they were asleep at the time. Over two hundred were killed, while a much larger number were wounded, and over one hundred taken prisoners. In this surprise the Missourians lost four men, and twenty wounded, and they captured three hundred and sixty muskets.

But the first important battle was fought at Carthage, on the 5th of July, 1861, between the Federal army, commanded by General Sigel, and the Missouri State troops, commanded by Governor Jackson. After one of the most spirited engagements of the whole war, General Sigel was badly whipped, and that, too, by a vastly inferior and badly equipped force. The next day after this battle, General Stirling Price arrived at Carthage, in company with Brigadier-General Ben. McCulloch, a famous fighting officer of the Confederate army, and also Major-General Pierce, of the Arkansas State militia. These accessions added about 2,000 men to the defensive army of Missouri.

The Abolition army under the several commands of Generals Lyon, Sigel, Sweeny, and Sturgis, had united at Springfield. The Missouri army started at once on the march towards Springfield, while, at the same time, the Abolition commanders quickly marched out their army to meet it. The Missouri force was a sorry sight for an army, in all but desperate fighting pluck. A subordinate officer drew the following humorous picture of its condition:

> We had not a blanket, not a tent, nor any clothes, except the few we had on our backs, and four-fifths of us were barefooted. Billy Barlow's dress at a circus would be decent, compared with that of almost any one, from the major-general down to the humblest private. But we had this preparation for battle, every one believed that he was fighting in a cause the most sacred that ever aroused the heroism of man.

This army consisted of five thousand three hundred infantry, with fifteen pieces of artillery, and six thousand horsemen armed with nothing better than flint-lock muskets and old shot guns, and very few cartridge-boxes. One long day's march brought this motley army to Wilson's Creek, or as it is also called, Oak Hill, eight miles from Springfield. Here they rested for the night; and the soldiers, notwithstanding their tedious march, "danced around their camp fires until a late hour." In this army there were about one thousand Cherokee and Choctaw Indians, some dressed in the regular Confederate uniform, and others in all kinds of fantastic uncivilized gear.

The Federal army, under Generals Lyon and Sigel, consisted at this time of about nine thousand men, well armed, among which was a thousand United States regulars, of the First and Second U.S. infantry, the Fourth U.S. cavalry, and Second U. S. dragoons. General Lyon, learning that the Missouri army was encamped at Wilson's Creek, struck his tents at about four o'clock in the afternoon, and marched slowly and silently along until he arrived within an hour's march of the enemy's camp, when he halted in a little valley, where his army slept upon their arms. The next morning, at daybreak they were again ready to march to the attack of the Missourians.

General Lyon now harangued his soldiers, telling them

that they were within a short hour's march of the enemy, and that he should that morning breakfast them in their camp. At sunrise he reached the position he wanted, and immediately opened the battle by attacking the Missourians at two points, on their right and left. He led the attack upon the right himself, while General Sigel was to attack the left and rear. After passing round a hill to get in position, General Sigel mistook a portion of General Lyon's force for the enemy and furiously began to pour shot and shell upon it, and kept up the mistake until General Lyon sent round a messenger to inform him of his mistake.

Though surprised, the Missourians under the command of General Ben. McCulloch, were instantly made ready for the battle, and entered into the fight, not only with courage, but with the reckless desperation of men who preferred death to defeat. In numbers and arms General Lyon had a very great advantage. He also had the still greater advantage of having effected the surprise of Ben. McCulloch's army. But this latter benefit did not seem very great, as the Missourians were instantly at work resisting the foe. It was a short but terrible conflict, in which General Lyon was killed, and his army beaten and put to a complete rout.

The retreat was conducted with a good deal of skill and energy by General Sigel. By forced marches he reached Rolla, a distance of about 175 miles in a little over three days, allowing his soldiers only three hours and a half sleep every twenty-four hours.

This entire defeat and rout of the Abolition army in Missouri was regarded as almost the finishing blow to that cause in the West. And so it might have been, perhaps, but for a disagreement between General McCulloch and General Price, in consequence of which General McCulloch took all the Confederate force under his command and returned to Arkansas, leaving General Price alone, with only the State troops of Missouri for the defence of that State. There is little doubt that, had General McCulloch remained and acted in conjunction with General Price and the State troops, Missouri would, in a short time, have been wholly cleared of the presence of the Abolitionists. Some time afterwards General McCulloch expressed his profound regret at what he called his "great mistake in withdrawing from Missouri."

Losing the support of the Confederate forces, General Price marched his State army of about five thousand men for the Missouri River, receiving reinforcements of citizens all along the line of his march.

Learning that the infamous bushwhackers and ruffians, Jennison, Jim Lane, and Montgomery, were near Fort Scott, with a force of marauders, plundering, burning, and murdering wherever they went, he marched directly for that place. Fifteen miles from Fort Scott, he met with Jim Lane, and put him to an utter rout and flight, and then continued his march on to Lexington, where Colonel Mulligan, with a Federal force, was strongly intrenched. At that place a desperate battle transpired, which, after fifty-two hours of uninterrupted fighting, resulted in the entire defeat and surrender of the Abolition force under Colonel Mulligan.

In General Price's official report of the battle, he said:

> This victory has demonstrated the fitness of our citizen soldiery for the tedious operations of a siege, as well as for a dashing charge. They lay for fifty-two hours in the open air, without tents or covering, regardless of the sun and rain, and in the very presence of a watchful and desperate foe, manfully repelling every assault and patiently awaiting my orders to storm the fortifications. No general ever commanded a braver or better army. It is composed of the best blood and bravest men of Missouri.

Just before this battle, General Fremont had been appointed by Mr. Lincoln to the command of the Department of the West. He inaugurated his advent in Missouri with the most ridiculous display of pomp, parade, and insolence. He behaved himself far more like an eastern bashaw than like a general in a republican country. He put forth a swelling order proclaiming "the abolition of slavery" and the confiscation of the property of all Missourians who adhered to the government of their State. So wildly did he behave himself that President Lincoln felt himself compelled to check his imprudence; and finally, he was, after a short reign, removed from his command, for military incapacity, and for permitting immense swindling of the Government by his subordinates.

While the battle of Lexington was going on, an army of jayhawkers, under Jim Lane and Montgomery, fell upon five hundred Missourians about thirty miles above Lexington, who, in an almost hand-to-hand fight, completely cut the jayhawkers to pieces, and thus made two victories for the Missourians on that day.

But these brilliant victories described in this chapter, were nearly the end of the triumph of the Missourians over the Abolition foe. An army of 70,000 men was ready to march under General Fremont, and as General Price had no force to meet such a tremendous army, and being without means of transportation for even the whole of the small force he commanded, and being almost out of ammunition, he was obliged to disband a portion of it, and make the best retreat he could. Fremont had his immense army already on the march, with the design of entirely surrounding the little force remaining under General Price; but the vigilant Missouri commander defeated his project by boldly sending out small forces to attack at two points the advance columns of General Fremont's army.

In this he was entirely successful, for he made such an impression upon the Abolition force that Fremont halted and began to ditch. But General Price gladly left the Abolition general ditching, and made the best of his retreat towards the Arkansas line. His whole command, now only 15,000 strong, crossed Osage River, which was much swollen by recent rains, in two rude flat boats constructed by his men for the occasion. Afterwards it took General Fremont sixteen days to get across the same stream on his pontoon bridges.

General Price continued his retreat to Neosho, a little town on the southern borders of Missouri, where Governor Jackson had assembled the State Legislature. At this place, after the people of Missouri had been plundered and ravaged for months by the marauding Abolition army, the Legislature passed an act of secession, and appointed delegates to the Provisional Congress of the Southern Confederacy. The State was literally driven out of the Union. We may say *fought* out of it. It was not the intention of the Legislature to pass an act of secession, until it found the State laws overthrown by the Abolition army under the pay of Mr. Lincoln's Administration.

The presence of the Federal army in Missouri, against which the State authorities struggled so long and so gallantly, was as great a crime on the part of Mr. Lincoln and the Black Republican party as the presence of the same kind of invading army would be in New York or in Massachusetts at the present time. The Missourians were all the time fighting for the preservation of their own laws, and the protection of their own State. And there was hardly a respectable native citizen of the State whose heart was not honestly and devotedly with General Price in his gallant but vain struggle to drive the marauding Abolition foe from its borders.

The State was literally overrun with such ruffians as Jim Lane, Montgomery, and Jennison, the former friends and associates of old John Brown in all his thefts and murders in Kansas. For many months before the Legislature passed the ordinance of secession, the native citizens of Missouri had been pillaged and imprisoned in the most cruel and brutal manner. The banks of the State were robbed of their specie. The dwellings of the wealthy were entered by freebooters in Federal uniform and stripped of their silver spoons, jewelry, ladies' wardrobes, and all other valuables. Their cattle were driven off, and either killed to feed the Abolition army, or given to the Germans who assisted that army to invade and plunder the native people of the State.

General Lyon, who was killed at the battle of Wilson's Creek, was a Connecticut Abolitionist of the most bitter type. He had neither pity nor mercy for any White man who was not an Abolitionist. He was an excellent military officer, but fanatical and cruel in carrying out his creed.

But under the military rule of General Lyon, the people of Missouri were not so badly off as they were under the brief but disgraceful reign of General Fremont. Fremont carried things with such a high hand that Mr. Lincoln was obliged in a short time to remove him. As I have before told you, he began by assuming the airs of some eastern bashaw or monarch. Some of his German officers imprudently let slip the idea that Fremont cared nothing for Lincoln or the United States, but that he was going to establish an immense German empire in the West. Perhaps this had something to do with Lincoln's very sudden removal of Fremont.

A gentleman describing a journey in Missouri at that time, writes as follows:

> God forbid I should exaggerate; and were I willing to do so, things are so bad that they could not be painted worse, with all the coloring in the world. My whole journey to this place has presented harrowing sights – widows, wives, children, and the aged, standing houseless by the wayside, their homes in flames and ruins. You will ask if they are Missourians who have done these things; you know the character of native Missourians too well to think they are. These destroyers are the valiant German and Dutch heroes of Sigel; runaways from battle-fields, who show their paltry spite to helpless little ones, whose fathers and brothers are fighting for freedom of thought, word, and action. Heaven forbid that the name of Missourians should be placed on such a record! Yet there are ambitious leaders among them, who care not who perish so they may rule. A German republic or empire is their dream, and already their general [Fremont] is assuming all the trumpery and airs of foreign courts – already he travels in state, has a German bodyguard, tricked out in what appears to be the cast off finery of a third-class theatrical wardrobe. When he travels on the river, an entire steamboat is not more than sufficient to accommodate the majesty of Fremont; guards pace before his door night and day; servants in gay livery hand round Catawba on silver waiters; grooms and orderlies flit about like poor imitations of the same class of servants in German cities, while the ruling language of the court is very low Dutch, redolent of lager bier and schnapps.

The suspicion that Fremont was secretly aiming at a German empire of his own in the Great West, gained some little confirmation from his manner of treating Mr. Lincoln's order for his removal. At first, for several days, he refused to be removed, but gave orders to all his subordinates to allow no one to reach his person. This was to prevent President Lincoln's order of his removal from being served on him. But after being satisfied that it would be a vain attempt for him to hold out longer, he yielded.

And after his removal, a considerable portion of his German soldiers mutinied, and refused, for some time, to do further service in the war.

It will probably never be known to what extent this scheme for a German empire under Fremont had progressed, at the time of Fremont's timely removal by Mr. Lincoln, but there is no doubt that those who were capable of sustaining the horrible despotism of the Abolition reign in Missouri were capable of enjoying the absolute rule of monarchy.

CHAPTER EIGHTEEN
Campaign in Western Virginia, and the Battle of Leesburg

Just before the great battle of Manassas, General McClellan had won a brilliant little victory in a battle at Rich Mountain in Western Virginia, and indeed General McClellan's whole campaign had been so generally successful that the Northern people looked upon him as altogether the best general on the Northern side. He was called the "Young Napoleon," and there was no end to the praise bestowed upon him, or to the confidence reposed in his generalship. But before he was withdrawn from Western Virginia to take command of the Army of the Potomac, the campaign in the former region was not, for some time, of a very spirited character on either side. After the Confederate General Garnett was so badly defeated by McClellan at Rich Mountain, General Wise, who had a small force in the Kanawha Valley, was obliged to fall back a hundred miles, to Lewisburg, a retreat which he effected rapidly, destroying all the bridges behind him to prevent the pursuit of the enemy.

General Floyd was sent to check the march of Colonel Tyler, who had invaded Western Virginia from Ohio. This Colonel Tyler was familiar with that whole region, having often, in former days, been over it buying furs. The confident Abolitionist said he would now "drive a big business in rebel skins." Colonel Tyler himself boasted that he intended to capture Floyd's whole command, and marched rapidly to meet him. An engagement took place near Cross Lanes, at which General Floyd whipped the boasting Abolition colonel very badly, capturing all his baggage, inducing his private wardrobe. The Colonel himself, it is said, was seen flying wildly a good ways ahead of his frightened and retreating command.

But General Floyd's good luck did not last long. His force consisted of less than 2,000 men, and he was, a few days after this decisive victory, overtaken by General Rosecrans, with a force of ten regiments of infantry and several batteries of artillery. With this formidable army General Floyd was attacked in his intrenchments. Confident in his superior numbers, General Rosecrans at once commenced an assault. But Floyd's men bravely stood their ground from three o'clock in the afternoon until dark. In five tremendous assaults Rosecrans' army had been completely resisted. But when the night fell and put a stop to active fighting, General Floyd withdrew his army across the Gauley River, by means of a hastily built bridge of logs, and made a successful retreat to Big Sewell Mountain, and thence to Meadow Bluff; securing his little army from all danger of being gobbled up by Rosecran's big force. Thus General Rosecrans, besides losing many of his men and several officers, was cheated of a victory of which he felt he was sure.

After the defeat and death of General Garnett at Rich Mountain, General Robert E. Lee was appointed to succeed him. General Lee made preparations as speedily as possible to go to the relief of General Floyd and General Wise, whose small commands were entirely checked by the comparatively large army of General Rosecrans. General Lee's army, in all, numbered about fifteen thousand men. With this force he marched directly to the aid of the Confederate forces in Western Virginia, and also to relieve the people of that region of the outrages inflicted upon them by the presence of the Abolition army.

When he reached the points held by Generals Floyd and Wise, he had in his command an army of nearly 20,000 men. He halted in sight of General Rosecrans, and for ten or twelve days offered that general battle. But at last Rosecrans disappeared one night, and retreated over thirty miles to the Gauley River. For some reason General Lee made no pursuit. It was already fall, and the deepening mud and the falling leaves in that mountain region advertised the approach of winter, and also the close of the campaign, for that season, in Western Virginia.

General Lee was withdrawn from this field of operations, and sent to superintend the coast defences of South Carolina and Georgia. There were, during the fall many brilliant skirmishes between detachments of the Federal and Confederate armies, but no great battle. But through all that section, all who did not profess sympathy with the Abolition cause, whether men, women or children, were treated with the vilest indignity and outrage wherever they were not protected by the presence of Southern soldiers.

For instance, there was a beautiful little village on the Virginia bank of the Ohio River, called Guyandotte. This place was suspected of having given a welcome to some Confederate cavalry who had been there and left; and when the inhabitants learned that it was the intention of the Lincoln army to destroy the town, they came out, both men and women, waving white flags in token of entire submission; but it was of no avail. The town was murderously assaulted and fired, and not only old men, but women and children might be seen jumping from the windows in wild attempts to escape from the devouring flames. One woman, with a pair of infant twins in her arms, rushed madly out of her burning house into the street, where she was instantly killed by a stray Abolition bullet, which penetrated her brain.

While events like these were going on in Western Virginia, McClellan was still busy in recruiting, repairing, and drilling the Army of the Potomac. And Generals Johnston and Beauregard were keeping watch of him from Manassas and its vicinity. In vain, during those long weary months, they tried to provoke another battle. Sometimes they would approach in force almost within cannon shot of Washington. But General McClellan could not as yet be provoked to risk another engagement. The South laughed at him, and the North scolded. But nothing could induce him to allow the Army of the Potomac to move again until he felt prepared for a sure victory.

So the summer and the fall wore away with no startling

event to relieve the long and tedious military stagnation of both the Federal and the Confederate Army of the Potomac, except the battle of Leesburg, which occurred near the end of October, 1861. Leesburg was an important position, as a key to the rich valley of the Shenandoah. At this place was a force of four regiments of Confederates under Brigadier-General Evans. General Stone had received orders from Washington to cross the Potomac River at Harrison's Island into Virginia. At the same time, Colonel Baker, a member of the United States Congress from Oregon, was despatched to take a command under Stone. Colonel Baker was a violent Abolitionist, but he won some distinction in the Mexican war, and was said to be a brave and gallant officer. He was put in command of all the Federal forces on the Virginia side of the Potomac, and ordered by General Stone to dislodge the Confederates from Leesburg.

Colonel Baker's force was four or five times as large as the little Confederate brigade at that place, and the people at Washington waited in confidence to hear that it was entirely gobbled up by Colonel Baker. But alas, it turned out to be another Bull Run affair on a smaller scale. The Confederates fought against such vast odds with a courage that amounted to desperation. Their whole number in the engagement was only 1800, but they fired and yelled and yelled and fired with such rapidity and with such deafening noise as to make it appear to the invaders that their number was ten times greater than it really was.

Colonel Baker's whole army at last gave way, and commenced a stampede down a hill that ended with the river's bank. In vain their gallant leader tried to rally his repulsed and frightened troops. They went pitching, tumbling, rolling down the steep banks. Throwing away their guns and knapsacks, they madly plunged into the river which they had just crossed flushed with the faith of victory. A large flat-boat loaded with the wounded and dying was swamped, and went to the bottom with its whole freight of life. Through all the disastrous fight, Colonel Baker displayed the most daring heroism and courage, and he was shot dead at the head of his troops while vainly trying to rally them to battle. The victory of the Confederates was complete;

while the loss of the Federal army was, in killed and wounded, 1,300; 710 taken prisoners, among whom were twenty-two commissioned officers, besides losing 1500 stand of arms and three pieces of cannon.

This affair at Leesburg produced another bitter disappointment and mortification at Washington, besides the deepest lament for the death of the brave Colonel Baker. So mad was the chagrin that it could only be appeased by some victim, and General Stone was arrested and went to prison without trial, specification, or charge; and after suffering many weary months of incarceration, he was let out, without even being informed why he was put in. He was ordered, from Washington, to advance across the Potomac into Virginia. That order had proved a great mistake and a great calamity, and it is supposed that poor General Stone was sacrificed in order to fix blame somewhere, so that the public attention would be drawn from the real authors of the mishap at Washington.

An incident occurred at the battle of Leesburg, which serves to illustrate the horrible character of the war, and how great ought to be the punishment of those who brought it upon our country. In the spring of 1861, two brothers in Kentucky who differed in politics parted, one to join the Southern, the other the Northern army. They shook hands, expecting never to meet again. After the battle was over, Howard, who had joined the Southern army, was looking for the bodies of friends who had fallen, when he stumbled over one showing signs of life.

"Halloa," said the object, in a husky voice, "Who are you?"

"I am a Southerner," said Howard, "you are one of the enemy. The field is ours."

"Well, yes, I have some faint recollection of a battle, but all I remember now is much smoke, a great noise, and some one knocking me down with a musket, and then I fell asleep."

Howard looked again, and lo! it was his brother Alfred, and he had himself knocked him down in the confusion of the battle.

CHAPTER NINETEEN
Campaign in Kentucky

I have to tell you many sad and painful things of the war in Kentucky. At the beginning of the war, the Legislature of that State passed a resolution against secession, and also against Abolitionism. It determined that it would remain neutral in the bloody conflict; that is, that it would not take sides with either party. While it justly condemned Abolitionism and all its bloody and inhuman plans, it would not withdraw from the Union, nor take any part with secession. There is no doubt that the most respectable portion of the people of Kentucky strongly sympathized with the South, but there was a numerous though less prominent class of people in the State who sympathized with the Lincoln party. But it was agreed that the State should remain entirely neutral during the war. It was not in the power of the State to prevent individuals from leaving its borders and going, as their inclinations led, either North or South. No doubt many did so; but still the official attitude of the State remained for some time faithful to its resolution of neutrality. This neutrality the Lincoln party professed to be satisfied with, and promised to respect it, but truth compels me to tell you that they broke the bargain the very first instant they had power to do so.

The friends of Mr. Lincoln were cunning, watchful, and vigilant. Not only watchful and vigilant, as unscrupulous men generally are in a bad cause, but they were full of hatred toward those who did not sympathize with the Lincoln party. They connived with the authorities in Washington to the illegal arrest of some of the most respectable and peaceable citizens of the State, whose influence they dreaded, and whose integrity they knew they could not corrupt.

Among these, ex-Governor Morehead was seized by the Lincoln authorities, and dragged out of his own house at midnight in the presence of his frightened family, and spirited away out of the State, in violation of the most sacred laws of the land. For a great many months he was kept locked up in Fort Lafayette, denied any trial – not even allowed to know why he had been seized, and refused the least privilege of communicating with his friends. Governor Morehead does not know to this day why he was thus seized. This cruel outrage on the part of the Lincoln Administration produced a perfect storm of indignation among all the most respectable people of Kentucky. The truth probably was that Lincoln wanted to get out of the way all the influential men in Kentucky who could not be swerved from the peaceful resolution to take no part with either side in the bloody conflict.

Soon after the seizure of Governor Morehead it was discovered that the Administration had hatched a conspiracy to seize the Hon. John C. Breckinridge, ex-Vice-President of the United States, Hon. Humphrey Marshall, ex-member of Congress, Hon. William C. Preston, ex-United States minister to Spain, Hon. Thomas B. Monroe, for more than thirty years District United States Judge, Captain John Morgan, and a good many more of the first citizens of Kentucky. Several of these gentlemen were apprized of the conspiracy against their liberty, if not their lives, in time to get off, and were obliged to throw themselves within the lines of the Confederacy for protection and safety. Messrs. Breckinridge, Marshall and Morgan no longer hesitated to take up arms against a power which had driven them from their peaceful homes.

About the time the above crime of driving peaceable citizens from their cherished homes was committed, it was discovered the Lincoln Administration was about to invade and seize Kentucky on a large military scale. There was a man by the name of Rousseau at Louisville, in that State, who was ready to sell himself to the cause of Abolitionism, and he was commissioned a general, with powers to get up a brigade to fight for Mr. Lincoln. At the same time it was discovered that the Abolition forces were about to seize upon Paducah and Columbus, important points in Kentucky, for the purpose of permanently holding the State. The Confederate general, Bishop Polk, discovered this plan, and instantly moved and occupied those places himself.

All idea of the neutrality of Kentucky was now at an end. The State became the scene of the wildest anarchy and violence. Wherever the Lincoln force prevailed there was no security for the property or the life of a man who was known to be opposed to the war. Governor Magoffin, who was sincerely desirous of preserving the neutrality and peace of his State, demanded that the Confederate troops under General Polk at Columbus should be withdrawn. General Polk replied that he would promptly comply with this request, provided the Abolition army should be withdrawn at the same time, and that guarantees should be given that it would make no more attempts to occupy Kentucky. But this proposition, which was agreeable to Governor Magoffin's sense of justice, was literally hooted at by Mr. Lincoln and his party. The truth is that the Lincolnites wanted Kentucky as a base of supplies and operation against the Southern States.

On the 14th of September, 1861, the Confederate General Zofficoffer wrote to Governor Magoffin as follows:

> The safety of Tennessee requiring, I occupy the mountain passes at Cumberland, and the three long mountains in Kentucky. For weeks I have known that the Federal commander at Hoskins' Cross Roads was threatening the invasion of East Tennessee, and ruthlessly urging our people to destroy our railroad and bridges. I postponed this precautionary movement until the despotic government at Washington, refusing to recognize the neutrality of Kentucky, has established formidable camps in the centre and other parts of the State, with the view first to subjugate your gallant State, and then ourselves. * * * If the Federals will now withdraw from their menacing position, the force under my command shall be immediately withdrawn.

Under the influence of William G. Brownlow, a vulgar and desperate man, known as "Parson Brownlow," there were

Lincoln clubs formed in East Tennessee, of a number of unprincipled and desperate characters like himself, who formed a conspiracy to burn all the bridges in their part of the State, especially on the line of the railroad. This was evidently a part of a general plan formed by the authorities at Washington, of making a strong invasion of the South through Kentucky and Tennessee.

General Polk still held his headquarters at Columbus, Kentucky, when an army commanded by General Grant, in numbers nearly three times as large as Polk's force, marched to attack him from Cairo. General Grant's army embraced a large land force, and gun-boats and transports to act in conjunction with it. It was said that General Grant had men enough to "surround the rebel army in Kentucky." It is affirmed that General Grant was never known to risk a battle, except when he led three or four times as many men as the enemy.

The battle between his and Polk's forces took place at Belmont, a little village near Columbus, on the 7th November. It was one of the fiercest little battles of the whole war. For four or five hours the conflict raged with the most deadly fury. At length the Confederate officers, Colonel Beltzhoover, Colonel Bell, and Colonel Wright, of General Pillow's division, sent word to their commander that their regiments had used up all their ammunition. General Pillow then instantly ordered the use of the bayonet. Accordingly a charge was made by the whole line, and General Grant's army was forced back some distance into a wood; but General Grant ordered up reserves, which in turn forced the Confederates back again to their old position. Twice again were Grant's soldiers forced back at the point of the bayonet, and each time the Confederates were obliged to yield again to the heavy reserve force brought against them.

At last General Pillow ordered his whole line to fall back, which it did in a most broken and disorganized manner. Grant's victory seemed complete. But just at this time reinforcements arrived under the command of Colonel Waller, and General Pillow rallied his men to the battle again. The whole conflict was opened again, if possible, with greater violence than ever, and this time the Confederates were entirely victorious. Grant's whole line gave way, and wildly fled before the hot pursuit and yells of Polk's army. Grant's forces took shelter in his gun-boats and transports, which were cut loose from their fastenings, and steamed up the river with the utmost speed. But they got off under the most murderous fire of the victorious Confederates, which produced such consternation on the boats that many soldiers were pushed overboard, or were left entirely at the mercy of the enemy.

In its flight, Grant's army left behind a great number of knapsacks, blankets, overcoats, mess chests, horses, wagons, and a large amount of ammunition and arms, all of which fell into the arms of the victorious Confederates. It is a remarkable fact, and one by no means creditable to General Grant, that, in his report of this battle, he dwells at great length upon his decided success in the early part of the day, but leaves out all direct mention of his complete defeat and rout afterwards.

But this brilliant victory availed little for the Confederate cause in Kentucky. The Black Republicans were already massing an immense army to operate in that State, and it was only a question of time when the State would be entirely in the grasp of the Abolition foe.

A few days after this Confederate victory at Belmont, the enemies of the Lincoln war in Kentucky enacted a very weak farce at a convention which met at Russellville on the 18th of November. After deliberating two days, this convention passed a resolution to form a provisional government for the State of Kentucky, with a view to joining the Confederacy. The patriotic motives of the members of this convention are not to be questioned. Their worthy object was to preserve the ancient liberty of the people of Kentucky, and to resist the Negro party, which was compassing the ruin of the State. But it was then too late. The die was already cast. The State was hopelessly involved in the net of Abolition treason. So many of it own citizens were either deluded or brought into the revolutionary plans of the Lincoln party, that further resistance, for the time being, was vain.

No doubt many of the citizens of Kentucky assisted the very army that was conquering their State, and preparing for the wholesale overthrow of their property, under the delusion that they were fighting for the Union. They have lived to see their error. They now see, and the most frank portion of them freely confess, that the object of the war was to free Negroes, and to overthrow the Union of sovereign States as it was formed by our fathers. It was a war led by men acting under the inspiration of the political principles of that old Puritan monarchist party of New England which tried so long to revolutionize this government in the early days of the Union, of which you have already had an account in this history. The conduct of the Black Republican Congress, and of the whole Black Republican party, since the close of the war, proves that the war was neither for the Union nor for liberty.

In November of this year an event occurred which may justly be regarded as the most humiliating in the eyes of foreign nations that had ever happened to our country. President Davis of the Confederate States had appointed as ambassadors to represent them in England and France the Hon. James M. Mason, of Virginia, and the Hon. John Slidell, of Louisiana. Both of these gentlemen had been United States Senators. They ran the blockade at a Southern port in the steamer *Nashville*, and arrived safely at Havana.

Here they took passage on the *Trent*, a British mail steamer for Europe. When only two days out, the United States steam frigate *San Jacinto*, Captain Wilkes, fired a shot across her bow, and having learned that Messrs. Mason and Slidell were on board, demanded that they be given up. The captain of the *Trent* protested that Captain Wilkes had no right to invade the flag of another power on sea any more than he had on land, but this plain and common sense view did not satisfy a little mind like that of Wilkes. He was determined to seize Mason and Slidell, which he did, and carried them to Fort Warren in Boston Harbor.

When the Abolitionists heard the news that these gentlemen had been arrested, their joy knew no bounds. There were no two men at the South whom they hated more intensely, for they were both able and uncompromising opponents of their wicked scheme of putting Negroes on an equality with White men. The

Abolition papers fairly boiled over in excess of joy. Congress endorsed the act by a vote of thanks, and dinners and testimonials were showered upon him as if he was the saviour of a country.

All this shows how mad was the popular mind at this time. People who had not lost their senses told these maniacs that Captain Wilkes had violated a plain law of nations, and that Mr. Lincoln would be forced to deliver the prisoners up. They hooted at the idea. In due time, however, John Bull was heard from. There was no parley. The word came, "deliver those men up or fight." It is useless to say that Lincoln and Seward backed down at once. It was a very disgraceful spectacle after all the boasting. The excuse given was that we were too busy fighting the South to attend to England at that time. "One war at a time," said Mr. Lincoln. He and Mr. Seward were both determined that nothing should interfere with their cherished designs against the Southern people. They preferred a war with their own brothers rather than any other that could be gotten up.

CHAPTER TWENTY
Closing Events of 1861, and the Beginning of the War

I have now given you the principal military events of the war up to the close of the year 1861. Thus far the tide of victory seemed to be in favor of the Confederates. Some events, however, not yet named, gave great advantage to the Abolitionists, as a basis of future operation.

A naval expedition, under the command of Commodore Stringham, started from Fortress Monroe on the 29th of August, to attack the Confederates at Hatteras Inlet, on the coast of North Carolina. This expedition was entirely successful, capturing fifteen cannon, 625 prisoners, and the Confederate Commodore Barron. On the 7th of November, Port Royal, on the coast of South Carolina, was captured by Captain Dupont. These events were a great loss to the South, as they gave the North excellent depots for naval and military operations.

There were also some military operations in Florida. A regiment of thieves and bruisers raised in the city of New York by "Billy Wilson," was sent to Santa Rosa Island, in the harbor of Pensacola, as a beginning of Abolition warfare in that direction. This regiment was surprised one night by a small force of Confederates, who set the New York bruisers flying, with their colonel, Billy Wilson, at their head. The Confederates, however, being few in number, were obliged to retreat, after burning the camp and all the clothing of Wilson's regiment. This retreat was made so suddenly that the Confederates were obliged to leave several of their wounded behind, who fell into the hands of the Wilson Zouaves, and by whom they were every one inhumanly murdered. When their dead bodies were recovered, they were all found to be shot through the head in a similar manner, besides several wounds in different parts of their bodies.

Nor were the Confederates long permitted to enjoy the fruits of their victories in Kentucky. General Zollicoffer's army was short of provisions, and he preferred to have it remain so to follow the example of the Abolition commanders, who seemed to enjoy plundering the inhabitants on the line of their march. To such straits was General Zollicoffer reduced, that his soldiers were obliged to live on a ration of beef and half a ration of corn per day. And the corn had to be eaten parched, as they had no meal, and no means of making any. But the soldiers submitted to this destitution without a murmur.

In this starving condition they fought a desperate battle at Mill Spring on the 19th of January, 1862. The Abolitionists were led by General Thomas. At first the Confederates were successful, and supposed they had won the day; but an accident turned their victory into an appalling and ruinous defeat. General Zollicoffer's brigade pushed forward to the very top of the hill, just over the brow of which it came upon an Indiana regiment under the command of the Abolition Colonel Fry. At first General Zollicoffer mistook this regiment for a portion of his own command. Colonel Fry's Federal uniform was covered by an India rubber coat, and General Zollicoffer rode to within a few feet of him before the mistake was discovered by either party. In a minute Colonel Fry raised his pistol and shot General Zollicoffer dead.

The fall of this brave officer produced a gloom that seemed for the moment to completely paralyze his soldiers, who were all of his own State, Tennessee, and were devotedly attached to him personally. General Crittenden, who was General Zollicoffer's senior in command, tried in vain to regain what had been lost since the earlier part of the battle. Retreat was inevitable. The half-starved Confederates seemed to abandon hope, and flew in confusion before the now victorious enemy.

Closing Events of 1861

Just after the events above described, General Grant ascended the Tennessee River, with a fleet of gun-boats and a powerful force to act in conjunction with them. He took Fort Henry without much resistance, and at once turned his attention to Fort Donelson, where there was a considerable Confederate force under Generals Pillow, Buckner, and Floyd. This was a point which nature had strongly fortified, and General Pillow determined to hold it to the last moment possible. General Grant's combined infantry and naval forces were a formidable host indeed.

Grant commenced his attack early on the morning of the 13th of February. He told his staff that he would enter the fort before noon. But the resistance of the Confederates astonished him. When the curtain of night fell upon the bloody scene, he really seemed to have the worst of it, notwithstanding his immense superiority of force. Of twenty gun-boats which he brought into the engagement, five were sunk or crippled. So badly was he punished, that he made no further assault in force upon the fort until three o'clock in the afternoon of the next day. He pushed his boats up to within a few hundred yards of the fort, and opened a murderous fire, which was met with a determination which appeared to him miraculous. His repulse was complete, and at the end of the second day's battle he was forced to fall suddenly back out of range of the Confederate guns, with his fleet frightfully shattered and torn to pieces. He was badly beaten, both in his naval and land forces. But reinforcements were pouring into him every hour by the thousand.

The whole Confederate force was but 13,000 at the commencement of the fighting, and this number had been greatly reduced in the terrible conflict. Grant had been every day reinforced, until he had about eighty thousand men – enough to surround the little Confederate army several times. Further resistance was useless. During the night after the third day's battle, it was resolved to surrender the fort. But General Pillow and General Floyd declared that they would not become prisoners, turned over their command to General Buckner, who sent a flag of truce to Grant for an armistice to negociate terms of surrender. A large number of General Floyd's command, and a few of General Pillow's, with all of Colonel Forrest's cavalry, succeeded in escaping through the enemy's lines during the night previous, and made their retreat towards Nashville. Tennessee. But the surrender of Fort Donelson rendered the surrender of Nashville, also necessary, as it left an uninterrupted passage for General Grant's gunboats up the Cumberland River to that city.

Nashville was evacuated in the wildest confusion. Consternation and dismay seized the inhabitants. Governor Harris imprudently rode through the city, shouting to the inhabitants that the Federals were coming. He hastily convened the Legislature, for Nashville is the capital of Tennessee, and adjourned to Memphis, to which place the State books and records were conveyed. Nashville was one of the most polite and cultivated cities of the South. It was the abode of wealth and refinement. Those who had known it before it fell into the hands of the Abolitionists, and who visited it afterwards, remarked that the saddest changes had taken place. All its previous beauty and refinement had vanished. The Abolition soldiers seemed to delight in violating the wonted propriety and decency of the place.

Nashville and vicinity was the scene of many of the exploits of that dashing Confederate officer, General John H. Morgan. At one time he dashed into the camp of a Federal regiment, and captured and carried off a train of wagons. At another time, with about forty of his men, he entered the town of Gallatin, about twenty-six miles from Nashville, while it was in the possession of the Federals, and marched directly to the telegraph office. He carelessly presented himself to the operator, and asked, "What is the news?"

The operator replied that, "It was said that the rebel scoundrel, John Morgan, was in the neighborhood," at the same time flourishing a pistol, saying, "I wish I could see the rascal."

Morgan replied, "Well, sir, I am Captain Morgan, and you are my prisoner." The valiant operator instantly wilted, and begged that his life might be spared. Captain Morgan told him that he should not be hurt, on condition that he would send such despatches over the wires as he should dictate. To this the operator was glad to agree.

Captain Morgan then sent various brief messages, and one among them to Prentice, the editor of the Louisville *Journal*, offering to be his escort on a visit he had said he would make to Nashville about that time. Captain Morgan amused himself in this way until the arrival of the cars from Bowling Green, when he, with his forty men, captured the whole train, taking five Abolition officers prisoners.

Captain Morgan often dressed himself in a Federal uniform, and performed some most amusing and daring feats. Once dressed in this fashion he was riding along in the vicinity of Murfreesboro, Tennessee, when he discovered six Federal pickets in a house, enjoying themselves, off of their duty. Having on the coat of a Federal colonel, he at once rode up to them, and roundly scolded the sergeant for being thus, with his men, away from their posts, and arrested the whole party. Supposing him to be a colonel in their army, they readily submitted, and delivered up their arms. He marched them into the road, and taking an opposite direction from the place where the Federal army lay, the sergeant said, "Colonel, we are going the wrong way."

"No," was the reply, "I am Captain Morgan, and you are my prisoners."

CHAPTER TWENTY-ONE
The Battles of Shiloh and Pittsburg Landing

While these events were going on in Kentucky and Tennessee, the war was progressing somewhat farther West and on the Mississippi River. In Missouri, not far from the borders of the State of Arkansas, at a place called Elkhorn, there was a severe battle on the 8th of March, 1862. The Federal forces engaged were under the command of Generals Sigel and Curtis, while the Confederates were commanded by Generals McCulloch, Price, and Van Dorn. The victory seemed to be with the Federals, because the Confederates were the first to withdraw, but the losses, both in killed and wounded, were the heaviest on the side of the Federals.

In this battle the brave Confederate commander, General McCulloch, was killed, and General Stirling Price was severely wounded. The death of General McCulloch was a great loss to the South, for he was one of the bravest and most dashing of all the officers in that service.

At this time the Abolition army began to make strong demonstrations on the Mississippi River. The State Legislature of Tennessee had removed from Nashville to Memphis. At Madrid Bend and at Island No. 10 in the Mississippi, above Memphis, were stationed Confederate forces as remote defences of that city. On the 15th of March, 1862, the Federals opened a furious bombardment upon both of these points.

The Confederate defences at these places had been constructed under the skillful supervision of General Beauregard, and were of very great strength. The Federals made the attack with five iron-clad gun-boats and four mortar-boats. The bombardment was kept up continuously night and day for fifteen days, without producing the least visible impression upon the Confederate works. In that time the Abolitionists fired three thousand shells, and expended over one hundred thousand pounds of powder, and the only damage they did was to kill one Confederate soldier. But the Abolitionists lost two gun-boats, or at least one was sunk and the other disabled. Such were the facts detailed in General Beauregard's official report to the Confederate Government.

But at this critical moment General Beauregard was called away to check a formidable movement of the Federals to cut off his communications with Richmond, by an immense land force of 80,000 men, under General Grant, and another of 40,000, under Buell.

The absence of General Beauregard from Island No. 10 was the cause of its speedy reduction. General McCall, who was appointed to the command of the post, was wholly incompetent for so responsible a trust. The Federals had, with miraculous energy and perseverance, cut a canal across the peninsula formed by the remarkable bend in the river, which was twelve miles in length, and which enabled the Federal gun-boats to get past the impregnable Confederate works at Island No. 10, without much difficulty, especially since the general who had taken Beauregard's place was not over shrewd and vigilant.

This canal was truly a miracle. I have said that it was twelve miles long, but this is the smallest part of the wonder. It had to be cut through a forest of large trees, which had to be "sawed off four feet under water." Through this canal two of the Federal gun-boats slipped past No. 10 on the night of April 5th, while the Federal commander, flag-officer Foote, adroitly held the attention of the Confederate general by an attack on the opposite side.

Now the Mississippi was held both above and below the island by the Federals, in large force at both points. There was nothing left for the Confederate commander to do but to get off

The Battles of Shiloh and Pittsburg Landing 147

as speedily as possible. This he did in the most unskillful and disgraceful manner. He spiked all his guns so imperfectly that they were in a short time unspiked and made serviceable to the Abolitionists. By this defeat the Confederates lost seventy cannon, most of them of the largest calibre, and a vast amount of powder, shot, shells, and other valuable munitions of war, besides about 200 of their soldiers taken prisoners. It was, under the circumstances, an irreparable loss to the South.

While these events were progressing on the Mississippi River above Memphis, the forces were gathering for an immense battle in Tennessee, about ninety miles east of Memphis. All the Confederate forces that were available were gathered under Beauregard at or near Corinth, which is situated at the junction of the Memphis and Charleston, and Mobile and Ohio railroads in the State of Mississippi.

At this time General Albert Sidney Johnston was also on the march with his army from Murfreesboro, to join General Beauregard at Corinth. The junction of the two armies of Beauregard and Johnston made a really splendid army, though probably much less in numbers than the force under Grant which was then encamped only a few miles away, upon the west bank of the Tennessee River. But it was not General Grant's intention to attack the Confederates until he was reinforced by Buell's army, which was then on the rapid march from Nashville to join him.

Generals Beauregard and Johnston, being apprised of this design, at once resolved to bring on the battle before Buell's army could arrive to reinforce Grant. Accordingly, on the morning of Sunday, the 6th of April, one of the greatest battles of the war was opened, with General Johnston the principal in command on the part of the Confederates. The battle commenced at daylight, and by six or seven o'clock was raging along the whole line of the two armies with terrific splendor. The Confederates fought with a desperation that seemed madness. Everywhere Grant's forces were driven back, although they fought with the greatest courage and determination. Their lines were continually broken, but they were constantly supplied with fresh victims. Thus the battle raged with unabating fury, the tide of victory, setting every where in favor of the South, when at two o'clock General Johnston was mortally wounded, while leading an assault at the head of his column. But the battle was already gained, and the dying hero breathed his last amid the wild shouts of the victory he had won. The news of General Johnston's fall was kept as long as possible from the army. Grant's forces were pushed back to the river. One after another of his positions were carried, until, by six o'clock in the evening, his whole line was forced back to Pittsburg Landing, where he was sheltered by his gunboats. All of Grant's encampments, with an immense amount of spoils, were in the possession of the Confederates, who were the undisputed masters of the field. They had three thousand prisoners, including one division commander, General Prentiss, and several brigade commanders, with many thousand stand of small arms, and vast quantities of forage, subsistence, munitions of war, and any quantity of means of transportation.

The number of General Grant's force in this great battle was 45,000 men. The number of Confederates was less than 38,000. The Confederates declared that they had to contend with Western troops, and said, "had we fought against Eastern or New England soldiers, we should have whipped them in half the time." General Prentiss, when he was taken prisoner, said to General Beauregard, "You have defeated our best troops to-day."

The Sunday night of this day's terrible battle, the Confederate troops slept on their arms in the Federal encampment. In the meantime, General Grant's army was in a most perilous condition. His reserve line was entirely destroyed, and his whole army crowded into a small circuit about Pittsburg Landing. They were driven to the very river's bank, and a surrender the next day seemed inevitable. But during the night Grant was reinforced by more fresh troops than Beauregard had in his whole command. Divisions under Generals Buell, Nelson, Crittenden, Thomas, and McCook, had all come just in time to save Grant's whole army from surrender.

At six o'clock on Monday morning, a hot fire from Grant told Beauregard plainly enough the story of the arrival of ample

The Battles of Shiloh and Pittsburg Landing 149

Federal reinforcements. In an hour's time another deadly battle, as fierce as that of the previous clay, was raging along the whole line. For four or five hours Beauregard's army repulsed every assault with marvellous valor, several times pushing precipitately back even the columns of fresh troops which were constantly hurled against them in such vast superiority of numbers.

An English officer in the Confederate service, writing a description of the battle, says:

> In some places we drove them by unexampled feats of valor, but sheer exhaustion was hourly telling upon both man and beast. Until noon we retained the ground heroically, but it became evident every moment that numbers and strength would ultimately prevail, so that although we had gained everything up to this hour, a retreat was ordered. Beauregard had prepared all the roads for this movement. There was no hurry or confusion, but everything was conducted as if in a review. We slowly fell back, leaving little of consequence behind, General Breckinridge and his Kentuckians bringing up the rear. We thus in an orderly manner fell back about two miles, and obtaining a favorable position for our small force, reformed line of battle, and waited several hours. The enemy did not stir; they seemed content to hold and not pursue, and did not remove five hundred yards from their original position of the morning. General John Pope was entrusted with the duty of following us up, but he acted very cautiously and fearfully, contenting himself with capturing two or three hundred exhausted and foot-sore Tennesseans, who lay down by the roadside.

With characteristic swagger and untruthfulness General Pope telegraphed to Washington: "As yet I have seen nothing but the backs of the rebels." The simple truth was that he did not venture near enough to see even their "backs."

This ended one of the most terrible battles ever fought either in ancient or modern times.

CHAPTER TWENTY-TWO
The Fall of New Orleans –
Infamy of "Butler the Beast"

Neither the people of New Orleans, nor the Confederate Government at Richmond had any fears whatever of New Orleans falling into the hands of the Abolitionists. But their dream of security was fallacious. An immense Federal fleet had long threatened that city, without venturing to make any demonstration against its defensive works at Forts Jackson and St. Philip.

But on April 17th, 1862, Flag-officer Farragut commenced bombarding the forts. His fleet consisted of forty-six sail, carrying two hundred and eighty-six guns, and twenty-one mortars. Many of these guns were of the most formidable size. General Duncan was in command of the forts. He had twelve gun-boats, one iron-clad, and a ram war-boat called the *Manassas*. He was regarded as one of the best artillerists in America. After a terrible bombardment had been carried on against him for one week, he telegraphed, on the 23d of April, that the Federals had made no impression upon his works. It is said that 25,000 thirteen-inch shell were thrown from Farragut's mortar-boats, without doing the least damage to the works.

But at half-past three o'clock on the morning of the 24th of April, Farragut's fleet steamed up the river, and, by an astonishing feat, absolutely ran the gauntlet between the two forts, placing the city of New Orleans completely at his mercy. General Lovell, the commander of the Confederate land forces, had a small force of Confederates in the city, but he was requested by the civil authorities to withdraw without making any fight, to save the city from the destruction of a bombardment. This General Lovell consented to do, after some hesitation, as it was certain that it would be impossible to remove the women and children in any time that would be allowed by the Federal commander. Besides, General Lovell had no force, and could get none, to save the city from either destruction by bombardment or surrender. It was therefore agreed between him and the mayor that the city should be surrendered, or rather left for the enemy to enter without resistance. For the Mayor refused to go through any ceremony of formally surrendering the city.

Flag-officer Farragut was very rude and haughty in his communications with the Mayor. For instance, the State flag of Louisiana floated from the City Hall, and Farragut sent word that it must be hauled down. This was not only an unreasonable but a very foolish demand, as the flag was the emblem of State authority, and not that of the Confederate Government. Mayor Monroe refused to haul down the State flag. The city was at the mercy of the Federal commander, and he could do what he pleased, but the flag would not be hauled down by the order of the city.

Several days elapsed in this correspondence between Farragut and the Mayor. Farragut threatened to bombard the city with all the men and women in it, if the State flag was not taken down. But no Louisianian could be found to tear down the State flag, even with these brutal threats of destroying the city continually coming from Farragut.

At length he was brought to his senses, probably by the fear that the transports freighted with General Ben. Butler and his army would arrive in time for that notorious character to share in the honors of first occupying the city. So on Tuesday morning, the first of March, Farragut gave up all he had been contending about with childish weakness for three or four days, and sent some of his own men to tear down the harmless State flag of Louisiana.

General Butler took possession as military governor of the city on the 1st of May. Then commenced a reign of insolence, despotism, and terror, such as was never before witnessed in any Christian or civilized country. Butler before the war was a lawyer of a great deal of bad eminence, in Lowell, Massachusetts. He was considered a man of considerable ability, but utterly destitute of integrity and honor. This reputation was a thousand times more than confirmed by his infamous rule in Now Orleans. Even women and young girls were subjected to the most scandalous treatment and torture at his hands.

The private citizens were plundered, not only of their gold, but of their jewelry, their silver-ware, and all articles of value Butler could lay his hands on. The elegantly furnished mansions of private and merely business citizens were in many instances stripped of all their most valuable articles, or taken possession of by some of the most brutal and shameless of Butler's officers, and converted into dens of debauchery and every other infamy.

Both men and women were savagely torn from their families and sent to dungeons for such things as laughing at Federal soldiers, and other harmless acts, which were never before treated as offences by any civilized nation. In some instances the dead were dug up by Butler's order, to see if rings and other valuable jewelry had not been left upon their person by the afflicted relatives. To such an extent were these horrid deeds practiced that the wretch obtained the cognomen of "Butler the Beast," by the common consent of mankind – a title which will stick to his infamous name as long as the memory of the war shall last.

An English officer in the Confederate service has the following remarks on the cruelty and brutality of General Butler's rule in New Orleans:

> The rule of General Butler in New Orleans has been forever rendered odious and detestable by his many acts of cruelty, despotism, and indecency. Nor shall I add more than say, that he has rendered himself contemptible to friends and foes throughout the civilized world. His general orders are a mass of cruelty and folly – an eternal monument of his base and indefensible character; and in his persecution of women he has shown his unmanly disposition and temper, beyond all former example.

He imprisoned a Mrs. Phillips on Ship Island, on the charge of laughing at the funeral procession of a Federal soldier.

The truth of the case was as follows: Mrs. Phillips (wife of Philip Phillips, formerly United States Senator from Alabama) was standing on her balcony; and when the *cortège* passed, many children in the next house, who had a dancing party, ran to the balcony, and all began to laugh. She was treated barbarously on Ship Island, and went deranged; but Butler laughed at her sufferings, but would not mitigate the punishment, saying that "all women were strumpets who laughed at Federal soldiers." He wished it to be believed that he was fearless, yet he wore armor under his clothes, slept on board ship, and was never for a moment without an armed guard, whether in or out of his house, while several pistols, ready cocked and capped, lay beside him, and sentinels walked within five paces of him. He had a large sign placed in his office in the St. Charles Hotel, with the inscription, "A she-adder bites worse than a male adder."

This was the first time in the history of the world whole people were imprisoned for the harmless folly of laughing at either the living or the dead. *Smiles* were never before punished as a crime. But the infamous tyrant who committed these crimes against humanity and law, will be repaid for all his barbarity, by having the contempt of the virtuous of all mankind while he lives, and by having his very family and friends shrink from the mention of his name, as "Butler the Beast," when he is dead.

His deliberate murder of a young man by the name of Mumford alone would stamp his name with eternal infamy. William B. Mumford had taken down a United States flag which some soldiers had placed there, and which was wrongfully there, because the city had not, at that time, been surrendered, nor formally occupied by the Federal army. And if it had been, the act of taking it down was an act of war, and not a crime. But it was in reality neither an act of war nor a crime. And besides, it was done before Butler had formal possession of the city. For this Butler ordered him to be hanged, and he was hanged. A more cold-blooded murder never took place, and the brave young man well said, when standing upon "Beast Butler's" gallows, "I consider that the manner of my death will be no disgrace to my wife and child; my country will honor them." And so it will, when the name of this brutal assassin is placed in history by the side of the most infamous criminals of the world.

CHAPTER TWENTY-THREE
Stonewall Jackson in the Shenandoah

At about the time of the entrance of Butler into New Orleans, there were some stirring events passing in the Valley of the Shenandoah, between Stonewall Jackson and the forces under the Federal General Shields. General Banks had been in that region all winter, but supposing that General Jackson had left the valley, he went off to Washington.

A correspondent who was with Jackson's army at this time, wrote as follows: "When I last put pen to paper I did not imagine that old Stonewall intended moving in such fearful weather; but when it was known that the general's servant had packed up, I knew we were all bound for a tramp somewhere." His Negro said:

> Whenever I misses massa a little while in de day, I allers knows he's prayin' a spell; whenever he's out all day, I knows we's going to move next day; but when he stays out and comes back to have a long spell of prayin', I knows dare's goin' to be a fought somewhar, mighty quick, and dis chile packs up de walibles and gets out ob de way like a sensible cullored pusson!

The same writer who relates this anecdote, gives the following interesting picture of the immortal Stonewall Jackson:

> "Stonewall" may be a very fine old gentleman, and an honest, good-tempered, industrious man, but I should admire him much more in a state of rest than continually seeking him moving in the front. And such a dry old stick, too! As for uniform, he has

none – his wardrobe isn't worth a dollar, and his horse is quite in keeping, being a poor, lean animal of little spirit or activity. And don't he keep his aids moving about! Thirty miles ride at night through the mud is nothing of a job; and if they don't come up to time, I'd as soon face the devil, for Jackson takes no excuses when duty is in hand. He is about thirty-five years old, of medium height, strongly built, solemn and thoughtful, speaks but little, and always in a calm, decided tone; and from what he says there is no appeal, for he seems to know every hole and corner of this valley as if he made it, or at least, as if it had been designed for his own use. He knows all the distances, all the roads, even to cow-paths through the woods and goat tracks along the hills. He sits on his horse very awkwardly (although, generally speaking, all Virginians are fine horsemen), and has a fashion of holding his head very high, and chin up, as if searching for something skywards; yet although you can never see his eyes for the cap-peak drawn down over them, nothing escapes *his* observation.

His movements are sudden and unaccountable; his staff don't pretend to keep up with him, and, consequently, he is frequently seen alone, poking about in all sorts of holes and corners, at all times of night and day. I have frequently seen him approach in the dead of night and enter into conversation with sentinels, and ride off through the darkness without saying, "God bless you," or any thing civil to the officers. The consequence is, that the officers are scared, and the men love him. What service he has seen was in Mexico, where he served as lieutenant of artillery. At one of the battles there his captain was about to withdraw the guns, because of the loss suffered by the battery, and also because the range was too great. This did not suit our hero; he advanced *his* piece several hundred yards, and "shortened the distance," dismounted his opponent's guns, and remained master of the position.

An anecdote is told of this great commander in one of his Shenandoah battles against Banks. Being dissatisfied with the manner in which one of his cannon was handled, he jumped from his horse, and giving the cannon a deadly aim with his own hands, he devoutly lifted his eyes to heaven, uttering this prayer, "The Lord have mercy on their guilty souls," and gave the word to "Fire."

Jackson's small force of only twenty-one hundred men was at a place called Kearnstown, when on the afternoon of the twenty-third of March, General Shields advanced upon them in great force. Jackson instantly formed his line of battle, with Brigadier-General Garnett commanding the left, while Ashby with his cavalry held the right, and Jackson himself the centre. The battle raged with fearful violence for four hours, during which time Jackson's little band contended with unparalleled gallantry against overwhelming numbers. But at seven o'clock in the evening he ordered a retreat, after having lost five hundred men in killed and wounded, three hundred prisoners, and two cannon.

General Shields made no attempt to follow him until the next day. Though defeated, General Jackson lost no baggage, and no officer of prominence in his command was killed. General Shields lost several officers, and was himself badly wounded in the arm by a shell. But he had achieved a great glory in defeating Stonewall Jackson, for he is, I believe, the only Federal general who has won that renown.

But the skill and successes of General Shields in the field did not save him from the persecution of the Abolitionists. He was blind enough to suppose that the object of the war was not to free Negroes, but to simply enforce the laws of the United States. He therefore did not use his army to steal Negroes, or to wantonly plunder and destroy the property of private citizens. And on this account the whole Abolition press literally howled at him, notwithstanding he had saved the Northern army in the Shenandoah from utter annihilation in consequence of the innumerable blunders of General Banks. But his faithful adherence to the rules of civilized war, together with his refusal to use his army to catch Negroes, caused Mr. Lincoln's government to give him the alternative of resigning or being removed.

When he came back to Washington, with his health shattered by his severe campaigns in the mountains of Virginia, he met with Senator Sumner, of Massachusetts, in the presence of Mr. Lincoln. Sumner at once began to upbraid him for his course in not allowing Negroes to come within the lines of his army. General Shields replied that he had discovered that a great number of the Negroes that thronged the Federal camps were simply spies, who remained within our lines just long enough to learn all they were capable of retaining, and then stole back to tell the Confederates all they knew.

He also stated that when he accepted a command, it was his understanding that the object of the war was not to free Negroes, but to preserve the Union. Sumner replied that, "If the object of the war was not to abolish slavery, there is no object of the fight commensurate with the vast expenditure of life and property, and I would go for stopping it to-morrow." This remark was made in the presence of Mr. Lincoln, and General Shields was surprised that he said not one word in contradiction of Sumner's statement that the sole object of the war was to free Negroes.

General McClellan, General Bud, General Fitz-John Porter, as well as General Shields, lost their commands, and were persecuted, because they insisted on conducting the war on the rules recognized by all Christian nations, and also because of their understanding that the object of the war was to preserve the Union, and not to free Negroes. Thus was the Northern army stripped of four of its very ablest generals, who were sacrificed to the black and piratical shrine of Abolitionism.

CHAPTER TWENTY-FOUR
Embarkation of the Army of the Potomac For the Peninsula – Evacuation of Yorktown – Battle of Williamsburg

While the events described in the last chapters were progressing, General McClellan was busy in perfecting the Army of the Potomac for a grand march against Richmond. For more than six months he had been wholly employed in perfecting that great army. The impatience of Congress, and the clamor of the Abolitionized people, had been continually raising the cry again of "on to Richmond." But General McClellan rather pompously and boastfully declared we "were to have no more defeats, no more retreats," and no amount of clamor could induce him to move before he was ready.

Early in the spring of 1862 he began to think of placing his tremendous army in the field of active operations. But a very great difficulty confronted him. The Black Republican leaders discovered that he was not an Abolitionist. They furthermore saw that he was so popular with the army that his views would naturally be to a great extent shared by it. Then some Democratic papers had mentioned his name in connection with the next nomination for the Presidency. It was at once seen that his very great popularity with the army would render him a formidable candidate. So they resolved upon his ruin, even if it cost the North the price of its whole army. Northern preachers declared that the best thing for the country would be McClellan's defeat.

Mr. Lincoln and his Cabinet were for having the Army of the Potomac go over the old Bull Run route on the way to Richmond. To this plan General McClellan was invincibly opposed. The question was finally referred to a council of the chief officers of the army, by whom General MeClellan's plan of the Peninsular campaign was almost unanimously recommended. But this was not the end of his embarrassments. A new Department of the Mountain, in Virginia, had been created to make a place for General Fremont. Notwithstanding that General had conducted himself so badly and foolishly in Missouri that the President was obliged to remove him from his command, the more violent leaders of Mr. Lincoln's party dogged the President until he made a new place for him And now they insisted that, notwithstanding General McClellan was just moving to try to take Richmond, ten thousand of his men under General Blenker should be taken from him and sent to Fremont's army away up to the mountains.

General McClellan so strongly remonstrated against this act – setting forth that he already had the smallest number of men he thought necessary for his great undertaking – that the President assured him that the men in Blenker's command should not be withdrawn from his army. Notwithstanding this solemn promise of the President he did order Blenker's division to be sent to Fremont only the day before McClellan was to start on his great campaign. For this act of faithlessness Mr. Lincoln pleaded the great "pressure upon him."

While General McClellan was solemnly reflecting upon this vacillation or treachery on the part of Lincoln, a member of his staff said: "General, the authorities at Washington are painfully afraid that you will succeed in taking Richmond, and therefore are stripping your army in the beginning." McClellan replied, "Such treachery seems impossible, and yet it does look like it."

But the preparations were fully made for the transportation of the Army of the Potomac to the Peninsula. The Peninsula is an isthmus formed by the James and York Rivers. It is from seven to fourteen miles wide, and about fifty miles long. To reach it the grand army went in transports down the Potomac to Fortress Monroe, which is seventy-five miles land march, over the Peninsula to Richmond. The van of the grand army started for Fortress Monroe on the 17th of March, 1862. Division after division left as fast as the transport boats could be loaded. It was a grand sight. The whole transport fleet consisted of over four hundred steamers and sailing vessels, which had to carry an army of one hundred and twenty-one thousand, five hundred men, with fourteen thousand animals, forty-four batteries, together with wagons, ambulances, pontoon trains and all the other vast appointments for so tremendous an army.

It took from the 17th of March to the 2d of April to transport this vast army from Washington to Fortress Monroe. It at once commenced its march towards Yorktown on the way to Richmond.

At Yorktown was a Confederate fort, which had just been re-enforced by General Johnston, the Confederate commander. General McClellan's plans for forcing those works were entirely frustrated by want of support from Washington. His intention was to make a naval and land assault upon the place at the same time. The naval part of the combined attack was to be executed by Flag-officer Goldsborough; and the land attack he assigned to General McDowell's corps. But Flag-officer Goldsborough wrote General McClellan that he could send no naval support to him and on the very day when he expected McDowell's corps he received an order from Washington that that part of his army had been detached from his command, and retained at Washington.

This was a heavy blow to McClellan. The same member of his staff who had addressed him on a former occasion in relation to the jealousy of the Administration, said: "You see how it is, General; it is certain that you are not to be supported in this campaign."

There was now nothing left for McClellan to do but to undertake the siege of Yorktown. This work he commenced at once. When on the fifth of May he had succeeded in finishing his works necessary to commence firing upon the fort, it was discovered that it was evacuated by the Confederates. This fact called forth many unfriendly remarks from the Abolition press. A siege which had been rendered necessary by the withdrawal of expected support from Washington, and had been executed with so much skill as to force the Confederates to evacuate the fort without risking a fight, was still the subject of unfriendly criticism in the government organs.

The Confederates evacuated Yorktown on the 3d of May. It was General Johnston's design to retreat with his whole army to the defence of Richmond. To General Longstreet was entrusted the duty of defending the rear of the army and of worrying the advancing columns of McClellan as much as possible. For this purpose General Longstreet made a stand at Williamsburg, about fifteen miles from Yorktown.

At Williamsburg the Confederates had somewhat extensive works, called Fort Magruder. Though it was no part of the Confederate plan of the defence of Richmond to hold this fort after McClellan had passed Yorktown, yet it was a good place to inflict some chastisement upon the invading army without any risk whatever to the Confederate army. So at this point on the fifth of May a bloody battle occurred. The Northern forces engaged were Hooker's division, Smith's division, part of Couch's, and Hancock's brigade, and the rear of the Confederate army, commanded by Longstreet.

The battle was opened by Hooker directly in front of Fort Magruder. The fort kept up only a sufficient show of resistance to thoroughly engage the attention of General Hooker, while the wily General Longstreet poured in a rapid succession of attacks upon his left flank, which gave Hooker more than he wanted to do all day, and which, but for the arrival of General Kearney's division at five o'clock in the afternoon, would have resulted in the destruction of General Hooker's whole division. During the battle the Confederates steadily but slowly forced back the invaders over two miles. Both sides fought with determined bravery. But Longstreet so skillfully handled his troops that he inficted a terrible punishment upon the Federals, with a comparatively small damage to his force. General Hooker's loss was one thousand seven hundred men, six field pieces, several thousand stand of arms and several hundred prisoners.

At nightfall the battle-field was in the possession of the Confederates. At two o'clock the next morning, after securing whatever booty the field afforded, Longstreet commenced to fall back towards the main body of the Confederate army, which was then many miles ahead of him.

The Federals made no haste to follow. They did not even enter Williamsburg in force until towards evening the next day, sixteen hours after the Confederates had left it. But as Longstreet was without transportation he was obliged to leave his wounded behind in Williamsburg. It is rather a mortifying thing to reflect upon that the Federal commander took occasion from this fact to claim a victory; when the plain truth was that Longstreet had turned round and dealt the advance columns of McClellan's army a terrible blow, and then pursued his march, with very little loss to himself, and considerable booty from the foe. Enough of such victories would not have left McClellan a single soldier to march back to Washington. The number of Federal soldiers engaged in the battle could not have been much less than forty thousand, while Longstreet had but twenty thousand in the fight.

The gallant Colonel Lomax of the Nineteenth Mississippi regiment was killed while leading a most daring charge against Dan Sickles' brigade; and his Negro recovered the body in the Federal lines, and carried it several miles on his back, and conveyed it to Richmond to the bereaved wife, to keep a promise he had made: *"that he would never let his master's body fall into the hands of the enemy."*

Up to the time that Abolition demoralization reached the Southern Negroes their hearts were with their masters and their masters' cause. In almost every town in the South they gave balls, parties and fairs for the benefit of the Confederate soldiers and sent thousands of dollars, of clothes, blankets, shoes, &c., for "Massa and de boys in Varginny." In Vicksburg the Negroes gave a ball which realized a thousand dollars, and freely gave it all for the Confederate cause. Indeed, it was their custom to boast "dat do Soofern colored man can whip a Norfern nigger wid de Yankee to back him."

CHAPTER TWENTY-FIVE
Doings of Stonewall Jackson in the Shenandoah Valley

Although the Northern newspapers tried to keep a good face on the fight at Williamsburg, there was a settling doubt on the minds of the people as to the way matters were going in the field. The initial battle in the campaign had evidently been adverse to the North.

But McClellan continued to push forward his columns, until by the 16th of May his advance divisions had reached the point known as the "White House," the head of navigation on the Pamunkey River, eighteen miles from Richmond.

General Johnston had already withdrawn his whole army behind the line of the Chickahominy River, and it was evident that he had determined to fight his great and decisive battle from the immediate defences of Richmond.

To act in conjunction with McClellan a fleet of Federal gun-boats, under the command of Commodore Rodgers, sailed up the James River. The fleet met with no opposition until it reached Fort Darling, on Drury's Bluff, about twelve miles from Richmond. But at that place, after a four hours' engagement with the guns of the fort, it was compelled to haul off with several of the boats badly damaged. Now we have the situation of all the Federal force acting for the taking of Richmond: the gun-boats on the James River twelve miles from the city, and McClellan's army resting on the Chickahominy, eighteen miles distant.

But here McClellan's offensive movements, as I shall show

you, really ended, and he ever after had to act on the defensive. The Federal forces, instead of being concentrated for a decisive battle, were scattered about at great distances from each other in four distinct armies. There was the Army of the Potomac on the Peninsula in Virginia, then in Western Virginia there was the Army of the Mountain, created expressly to make a command for Fremont, to stop the ceaseless threats and clatter of the more violent of the Abolitionists. Then there was the Army of the Shenandoah, under General Banks, and the Department of the Rappahannock, under General McDowell.

Now when the authorities at Washington saw the position in which they had placed McClellan's army they began to feel the necessity of doing something for the protection of Washington. For it was evident that, if McClellan's army was destroyed, there would be nothing to prevent the whole Confederate force from marching directly on Washington, as Richmond, in that event, would be effectually relieved from danger.

It was therefore resolved, at this eleventh hour, to consent that General McDowell should march to reinforce McClellan on the Chickahominy. But some of the "Republican" papers were careful to say beforehand that, if the army of the Potomac should prove successful, it would be through the hand of General McDowell: notwithstanding that they had before abused that General for the defeat of Bull Run.

General McDowell, at the time we were speaking of, had an army of thirty thousand, at Fredericksburg. For the purpose of enabling him to march to attack Richmond with McClellan, General Shields' division of ten thousand men was ordered from the army of General Banks to go to McDowell, which made his effective force over forty thousand men.

The 26th of May was set as the time when McDowell's column was to move. But before it had been pushed more than ten miles from Fredericksburg, the shrewd commander at the head of the Confederate army, General Joseph E. Johnston, quickly saw the nature of the movement, and it was easy for him to stop it. He had only to give the word to Stonewall Jackson, who was already up in that region to make one of his clashing

Doings of Stonewall Jackson in the Valley 169

campaigns down through the valley again to put a stop to all reinforcements to McClellan from that quarter, or any other.

At this time Banks' army was at Harrisonburg. Fremont was at Franklin, on the other side of the mountains, in Western Virginia. But a brigade of his department, under Milroy, was on its way to reinforce Banks. Jackson, in the first place, by a rapid march of seventy miles threw his gallant force against the command of Milroy and Blenker combined and drove it back.

General Fremont rushed to their assistance, but Jackson, leaving some cavalry to deceive Milroy, suddenly retraced his steps, and joined General Ewell, whom he had left in the valley with ten thousand men. General Banks, supposing that Jackson was engaged over the mountains in Western Virginia, was quietly making his way towards Fredericksburg, unconscious of danger. On the morning of the 22d of May, however, Banks heard Stonewall Jackson's guns in his rear.

Ewell was sent to seize Winchester, General Banks' great depot of army stores, while Jackson attacked his advance at Front Royal. Banks was not only completely outwitted, but seemed to lose all self-possession. He did not retreat, he flew, and never stopped until he got on the north bank of the Potomac. It is said he made the remarkable time of fifty-three miles in forty-eight hours. Immense stores of all kinds fell into the hands of the Confederates. It was one of the most brilliant exploits of the war, and made the name of Stonewall Jackson famous.

When the authorities at Washington heard that Stonewell Jackson was at Winchester, and then up at Harper's Ferry again, they were wild with another alarm, and instantly ordered McDowell to face about, and instead of marching to attack Richmond, to fly up the Shenandoah to protect Washington. President Lincoln had been heard to boast that he had "set a *trap* for Jackson." But now he was trembling with the fear that he should fall into the trap himself.

Now there was a combined force of thirty thousand men, under Fremont and Shields, in a grand chase to catch Jackson, with his sixteen thousand. But he outwitted all his pursuers. Fremont intended to go down on one side of the Shenandoah

River and Shields on the other, and thus cut off Jackson's retreat. Ashby's cavalry, however, held Fremont in check. It was during this retreat that General Turner Ashby, one of Virginia's most chivalric sons, fell while leading a gallant charge at the head of his command. Jackson kept on in his course until he arrived at Cross Keys, where he turned upon Fremont, soundly whipped him, and then crossed the Shenandoah River at Port Republic, burning the bridge behind him, and, falling like a thunderbolt upon Shields' command, almost annihilated it.

Thus ended Jackson's brilliant Valley campaign, and with it ended all idea of the frightened Mr. Lincoln of sending reinforcements to McClellan. Jackson's little army had become so "everywhere present" that the Abolitionists at Washington began to shake as soon as they heard the name of Stonewall Jackson mentioned.

CHAPTER TWENTY-SIX
Battle of "Fair Oaks," or "The Seven Pines," and "Gaines' Mills"

General McClellan's situation on the banks of the Chickahominy was a critical, if not a painful one. Whether from necessity or over-caution, he was certainly painfully inactive. The disappointment in not receiving the co-operation of McDowell's army might well have paralyzed him, for he would never have been caught in the situation he found himself placed in, had it not been a part of the plan of the attack upon Richmond from that point, that McDowell should be sent to co-operate with him.

General Johnston having succeeded in his skill fully devised trick to prevent the union of McDowell's with McClellan's forces, determined at once to strike a decisive blow by an attack upon McClellan in his situation at Seven Pines and Fair Oaks Station, on the banks of the Chickahominy River. The attack was to commence on the morning of the 31st of May. To General D. H. Hill and General Longstreet was entrusted the attack upon McClellan's front, while General Huger was to assail his left flank, and General G. W. Smith his right. Smith, Longstreet, and Hill were all promptly in position at eight o'clock, but they had been ordered to wait and not begin the attack until they heard Huger's forces firing on the left. They waited impatiently for two hours for the signal gun of Huger. The cause of his delay was a difficulty in crossing the river, a fact which was at the time unknown to Generals Longstreet and Hill.

At ten o'clock General Hill advanced and opened the battle by attacking McClellan's front, which was pretty well entrenched, and therefore the assailing Confederates met, not only a determined resistance, but a most murderous fire. Soon, however, a brigade of Johnston's army succeeded in gaining a position partially in the rear of McClellan's redoubts or breastworks, and commenced a furious flank-fire upon them, which in a short time drove the Federals out, leaving their guns in the possession of the Confederates.

But all this time nothing was heard of Magruder; and General Gustavus W. Smith, who was to attack McClellan's right flank, in consequence of the course of the wind, heard nothing of the musketry of Hill and Longstreet, and did not learn until four o'clock in the afternoon that a battle had been going on all day. He had been all the time nervously waiting for Magruder's signal gun to begin the battle. But when he learned the facts, he immediately threw his men forward with such force and fury as to drive everything before them.

The most desperate courage was displayed by both armies; but the results of that day's terrible battle were in favor of the Confederates. But General Johnston, the commander-in-chief of their forces, was so severely wounded that it was a long time before he was able to take the field again.

An English officer in the Confederate service, from whom I have before quoted, says of this battle:

> As I rode through the enemy's camp, viewing the destruction on every side, I met Frank, one of Longstreet's aids, looking as blue as indigo.
>
> "What's the matter, Frank? Not satisfied with the day's work?" I enquired.
>
> "Satisfied be hanged," he replied. "I saw old Jeff. Davis, Mallory, Longstreet, Whiting, and all of them, a little while ago, looking as mad as thunder. Just to think that Huger's slowness has spoiled every thing! It is true, Longstreet and Hill fought magnificently, as they always do, and have gained a brilliant victory; but had Huger obeyed orders we should have demolished the enemy. As it is, their right is routed and demoralized, and we have gained nothing more than a brilliant victory."

Battle of "The Seven Pines" and "Gaines' Mills"

In General Johnston's report of this battle, he says:

> We took ten pieces of cannon, six thousand stand of arms, one garrison flag, four stand of regimental colors, a large number of tents, besides much camp equipage and stores. Our loss was four thousand two hundred and eighty-two killed, wounded, and missing; that of the enemy is stated in their journals to have been ten thousand, although no doubt that figure is far below the truth.

President Davis issued a short congratulatory address to the army which had so gallantly won this victory, closing with these words:

> You are fighting for all that is dearest to man; and though opposed to a foe who disregards many of the usages of civilized warfare, your humanity to the wounded and the prisoners was the fit and crowning glory of your valor. Defenders of a just cause, may God have you in his keeping.

On the 12th of June, just twelve days after this battle, which was followed by the retreat of McClellan's army, General Ben. Butler issued the following impudent and lying bulletin in New Orleans: "On May 31st, Richmond was evacuated, and General McClellan took possession of the city! General Banks had driven Stonewall Jackson headlong to the foot of General McDowell, who before this has probably kicked him over the border. So ends the drama! – it is enough."

I am ashamed to confess that this is only a specimen of the misrepresentation and falsehood with which the people were insulted by certain of the Northern press and Northern generals during the whole progress of the war.

After the wound of General Johnston, General Robert E. Lee, who was then acting as chief of the war department in Richmond, was appointed to Johnston's place as commander-in-chief of the Army of Northern Virginia, though the immediate command of the forces in the field fell upon General Longstreet when Johnston was disabled.

The battle-field of "Fair Oaks" or "Seven Pines" is only

six miles from Richmond, and so after the Confederate General had delivered his severe blow, he retired his army within the lines of the defences of that city, and McClellan's troops at once reoccupied the ground from which they had been driven by the day's battle.

After this battle some time elapsed without any active operations on either side worth mentioning. But in this pause General Lee was busy in preparing to deal a decisive blow to the invaders. He decided to concentrate all the available force of the Confederate armies at Richmond. This plan involved the withdrawal of Jackson from the Shenandoah. To put McClellan and the authorities at Washington off their guard he made a feint of reinforcing Jackson in the Shenandoah valley at the very time he was bringing his whole force to Richmond. This movement he cunningly masked by detaching a division, under General Whiting, and sending it off to join Jackson. At once the rumor flew over the North that Lee was preparing to invade Washington. Lincoln, McClellan, Congress, and everybody in the North were deceived; for all this time Jackson with a force now increased to twenty-five thousand men was secretly and rapidly marching to reinforce Lee at Richmond. So skilfully did Jackson conceal his march that neither Banks, Fremont, nor McDowell had any idea that he had left the valley of the Shenandoah, and were all the time making prodigious preparations to keep him off of Washington.

Gen. Robert E. Lee

In the meantime Lee sent that bold cavalryman, General J.E.B. Stuart, with fifteen hundred troops, to make a raid round the whole circuit of McClellan's army. This bold undertaking was a perfect success. The whole North was startled with a report that Lee was in McClellan's rear. And Lee was put in possession

Battle of "The Seven Pines" and "Gaines' Mills" 175

of a perfect knowledge of the position of the invading army, and at once ordered a general forward movement.

General Jackson had already arrived at a point where he could sustain the attack commenced by the rest of the Confederate forces. On the afternoon of the 26th June, General A.P. Hill crossed the Chickahominy River at a place called Meadow Bridge, while the divisions of Longstreet crossed at Mechanicsville Bridge, with the intention of marching down the north bank of the river together for a general attack upon McClellan's lines.

But they had no sooner crossed the river than they were confronted by General Fitz John Porter's corps which held a strongly intrenched position. A short but bloody conflict took place at this point, in which the Confederates were repulsed with fearful loss, for the number of men engaged. The engagement did not cease till nine o'clock at night, when each side occupied the same position that it did at the opening of the engagement.

The next morning at day break the Confederates renewed the attack upon McClellan's forces, then posted at Gaines' Mills. This position was admirably chosen and heroically defended. All day the waves of battle surged to and fro, and thousands of brave men on both sides bit the dust. The sun was just sinking down in the West as if to hide its face from the ghastly scene. The Confederates greatly exhausted had sought the cover of a piece of woods, and McClellan apparently mistaking their silence for defeat moved a heavy mass of infantry to their attack. The advance was beautiful. The long lines of splendid infantry, sent up cheer upon cheer as they advanced. The Confederates crouched closely to the ground, and when the Federals arrived within a hundred yards, they poured a deadly volley in their close ranks, then rising with unearthly yells, and dashing through the smoke of battle fell upon them with the bayonet, the pistol and the bowie knife. The Federal columns fled in confusion.

The battle, however, was not ended. McClellan's artillery still occupied a commanding hill and was sweeping the field with canister and grape. The wise forethought of Lee had provided for this emergency. The gallant Texas brigade of General Hood had been held in reserve. All at once a wild shout arose! It was the

Texans with their gallant commander on foot, leading them in the final charge. On they came like an avalanche. Nothing could resist them. They charged among the redoubts and guns, and soon McClellan's line was broken beyond recovery. A hand to hand conflict ensued. Clouds of dust, smoking woods, long lines of musketry, the deafening roar of artillery, were mingled in the wildest confusion, but the Confederates were victorious. Slowly, and sullenly the long dense lines of McClellan retired under the cover of the darkness.

Scarcely had the roar of the cannon ceased at this point before the sound of Stonewall Jackson's guns broke upon the ear. He had fallen upon McClellan's rear almost while that officer had been dreaming that he was in the Shenandoah. His line of retreat was cut off! Thus ended the battle of Gaines' Mills.

The same English officer whom I have often quoted in this history has made the following remarks upon the results of that terrible battle:

> The field was a rich booty. I myself counted fifteen magnificent brass and bronze field-pieces, with caissons and horses and dozens of cannoneers exactly as they were left by their vanquished owners. Camps, clothing, thousands of prisoners, and immense quantities of small arms, banners, drums. Many of our

The charge of the Texas Brigade at Gaines' Mills.

troops lay fast asleep where they had halted, some of them using a dead Federal for a pillow! The destruction was awful; and if many guns fell into our hands, the heaps of blue-jackets around them told that they had been bravely defended. Many horses were shot; and the enemy finding themselves unable to carry off the pieces, had deliberately cut the throats of the uninjured animals to prevent them from falling into their hands. The ground around the cannons was dyed purple. Judging from the placid countenances of many, I thought they were only sleeping; but on closer inspection invariably discovered a small hole in the side of the head, made by the unerring bullet of our sharp-shooters!

But if Lee had won a great victory, it had been at an immense sacrifice of life, and the loss of some of his bravest officers. Among them, Major Robert Wheat fell while gloriously charging at the head of his Louisiana Battalion. With tones of anguish it was whispered around by his comrades: "Poor Wheat is gone." His dying words were: "The field is ours, as usual, my boys. Bury me on the battle-field."

Alas, how many such brave and patriotic men have fallen in this cruel and wicked Abolition war? How many happy homes made desolate? How many kind hearts broken? Will the just Maker of men ever forgive the fanatic wretches who brought about this unnatural, this terrible conflict?

CHAPTER TWENTY-SEVEN
McClellan's Retreat

With this last defeat all General McClellan's plans for taking Richmond were suddenly brought to an end, and his genius was taxed to keep his whole force from being gobbled up by Lee's victorious army. There was no alternative left but to retreat through the great swamp to the banks of the James River, where he could enjoy the protection of his gun-boats – those friendly supports which had so often saved General Grant from annihilation in the Western campaigns.

This retreat for the James River was therefore commenced immediately, and was conducted, as the Confederate commanders confessed, with consummate skill. After McClellan succeeded in getting the remains of his army to the James River, the Confederate General Hood remarked: "If Grant, or any other Federal general, except McClellan or Sherman, had had the conducting of that retreat, we should have caught the whole army."

Lee vigorously pursued the retreating Federals. His advance column overtook a portion of McClellan's rear on Sunday, the 29th of June, at Savage's Station, on the York River railroad. A sharp four hours' battle took place at this point. The Federals had strongly entrenched themselves for the purpose of checking pursuit, and as soon as Lee's column came within range, they poured forth a murderous fire. After three or four hours of desperate fighting, the Federals were driven out of their trenches, and made double quick retreat to overtake the rest of the army. The Confederate General Griffiths, of Mississippi, a skillful and heroic officer, was killed in this engagement.

At daybreak the next day, Monday, June 30th, the pursuit of the retreating Federals was resumed by Lee's victorious army. But McClellan was conducting that retreat with matchless energy and skill, and Lee's forces had not proceeded many miles when they were surprised at a place called Fraizer's Farm by a portion of McClellan's army which was skillfully covered by some sedge pines, which completely hid it from the view of the pursuing hosts. At the very first fire batteries of sixteen heavy guns opened upon the advance columns under General Hill. Instantly the Confederates rushed bravely forward into the very jaws of death. From several lines of battle they received the most murderous fire of musketry. The battle, though short, was one of the most deadly of the war.

Swinton, in his excellent history of *The Campaigns of the Army of the Potomac*, says of this conflict:

> Finally Randall's battery was captured by a fierce charge made by two [Confederate] regiments, advancing in wedge shape, without order, but with trailed arms. Rushing up to the muzzles of the guns, they pistoled or bayoneted the cannoneers. The greater part of the supporting regiment fled; but those who remained made a savage hand-to-hand bayonet fight over the guns, which were finally yielded to the enemy.

It is truly appalling to think of the slaughter of so many brave men on both sides, and all for the sake of forcing upon the Negro a condition which he neither asked for nor knew how to enjoy.

The following is a story which an English officer gives of a talk with an old Negro the day after the battle of Fraizer's Farm:

> Returned from viewing as much of the field as was possible in the darkness, I observed a light in Fraizer's house, from which also there was smoke ascending. Feeling somewhat cold, and, as I expected, found it occupied by many of the wounded. Before the fire sat a middle-aged Negro, wrapped up in a blanket and shivering.

"What's a-miss, uncle," taking a coal to light my pipe.

"Do Lor' bress you, massa! de chills, de chills.'"

"Were you here, uncle, during the fight?" I asked, taking a stool.

"No, sar! dis chile was in de woods! de best place, I tink, when dem ar bullets come a-whistling an' singing roun' yer head. Was I scart, oh? I tink I was scart – it was worse nor half-a-dozen scarts to this darkie. Well, you see, massa, it was dis way. When ole massa hert the Lincumbites was comin roun dese diggins, 'Pete,' says he, 'I'se gwine to Richmon, and I wants you ter see to things, an' mind de Lincumbites don't run off wid anything; they won't hurt you,' says he, 'but if dey only catches me, I'm a gone chicken.'

"Weel, massa, one ebenin while I eat supper, up comes a whole lot of Lincumbites, and says dey, 'Whar's de master, nigger?'

"'In Richmon,' says I, an' went on eatin; but a big fellow says to me, 'Hi, nigger, yer wanted out here,' and I went out. 'How many chickens has yes got?' says one. 'Who's dem turkeys 'long to?' says another. 'If yer don't bring me some milk, I'll burst yer head,' says one in de crowd. 'Pull dat bed out here,' says another. 'Tuch him up wid de bayonet,' says another, and case I couldn't begin to speak to 'em all, somebody kicks me on de shin, and I runs in de house. One of de men wid traps on shoulders comes and makes 'em kind o' quiet, but I find out dey hab stolen my supper, and de bed, and de chairs, and didn't leave me my ole pipe!'

"If dis is de Union folks, tinks I, dey won't suit dis darkie, sure! So after dey stole all de chickens, and de turkeys, and de cabbage and taters, I tought it was about time for dis chile to leave. So I packs up two or tre things in a handkercher, and puts out.

"'Halt dar!' says a big feller, wid a gun. 'Where's yer gwine, darkie,' says he.

"'I gwine to Richmon,' says I, 'to massa, to get something to eat.'

"'O, yer tick-headed nigger,' says he, 'doesn't yer knew we's de great liberation army ov de norf, and come to set all de niggers free?'

"'I'se a free colored pusson, any how,' says I, 'and kin

go anywhere I'se a mind,' and was gwine to pass him, when he hits me wid de gun, and two sodgers seizes me by de scruff ob de neck, and hauls me up before de kernal.'

"'Where did you cotch de contraban'?' says he, smoking a cigar, big-like, and frowing out his legs.

"'I'se a free man, sar,' says I.

"'Hole your tongue,' says he, getting kind o' red; 'if dese people doesn't know de blessin' of liberty, dey must be taught, dat's all. Take him off to do guard house, sargent,' says he, and kase I said I'se free, de sargent begins and kicks de cloth out ob my pants.

"'And dare dey hab me, massa, more nor a week, feedin' me and lots ob odder darkies on black beans and pork massa's hogs won't eat. But when I hears de firing going on – now's de time for dis chile, says I, and I gets out ob de way right smart for an ole darkey. Fust I gets to de right, but de bullets fly so mighty thick I runs off somewhar else; den one oh de big screechin' things comes along, and I begins to say my prayers mighty fast; den while I lay behind a tree, our folks comes up, makin' a big noise, and I lays berry close to de groun'; but I get mighty scart, and runs clar into de swamp, and dar I stays until just now, when I crawls home agin, shiverin' in every jint. Don't talk to me, massa, ob de norf. I knows how it is – dey only wants to work de life out oh de colored folks, and den dey gives 'em deir free papers, to let 'em starve. Dey can't fool dis chile – he knows more nor he wishes to know 'bout do great norfern liberation army.

"De darkies better stay wid ole massa, and lib as he libs, and hab doctors to look afer 'em, and hab dimes to spend. Dem Yanks is big fools, and dey tink they's good as us, but dey ain't half as good as some darkies, if dey is White folks and talk big!"

Now this old Negro was a fair specimen of the spirit with which the darkies generally regarded the Abolition army. They were a thousand times more happy and contented than they will ever be again. It was hard work to teach them to hate their masters. It has cost us nearly a million of White men's lives, and four or five thousand millions of dollars, to force upon them what they did not want, and what they can never learn to use with benefit either to themselves, or to the superior White race.

After the last battle, at Fraizer's Farm, McClellan retreated during the night to a point where the right wing of his army rested under the protection of the Federal gun-boats in James River. His front was strongly intrenched in an admirably chosen spot at Malvern Hill. Never was a position better calculated for defence, or for delivering a terrible blow to an attacking force. This was McClellan's last stand, for he could go no further, except to fall entirely back to the bank of the River, under his gun-boats.

The Confederate forces at the battle of Malvern Hill were under the command of General Magruder, who ordered his infantry to charge in the very face of McClellan's formidable breastworks, behind which a hundred cannons, of the heaviest calibre, were in position to rain a perfect shower of grape and canister down through the open space, over which the Confederates must pass to reach them. But, at Magruder's mad command, the brave fellows rushed forward at full run, while instantly they were met by a murderous fire from McClellan's breastworks, which mowed them down like grass.

They were not merely repulsed, they were murdered. Again Magruder ordered fresh victims for the same slaughter, and again the gallant men rushed forward only to be killed. Still a third time the foolish command was given for more men to take the place of so many already slaughtered in the fruitless attempt. A soldier who was in McClellan's army at that time says:

> I never saw such courage as those Confederate boys displayed at Malvern Hill. We were in a position where we could mow them down just like winrows, but on and on they kept coming, until the heaps of their dead might have been used as breastworks, could they have been reached without meeting the same certain death of their gallant comrades who had gone before!

Thus the work of death went on until the merciful darkness put a stop to the slaughter. McClellan's works had not been carried, but the Confederates occupied the field, and pushed forward their pickets to within a hundred yards of his guns.

During the night McClellan withdrew as secretly as possible, and retreated to the bank of the River at Harrison's Landing, a position which was covered by his gun-boats.

This was the last battle of his disastrous retreat, and the end of his Peninsular campaign. Never before had so many stupendous plans miscarried. Never such great expectations brought so poor a termination. Instead of taking Richmond his whole army narrowly escaped destruction, and nothing at last saved it from being captured but the gun-boats in James River.

Some idea of the spirit which animated the Confederates may be judged of from the following incident. Major Peyton, a Confederate officer, while leading a regiment in one of the charges at Malvern Hill, had a young son, only fifteen years of age, struck down by a cannon ball. The boy in his agony cried out: "Help, father, help me!"

"When we have beaten the enemy," was the father's stern reply. "I have other sons to lead to glory. Forward men!"

But a few minutes elapsed before another cannon ball lay the father bleeding by the side of his son.

Never did a more gallant people draw a sword than these Southern men.

CHAPTER TWENTY-EIGHT
The Inauguration of a Reign of Plunder and Arson

After the failure of the Peninsular campaign Mr. Lincoln issued a proclamation calling for 300,000 more soldiers. The people of the North were generally discouraged, that is, the Abolitionists and all who sympathized with them began to doubt their ability to subjugate the South. The Black Republican press was bitter and abusive. It was hard work to raise more soldiers, and it was only by paying immense bounties that any recruits could be obtained.

But there was, however, a fresh hope dawning in the bosoms of the Abolitionists. Hitherto McClellan's commanding influence enabled him to impart a certain moral restraint upon the army, and to keep its action somewhere within the rules of civilized warfare.

But that influence was now gone. The war was to be changed to an almost universal crusade for theft and plunder. Revenge and cruelty were to take the place of civilized warfare. By a general order from Washington the military commanders were directed to seize all the property they could find belonging to citizens of the Southern Confederacy. This order caused all Europe to look upon the North with a degree of surprise and contempt, for it was a violation of the rules of civilized war.

While McClellan's campaign on the Peninsula was progressing, all the fragments of the Abolition armies in Northern Virginia, under Banks, Fremont, and McDowell, which had from time to time been cut to pieces by Stonewall Jackson, were consolidated into one army, under the command of General John Pope. This was called the "Army of Virginia." The plan of forming this army was in the first place started by the more ultra of the Black Republicans, with the hope of checking the popularity of General McClellan, upon whom they were convinced they could not depend, to carry out the uncivilized plan of warfare now determined on. They had also cherished hopes that this army might work its way round and snatch from McClellan "the glory" of taking Richmond. This accounts for the evident satisfaction expressed by some of the more open-mouthed of these Abolitionists when it became evident that McClellan would not take Richmond.

Pope inaugurated his campaign by a general order entirely worthy of his own brutal nature and of the savage instincts of those who had commissioned him. Pope's appointment to the command of this new "Army of Virginia" was dated June 26th, the day before McClellan's battle at Gaines' Mills. The infamous order above referred to was dated July 23d, 1862. It commanded all his subordinate officers to immediately arrest all citizens of the Confederate States within their reach, and make them take an oath of allegiance to Lincoln, and give satisfactory security for keeping it, or be banished from their homes and driven farther South, and, if they ventured to return to their homes, to be treated as spies, that is, to be shot.

The object of this barbarous order was simply to get hold of the private property of the Southern people. His order was couched in the most bombastic language, declaring that his headquarters should be in the saddle, and ridiculing all such ideas as lines of retreat and base of supplies. This was intended as a cut at McClellan, and was greatly relished by all the shallow people who could be taken by the swagger of such an ignorant gasconader.

He also declared that his soldiers should not be employed in guarding "rebel property." This was looked upon as general order for arson and plunder. It gave great delight to all those malignant creatures known as "radicals." Indeed, Pope's brutal order, which was most congenial to his own bad heart, was evi-

The Inauguration of a Reign of Plunder and Arson 187

dently inspired by the leading Black Republicans of Washington. But General McClellan at once saw that such an order, proceeding from the commanding general of the new Department of Virginia, would be regarded as a general license for plunder and robbery, and would result in the overthrow of all discipline, and therefore of all efficiency in the army.

So to save his own army from demoralization from such a cause, he immediately issued an order of an entirely different character, in which he used the following words:

> The idea that private property may be plundered with impunity, is, perhaps, the worst that can pervade an army. Marauding degrades as men and demoralizes as soldiers all who engage in it, and returns them to their homes unfitted for the honest pursuits of industry. The General commanding takes this occasion to remind the officers and soldiers of this army, that we are engaged in supporting the Constitution and laws of the United States, and in suppressing rebellion; that we are not engaged in a war of rapine, revenge or subjugation; that this is not a contest against populations, but against armed forces and political organizations; and that it should be conducted by us upon the highest principles known to Christian civilization.

Three weeks from the date of this order General McClellan was virtually removed from command. Creditable as it was to him, as a man and a general, it cost him his command; and the brutal and ignorant Pope was, for the moment, the pet and hope of Mr. Lincoln and his party.

Nor can we be surprised at this, for McClellan had, in his order, entirely misstated the objects of the war. He had correctly set forth the rules of civilized warfare, and had well defined *his own* idea of the objects of the war; but his notions of the objects of the war and those of Lincoln and his party were widely different. It *was* "a war of rapine, revenge and subjugation;" it *was* a "contest gainst populations," and it was not the design of those who were waging it that it "should be conducted upon the highest principles known to Christian civilization." This was General McClellan's idea, but it was not the idea of Lincoln, Seward, and the party they represented.

No one, therefore, can be surprised that McClellan lost his command after the publication of the humane and enlightened order to his army. Between him and the leaders of the war, there was certainly a very great conflict of opinion. Just as much of a conflict as there is between civilization and barbarism, or between cruelty and humanity, or vice and virtue.

So McClellan's army was taken from him, and was removed from the Peninsula and sent to act in conjunction with Pope. At the same time, General Halleck, an old army-officer, who had been, up to this time, employed in the West, was brought to Washington and placed in the position of Commander-in-chief, much to the disgust of nearly every one of the best officers in the Northern army. But the "malignants" at Washington must have a fit tool of the despotism and cruelty which were now to be the fixed policy of the Administration. McClellan could not be used for such a tool; Halleck and Pope could.

One of Halleck's letters closed with these brutal words: "Our armies will ere long crush the rebel lion in the South, and then place their heels upon the heads of sneaking traitors in the North." By *sneaking traitors* he meant all the patriotic men who loved the Union our fathers made and refused to be roped into the bloody ranks of Abolition despotism.

Governor Stone of Iowa in a public speech at Keokuk said:

> I admit this to be an abolition war and it will be continued as an abolition war so long as there is one slave at the South to be made free. I would rather eat with a nigger, drink with a nigger, live with a nigger, and sleep with a nigger than with a Democrat.

Such vulgar language shows the hate and bitterness that filled the hearts of the Abolitionists. About this time the Abolition papers were filled with articles asserting that the war would never be successful until Mr. Lincoln declared all the Negroes of the South free. Of course he could not free the Negroes until *after* he had conquered the Southern people, for they would not, until then, be within his control. But still the Abolitionists were clamorous for the act to be done. Mr. Lincoln and Mr. Seward, however, were not yet ready to throw off the thin mask of conservatism under which they commenced the war. But they had wrought up the Northern people to a pitch of fury and made them ready to endorse the cruel and inhuman mode of warfare we have described, and the next step was soon to follow.

CHAPTER TWENTY-NINE
The Second Battle of Manassas or Bull Run

  General Pope's reign of plunder and persecution was of short duration, as was also his insolent boasting. He had been reinforced by a considerable portion of McClellan's army, and had certainly men enough under his command, if he had possessed the skill to handle them. But unfortunately for him General Lee had despatched Stonewall Jackson to look after him.

  When Jackson's force left Richmond for the Rappahannock again, which had already been the scene of so many of his victories, some of the Confederate officers sarcastically said: "Lee's short of rations again! Jackson's detailed to go to the commissary!" By the "commissary" was meant General Banks, for Jackson for some time supported his army off of stores taken from that general. Hence Banks was called "Jackson's commissary" by the Confederate soldiers.

  And it so happened that, in this new campaign, Jackson first struck that portion of Pope's army which was stationed under Banks, at a place known as Cedar Mountain. A battle took place on the afternoon of the 9th of August, which, after a fierce fight, resulted in the total defeat and rout of the Federals, who, however, were not followed more than two miles when Jackson ordered a halt for the night.

  Jackson's force in this battle was 8,000. That of the Federal general was 15,000. The Confederates lost six hundred killed, wounded, and missing, while the Federals lost about two thousand. Jackson captured five hundred prisoners, fifteen hundred stand of arms, two Napoleon guns, twelve wagon loads of ammunition, and several wagon loads of new clothing. It was quite true that Banks had been acting as Jackson's commissary again.

General Pope, who had boasted that he should make his head-quarters in his saddle, was completely out-manœuvred and entrapped every way. One night General Stuart swept round his camp and burned it, capturing three hundred prisoners, and very nearly captured Pope himself. All of his public and private papers fell into Stuart's hands, not even excepting his coat and pantaloons.

I forgot to mention that in the battle of Cedar Mountain, that Jackson's victory was not gained without a great and irreparable loss, in the death of General Charles H. Winder, who was one of the bravest and most gallant men in the Confederate army.

The next heard of Stonewall Jackson after the battle of Cedar Mountain was that, with a force of 20,000 men, he was far up the valley towards the head-waters of the Rappahannock River, where he had been sent by Lee on one of the most adventurous, if not dangerous, undertakings of the whole war. The object was to actually get in the rear of Pope's army, cut off his communications, and destroy his stores. The danger of this experiment was that it would place Jackson's army between two great Federal armies, Pope's on one side, and that of the immediate defences of Washington on the other. This very plan shows that Lee held the generalship of both Halleck and Pope in great contempt.

Jackson's army was marched with such secrecy and rapidity that his own officers could not comprehend the nature of the movement.

Said one of these: "Let us look facts fully in the face. Here we are marching in the rear of an enemy more powerful than ourselves, far from all supports, liable to be broken up by superior numbers from Washington, on the one hand, or literally annihilated should Pope face about."

Another replied: "'Tis just like him; no one can imagine what he is about; it was so in the valley and elsewhere – plenty of marching and fighting, and mighty little to eat, except what we chanced to capture."

Replied a third: "As to rations, I know not what we shall do; we are on half allowance now, and to-morrow we shall have to fast and fight as usual. I heard that the commissary-general spoke to Jackson about it, but he simply replied, 'Don't trouble yourself, the enemy have a superabundance – their depots are not far ahead.'"

Events proved that Jackson's estimate for abundance to eat was right, for a few hours' march brought his army to a place called Bristoe's Station, which was the first railroad depot connecting with Pope's rear. On the sudden appearance of the Confederates, Pope's guards escaped towards Manassas, and spread the alarm. Manassas was an immense depot of Federal stores of all description. In a few hours Jackson's army was luxuriating in this vast depot of abundance. Every thing was captured without even a skirmish. Jackson found himself in possession of "nine cannon, seven full trains heavily laden with all kinds of stores, ten first-class locomotives, fifty-thousand pounds of bacon, one thousand pounds of beef, two thousand barrels of pork, five thousand barrels of superfine flour, vast quantities of hay, oats, corn, thirty thousand loaves of bread, an immense amount of hard bread, and all kinds of ammunition, etc."

The telegraph was found to be in good working condition, and the rejoicing Confederates telegraphed to Alexandria, which was the largest Federal depot of war stores, calling for an immediate supply of artillery and wagon harnesses, with other like things which the Confederates most needed. The Federal commandant, having no suspicion that the despatch was from Stonewall Jackson's men, sent forward a heavily laden train, with all the articles called for, and these all fell into the hands of the Confederates.

All this mischief had been done by Stonewall Jackson, when Pope had no suspicion that he was within sixty miles of the place. In the meantime General Lee was hurrying the march of the main body of his army to support the new position gained by his advance, under General Jackson, on the very spot at Manassas where the first great battle of the war had taken place two years before.

General Pope also had been aroused to the true state of things, and at once hurried forward his whole force to the same point. In a characteristic bombastic speech to his army, he boasted that he should "bag Jackson this time!"

Jackson had made the best of the brief time in throwing up defensive works, and preparing for the fierce conflict which he knew must soon come. It was no part of his plan to retreat, and indeed it was Lee's instruction for him to keep his position until he should arrive with the main army.

On Wednesday, the 27th of August, 1862, a portion of Pope's advance, without knowing, came within reach of Jackson's guns at Manassas Junction, and was driven back in confusion. All the next day Pope's army was pouring around him. That night Jackson removed his whole force from Manassas Station to the old battle-field of Manassas, where he was a little nearer to Longstreet's division, which he knew to be approaching in the direction of Thoroughfare Gap, and where he would also have a better position for either attack or defence. There was skirmishing and a good deal of pretty serious fighting all day Friday, August 29th, but the decisive battle did not take place until Saturday morning. Lee's whole army had arrived and was in position for another terrible battle on the old blood-stained field of Manassas. General Pope threw forward a heavy force upon Lee's right, when that wily commander at once fell back with that portion of his array for the purpose of leading General Pope to suppose that he was retreating. The shallow Pope fell into the trap, and in his great joy, telegraphed to Washington that Lee was "retreating to the mountains." The news was flashed all over the North, and the bulletins of the newspapers were blazing with tidings of a great victory won by Pope over Lee.

In the meantime Pope drove forward what he supposed to be a pursuit of the flying Confederates; but, as the result proved, drove his own army into the jaws of destruction. He had gone in this *pursuit* but a short distance, when he met the most deadly fire from nearly all Lee's artillery, which was concealed in the forest. Instead of retreating, Lee had simply withdrawn his left flank, while his right remained intact, and therefore the commencement of General Pope's pursuit was really the beginning of the most dreadful and decisive battle of the campaign. The conflict was bloody but short. It was Bull Run over again. Speaking of the way the Confederates fought, a Northern correspondent. says: "They came on like demons emerging from the earth." The Federal army was not only defeated – it was routed, and the disorganized mass of soldiers had to trust for safety to their own heels or horses.

General Pope did not stop his flight until he was safe within the defences of Washington. A correspondent in his army for a Baltimore paper put his loss at 32,000 men, killed, wounded and missing. Lee paroled 9,000 prisoners.

Thus ended poor Pope. Never did a man set out with so much bombast and swagger, and never did any man fall so fast and so low. Even the brutal school of Abolitionists who had placed such hopes in him, and who had rejoiced so much at his inhuman programme for the war, were heartily ashamed of him. He fell to rise no more. He is to this day the laughing-stock of men.

CHAPTER THIRTY
Lee in Maryland – Battle of Antietam

With the ridiculous failure of General Pope, the "Army of Virginia" which had been created to blot out "the Army of the Potomac," passed out of existence, and the old name of "the Army of the Potomac" was a power again, and McClellan was reinstated in command.

It was a bitter pill for the Administration to take, to put forward General McClellan after they had so publicly insulted and belittled him. But the cry of "Washington is in danger!" was reverberating over the North. Mr. Lincoln and his Cabinet were trembling with fear. And it was seen that the army demanded McClellan again.

For although he had not, at this time, been formally removed, he had been put under a cloud, a fact which caused a universal discontent in the Army of the Potomac especially. Indeed, there was no alternative for Lincoln but to reinstate McClellan.

Virginia had been cleared of Federal troops, and Lee was preparing to march into Maryland with a view of pushing his army into Pennsylvania.

The result of Pope's campaign had really been to put the Administration at Washington completely on the defensive.

On the fourth day of September, General Lee actually crossed the Potomac River into the State of Maryland. Whether General Lee had any object in this movement further than to possess himself of the immense Federal army stores at Harper's

Ferry, and to replenish his commissary department generally, is very doubtful. Lee invaded Maryland with three army corps, commanded respectively by Generals Jackson, Longstreet, and Hill.

Jackson was to march directly for Harper's Ferry, while Hill and Longstreet were entrusted with the responsibility of watching and holding in check General McClellan in any effort he might make to protect the Federal force at Harper's Ferry.

General McClellan had only been reinvested with command twelve days when this movement on Lee's part was made. To keep McClellan from reaching Harper's Ferry, Longstreet was directed to march directly to Hagerstown, in Maryland, and there to wait until McClellan's movements should develop. Immediately General McClellan moved his entire force in the direction of the mountains which Lee suspected he would, and to provide for which Lee sent General D. H. Hill to check him. Hill's instructions were to hold a certain point at all hazards until Jackson had reached Harper's Ferry. That point is known as Boonsboro' Gap. At this place a severe battle occurred. At first the Confederates, being greatly outnumbered, were being terribly pressed, and the Confederate General Garland was killed, but at length reinforcements arrived under General Longstreet, and the fighting was desperate on both sides. When night shut down upon the bloody scene the two opposing armies occupied the same position they did in the morning at the opening of the battle.

But the Confederates had gained their object, which was to prevent reinforcements from reaching Harper's Ferry.

While the battle was progressing at Boonsboro' Gap, General Jackson was capturing Harper's Ferry. During the night he placed his heaviest guns in position, and in the morning opened upon the place from all directions. At half past seven, A.M., the place surrendered. The Federal commander, Colonel Miles, had one of his hips shot away in the engagement.

Jackson took twelve thousand troops, twelve thousand stand of arms, seventy-three pieces of artillery, and over two hundred wagons. This surrender took place on the 14th of September. General Lee, perceiving that McClellan was massing his whole force, united his army as far as practicable at a point near Sharpsburg, about eight miles to the west of Boonsboro' Gap. At this place occurred, on the 17th of September, the memorable battle of Antietam, which takes its name from the beautiful valley where it was fought. General Lee was strongly posted, but he had not over forty-five thousand men, while the Federal army numbered nearly a hundred thousand. McClellan commanded in person, while under him were Generals Burnside, Porter, Hooker, Sumner, Franklin, Meade, Sedgwick, and Pleasanton, commander of cavalry.

The battle was opened by an assault upon Lee's left which was held by Stonewall Jackson. Hooker led the attack with eighteen thousand men well posted in the high grounds where Jackson lay with a force of only four thousand. In that day's terrible fight nearly one half of these brave fellows were left dead upon the field of slaughter. The whole force of both armies was soon at work in one of the fiercest conflicts that occurred during the war. The very earth shook all day with the terrible shock of battle. The tide of success was now with one side, and now with the other, until each must have welcomed the friendly night which put a stop to the horrible slaughter.

The Federal historian of the Army of the Potomac, Swinton, admits that the fortunes of this day's dreadful fighting were rather with the Confederates, notwithstanding the vast disproportion of numbers, and his opinion is sufficiently sustained by the fact that during the night, McClellan disappeared from the front, leaving his dead unburied on the sanguinary field where they had poured out their blood so heroically.

The loss of the Federals in this battle was, in killed and wounded, twelve thousand five hundred men. That of the Confederates was over eight thousand. All day of the 18th of September, both armies were too much exhausted to renew the deadly strife. And during the night of that day General Lee withdrew across the Potomac, without an effort on the part of McClellan to prevent him. On the 20th General McClellan commenced to cross the river into Virginia, but no sooner was one column across than it was badly repulsed and driven back into the river by General A.P. Hill.

Thus ended all attempts to follow up Lee with the immense stores he had gained by his brief campaign in Maryland. Of Lee's return to Virginia, an Abolition paper bitterly said:

> He leaves us the *débris* of his late camps, two disabled pieces of artillery, a few hundred of his stragglers, perhaps two thousand of his wounded, and as many more of his unburied dead. Not a sound field-piece, caisson, ambulance, or wagon, not a tent, a box of stores, or a pound of ammunition. He takes with him the supplies gathered in Maryland, and the rich spoils of Harper's Ferry.

If General Lee's intention in passing into Maryland was simply to gather supplies, his campaign was a great success; but if, as was and is generally believed, he meant to make a stand on that side of the Potomac, as a base of operations against the North, then he signally failed. For the battles which McClellan had delivered against him, though not victories, had caused him to recross into Virginia, and give up the invasion of the North.

But the campaign cost McClellan his command. The Abolition leaders, who were but too glad of an opportunity to destroy him, seized upon the fact that Lee, with his inferior force, had done so much damage, and escaped safely back into Virginia. One day, while McClellan was sitting in his tent at Beckertown, conversing with General Burnside, he received the following despatch from Washington:

> General Order, No. 182.
>
> War Department, Adjutant-General's Office,
> Washington, Nov. 5th, 1862
>
> By direction of the President of the United States, it is ordered that Major-General McClellan be relieved from command of the Army of the Potomac, and that Major-General Burnside take the command of that army.
>
> By order of the Secretary of War.

McClellan coldly read the dispatch, and, handing it to Burnside, said: "Well, Burnside, you are to command the army."

Thus ended General McClellan's military career in the great Abolition war.

Just previous to the removal of General McClellan on the 22d of September, Mr. Lincoln had issued what he called his "preliminary Proclamation of Emancipation," that is, he announced that if "the rebels," as he called them, did not submit on or before the 1st day of January, 1863, he would issue an edict, "freeing all their slaves, and would pledge the Government to maintain that freedom." Of course Mr. Lincoln had no more right to do all this than he had to issue a decree making himself Dictator for life. I have shown you on page 113 how solemnly he declared that the war was prosecuted "to preserve the rights of the States," and now when only a year had elapsed, he completely falsified his own word.

No man ever lost such a glorious chance for immortality as General McClellan did when he did not resign his commission in the army upon this announcement being made. Thousands of brave and gallant boys had enlisted under the solemn promise first made by Mr. Lincoln, and if General McClellan had set an example of resigning, it would probably have produced such an effect in the army that the Abolitionists would have been compelled to withdraw it. If they had been thus forced to give up their Negro freedom idea, we should soon have had peace, for they would never have prosecuted the war for any other purpose.

General McClellan, however, did not resign. Yet the effect of the proclamation in the army was very great. We shall refer to it in another chapter.

After the battle of Antietam, Mr. Lincoln had visited the battle-field, and an incident, entirely authentic, is related, showing with what levity and indifference he viewed the scene of the dreadful carnage and slaughter.

"There," said McClellan, who was riding by his side, "we buried eight hundred gallant and noble follows."

Mr. Lincoln, scarcely glancing at the spot, exclaimed, "Mac, did you ever hear Major P. sing Old Dan Tucker?"

The general shook his head in evident sorrow at such desecration of the newly-made graves about him, when Mr. Lincoln, calling to Major P., who was riding a few rods in the rear, insisted that he should sing "Old Dan Tucker" for General McClellan, and it was done.

If this statement was not authenticated beyond doubt, I should hesitate to put it in here, for never before over the fresh graves of a battle-field did one whose heart ought to have wept tears of blood, indulge in such unfeeling, such unholy jests.

CHAPTER THIRTY-ONE
Bloody Doings in the West

     It is necessary to go back a little to give some account of the way the war was progressing in the West.

     On the very day when Lee won the great victory at the second battle of Manassas, there was a battle going on at Richmond, in the State of Kentucky. The Abolition government at Washington had never relaxed any of its energy in that section. Indeed its military movements in that section were quite equal to those in Virginia in magnitude. The stupendous project had already been formed of driving out the Confederate forces from Kentucky, Tennessee, and all the States west of the Mississippi, and then of cutting down through the Gulf States into the very heart of the South. Grant was "pegging away," as Mr. Lincoln would say, in Mississippi, McClernand and Buell in Kentucky and Tennessee, while there was another Federal army operating in Missouri and Arkansas.

     It was necessary for the Confederate Government to do something to distract the plans which were gradually ripening for the subjugation of these more Southern States. The scheme hit upon was to make some bold raids through Kentucky, and threaten Cincinnati and the State of Ohio, for the purpose of dividing the strength of the Federals, which was setting so strongly South.

     Early in the month of August, the Confederate commander in Kentucky and Tennessee, General Kirby Smith, ordered a strong force to move northward, for the purpose of carrying out the scheme above stated. On the 29th of August it reached the little town of Richmond, where lay a considerable Federal force under General Nelson. A severe battle followed, in which the Abolition army in that region was quite as badly whipped as it was at Manassas in Virginia the same day.

This defeat of Nelson at Richmond left General Smith a clear track through Kentucky to Lexington, at which city he arrived on the 4th day of September. As his army passed through Lexington it received the wildest display of welcome, especially from the ladies. The rule of the Abolition commanders in that region had been brutal in the extreme, and Smith's presence was therefore hailed as a sign of protection and safety from further outrage. When General John Morgan's cavalry, which was in Smith's command, reached the city, it is said that the demonstrations of welcome were perfectly deafening. In that place this gallant officer was again in the presence of his own neighbors and friends.

When it became known in Cincinnati that General Smith had won the battle of Richmond and penetrated as far towards the Ohio line as Lexington, the people of that city were wild with fear.

The whole city instantly became a camp. People going from their houses to their places of business, or from their places of business home to their meals, were seized by the Abolition officers and pressed into the army.

At the same time that General Smith entered the State of Kentucky from the line of Richmond, General Bragg came into the State with another Confederate army in a more easterly direction, from Knoxville and Chattanooga. But General Smith's orders in marching so near to the Ohio line were to menace, not to attack. After making this demonstration he was to fall back to cooperate with Bragg's army.

This cunning demonstration of the Confederates in Kentucky had the desired effect. It caused the Federals to evacuate East Tennessee and Northern Alabama.

On the 17th of September, General Bragg fell upon a force of Abolitionists at Mumfordville, and captured about five thousand prisoners, with a loss of less than a hundred of his own men. On the 8th of October he had a severe battle with nearly the whole Federal army in Kentucky, at Perryville, which was not a decided victory to either side, though Bragg claimed a victory. He captured fifteen pieces of artillery and took a large number of prisoners. But his mistake was in risking the battle at all with only part of his own army, for the commands of neither General Smith nor that of General Withers were with him at the time.

Ascertaining that the Federals had been reinforced during the night, General Bragg withdrew early the next morning to Harrodsburg, where he met Generals Smith and Withers.

While Bragg was thus backing and filling, and losing his opportunity, General Buell's army was swelling to dimensions so far beyond that of the Confederates that it became evident that he must beat a retreat.

This he commenced on the 12th of October, carrying with him an immense amount of stores and munitions of war. It was painful to witness the dismay of the Democrats and better sort of people of the region round about Lexington when they saw that they should no longer enjoy the protection of the Confederate army. Women and children were everywhere seen crying and wringing their hands. They declared that they preferred to die rather than again be subjected to the brutality and cruelty of the Abolitionists.

Thus ended that Confederate campaign in Kentucky. Though it had done some gallant fighting and won no mean victories, yet it was nearly fruitless of the great advantages it might have won had General Bragg pushed his opportunity as Stonewall Jackson, and other Confederate commanders, would, no doubt, have done.

The people of Kentucky were in a strangely divided and unhappy condition during the whole war. Men like George D. Prentice, the editor of the Louisville *Journal,* a prominent paper in that State, took strong sides with the Abolitionists.

While professing to hate Abolitionism, they threw all their influence in its favor, and gave the strongest support to a man who had no other object but the abolition of "slavery," and the subversion of the democratic form of government established by the great men of the Revolution.

While the events above described were taking place in Kentucky, active scenes were transpiring further South. General Rosecrans, a Federal commander of what was called the Army of the Mississippi and Tennessee, was entrenched, with forty-five thousand men, at Corinth. The Confederate commands of Generals Van Dorn and Price united and marched to Corinth, for the purpose of engaging Rosecrans. It was a desperate and foolhardy undertaking to attack an entrenched army so greatly superior in numbers. The Confederate forces were under the command of General Van Dorn. The battle was opened on Friday morning, October 3d, 1862. Under General Van Dorn were Generals Price, Lovell, Maury, and Herbert. Van Dorn's assault was made with tremendous power, The Federals were pushed slowly back for nearly two hours under the admirably handled batteries of General Lovell's corps.

But Rosecrans had been driven into his fortifications. Still the Confederates drove him beyond his first line of fortifications, back within his second. This was the condition of the two armies when night put a stop to the fearful carnage. Van Dorn was elated and telegraphed to Richmond that he had gained a great victory. But he knew not yet the strength of Rosecrans' works.

The next morning before daylight (General Van Dorn still commanding), General Price commenced firing with his artillery, at a distance of only four hundred yards in front of the enemy's entrenchments. Soon Lovell, Price, Maury, and Herbert were all hotly at work. The Confederates fought with the same desperation they had displayed the previous day, but it was a useless struggle. After performing prodigies of valor, and after a horrible slaughter of some of the bravest men that ever entered a battlefield, Van Dorn ordered his troops to fall back. But this order was not given until three o'clock in the afternoon. From daylight to this hour he had kept his little army in one of the fiercest and most unequal combats ever witnessed. But when he gave up and fell back, Rosecrans made no attempt to follow him, which showed that he, too, had had enough of fighting for the time.

While these bloody scenes were being enacted in Tennessee, the northwestern portion of the State of Missouri was the theatre of the most horrible guerrilla warfare. Under the despotic rule of General Schofield, and the murderous cruelties of an infamous scoundrel by the name of Colonel McNeil, the people of that section had been goaded into uncontrollable madness.

One act, of the many atrocities of McNeil, will forever stamp his name as one of the most hardened wretches that ever lived. A so-called Union man by the name of Andrew Allsman was missing. McNeil issued an order that unless Allsman was found in ten days he would shoot ten Confederate prisoners. The ten days elapsed and Allsman was not found. In vain the citizens and the Confederates protested that they had not harmed him, and knew nothing of his whereabouts. But McNeil was determined to have a feast of innocent blood. So he took ten innocent citizens of Missouri to slake his cannibal appetite. In vain did their wives and friends plead! The ten men were inhumanly slaughtered as a revenge for the absence of the one man Allsman. Afterwards the man Ailsman turned up alive and well!

He had been absent of his own will and motion. But the ten innocent men were in their graves, as an everlasting monument of the infamous cruelly and butchery of Abolition rule in Missouri.

This wretch McNeil, it is said, is still living and is now one of the leading spirits of the Abolition party in the State of Missouri. He is a fit instrument of the abominable despotism of the Abolitionists of that State, where clergymen, who refuse to take a certain illegal and ridiculous oath, are ruthlessly dragged out of their pulpits, and incarcerated in dungeons, or forbidden, under the most outrageous penalties, to preach the Gospel of Christ.

When these scenes are rehearsed, in future times they will be regarded as the darkest and bloodiest events that disgrace the history of mankind. They have already caused the name of the United States to be repeated with a chill of horror throughout the civilized world.

CHAPTER THIRTY-TWO
General Burnside's Bloody Campaign

We now return to relate the progress of the war in Virginia. After it was known that Burnside had succeeded McClellan in the command of the Army of the Potomac, the Abolition press struck up the old cry of "On to Richmond." Burnside was the new pet of the hour. All at once the Abolitionists discovered that he was just the man for the occasion. Though nobody ever imagined that Ambrose Burnside was anything more than the most common of common place mortals, now he was pushed into notice as a very great man. We shall soon see what very small timber is sometimes used to make great men.

On taking command General Burnside at once applied himself to the task of changing the base of the army to Fredericksburg, on the Rappahannock River. This strange movement astonished the authorities at Washington, as they could not possibly see the object of it. He, however, persuaded them that he had discovered the true plan to defeat Lee and take Richmond. This plan was to leave a small force to make a show of crossing the Rappahannock, near Warrenton, as a feint to deceive Lee, and make him believe that the Federal army was about to throw itself into Virginia, and then by a rapid march to throw his whole army across the river at Fredericksburg. This movement General Burnside thought would catch Lee in a trap. Though even in case his trick were successful nobody but the cunning Burnside could see the *trap*. The idea of Ambrose Burnside attempting to catch Robert E. Lee in a *trap* carries with it a certain amount of amusement.

The whole nature of Burnside's movement was as well known to Lee as it was to himself. But the Confederate commander did effectually deceive Burnside by making him believe that he had sent a large portion of his forces down the river.

General Burnside commenced throwing his pontoon bridges across the Rappahannock at Fredericksburg on the night of the 10th of December. The whole movement was visible to the eye of Lee's troops posted on the bluff which overlooked the whole town on the river.

Lee designedly made but a feeble resistance to Burnside's crossing, just enough to impress that weak man with the idea that none but a small Confederate force was in his front; for Lee was just as anxious to get Burnside on his side of the river as Burnside was to get there.

The whole of the 12th day of December was occupied in the passage of Burnside's army across the Rappahannock, and at night he occupied Fredericksburg. The news flashed over the North of Burnside's great victory; he had successfully crossed the Rappahannock and had taken Fredericksburg! The Abolitionists and their sympathizers were wild with joy. It was said that "the right man had been found at last." Large sums were bet that Burnside would be in Richmond in ten days. How far it was to Richmond, or how he was to get there, were questions which they did not think upon. Their wild imagination *jumped* him into Richmond.

Burnside imagined that on the morning of the 13th of December, after his troops had enjoyed so quiet a night in Fredericksburg, he should make short work with what he believed to be the fraction of Lee's army before him, if indeed Lee did not fly during the night. He little comprehended the fact that the whole of Lee's army was anxiously waiting to receive him.

The sun that morning rose clear, but a dense fog hung over the town of Fredericksburg until nearly nine o'clock. Lee's men on the bluffs and hills around could distinctly hear Burnside's officers commanding and marching their men about in the fog. As soon as this foggy veil lifted, Burnside ordered his men to attack. Lee at first returned the fire slowly and on certain points of his line gradually fell back for the purpose of drawing Burnside's army out into the inevitable jaws of death that awaited it. Lee was personally on the battlefield all day. When the firing began in the morning he might have been seen quietly riding along the whole front, and finally taking up his position on the extreme right of his lines, where Stuart's horse artillery was posted, and which was already hotly at work with Burnside's left flank, commanded by General Franklin.

But Burnside was himself two miles from the battle-field, on the other side of the river, viewing the scene with a glass from the top of the "Phillips House."

It must have been an awful sight to him, for his men were not only shot, they were mowed down. Every charge they made was repulsed with the most terrible slaughter. Actually his army was not so much fighting as being murdered. No men ever fought more gallantly, and no brave fellows were ever slaughtered more mercilessly in consequence of the stupidity of the general commanding. Lee had so placed his army on and around those heights that whichever way the invaders turned they met sure destruction. Lee's whole force was only eighty thousand men, while Burnside's army numbered one hundred and fifty thousand men. But had it been three hundred thousand the results of that day's battle would have been the same. The more that Burnside saw how his attacks were repulsed, the more determined he seemed to be that his men should be slaughtered. Towards night he became so irritated that no one received a civil answer from him.

Nearly all of his division commanders were able and experienced generals, and they fought with a heroism that won the admiration of even the enemy. General Hancock led five thousand men into the fight in the morning, and before it closed he had lost two thousand and thirteen, of whom one hundred and fifty-six were commissioned officers. Burnside's total loss was twelve thousand three hundred and twenty-one, killed, wounded, and missing. An English officer, who was in this battle on the Confederate side, in giving a description of it says: "Our total loss was two thousand." The same writer says:

> Again and again were the Federals re-formed, and ad-

vance succeeded advance as fresh regiments rushed over heaps of slain, to be themselves torn in an instant into mangled and bleeding shreds. The position was unassailable – a sheet of flame streamed across our whole front, and destroyed everything mortal that approached it. The sight was horrible. It was not a scientific battle, but a wholesale slaughter of human beings for the caprice of one man [Burnside] who, two miles across the river, sat upon the heights, glass in hand, complacently viewing the awful panorama below.

Thus ended Burnside's horrible slaughter. It ought not to be called a *battle* on his part – it was a *slaughter-pen.* This new road to Richmond had ingloriously terminated in a grave-yard.

For two days Burnside's mangled and bleeding army lay quiet in the valley, without making any attempt to renew the engagement. It has been a matter of surprise that Lee did not follow up his victory by attempting to drive the Federal army across the river, by which he might have captured a considerable portion of it, had the attempt been made at daylight the next morning. But he probably supposed that it was Burnside's intention to renew the fight, in which case he expected to be able to pretty nearly annihilate the Abolition army, without any considerable loss of his own men. This saving the lives of his men seemed always to be a paramount study of the Confederate commander.

But, in the darkness of the night of the second day after the slaughter, Burnside withdrew his whole force over the river, and was safe from the reach of Lee. In one day he had won an immortality of shame. If Pope had proved himself a *failure,* Burnside had proved himself a disgrace to the profession of arms.

And the shocking vandalism of his army in Fredericksburg proved that he was *morally* as deficient in the qualities of general as he was *intellectually.* The town was literally sacked and pillaged. It was barbarously destroyed. Even the churches were wantonly defaced. Arson, robbery, the insult and torture of women and children, were the only monuments of Burnside's generalship.

The army correspondent of the New York *Tribune* rejoiced in giving the following record of Abolition barbarity:

The old mansion of Douglas Gordon – perhaps the wealthiest citizen in the vicinity – is now used as the headquarters of General Howard, but before he occupied it, all the elegant furniture and works of art had been broken up and smashed by the soldiers. When I entered it early this morning, before its occupation by General Howard, I found the soldiers of his fine division diverting themselves with the rich dresses found in the ladies' wardrobes; some had on bonnets of the fashion of last year, and were surveying themselves before mirrors, which an hour afterwards were pitched out of the windows and smashed to pieces upon the pavements; others had elegant scarfs bound round their heads in the form of turbans, and shawls around their waists.

The soldiers had also helped themselves to all such things as spoons, jewelry, and silver plate. Never since the march of the Huns and Vandals was an army permitted to commit such robberies of private property.

It would be certain death for soldiers to commit such thefts under a general who meant to conduct the war upon the recognized rules of civilized warfare.

After his disgraceful defeat, General Burnside floundered about in the mud up and down the banks of the Rappahannock for nearly a month, when he became satisfied that many of the officers in his army held him in great contempt, and he determined at once to make an example of them for daring to distrust his ability.

So he, with one bold stroke, dismissed from the service of the United States, Generals Hooker, Brooks, Newton, and Cochrane; and removed from command in the Army of the Potomac, Generals Franklin, W.F. Smith, Sturgis, Ferrero, and Colonel Taylor.

On this order the madman posted to Washington, and demanded of the President an approval of his removal of all these officers, or accept his own resignation. Of course the President could not hesitate a moment, so he immediately accepted Burnside's resignation, and appointed General Hooker to his place as commander of the Army of the Potomac.

Thus, exit Burnside!

CHAPTER THIRTY-THREE
Mr. Lincoln's Campaign in the North

I propose to refer to the course which Mr. Lincoln's Administration pursued towards all in the North who differed from it. It has always been held that it was not only the right, but the duty, of every citizen to oppose the policy of any Administration when he thought it wrong. Indeed, every patriotic person will work with zeal and energy to change any existing Administration whose policy he thinks ruinous to the country.

It was soon discovered, however, that Mr. Lincoln did not intend to allow any opposition to his policy. His organs called his administration of the Government the Government itself, and accused everybody of "opposing the Government" who protested against his unconstitutional acts. The war he was waging was not so much a war against the South as it was against the democratic and republican principle of government. Hence he was determined to put down the spirit of liberty wherever he found it.

The first warfare on these principles in the North which Mr. Lincoln indulged in was an assault on the freedom of the press. In July, 1861 he ordered that all the leading Democratic papers in New York city be denied circulation in the mails. This was one of the most arbitrary and tyrannical acts ever committed, but, strange to say, it was generally endorsed by the Abolition newspapers, though their editors had been howling themselves hoarse for years in favor of a "free press."

This act was followed by a general attack upon the Democratic press all over the North. As if by a preconcerted signal the

Abolitionists excited mobs to attack and destroy Democratic printing offices wherever there was one that protested against Mr. Lincoln's usurpations. In some cases Democratic editors were killed, in others badly injured, and in a great many instances their offices were destroyed and their types cast into the street.

I am glad to say, however, that in some cases these cowardly mobbers got what they richly deserved. One of these mobs attacked the office of *The Democrat,* a paper published at Catskill, New York, when Mr. Hall, the editor, getting a hint of their approach concealed himself in his office, and as they began to pelt the windows with stones and brickbats he took deliberate aim and fired a whole charge of small shot right into the thighs of one of the leading mobbites. He jumped and yelled fearfully, and his companions, not expecting such a reception, ran away as fast as their cowardly legs could carry them.

I only regret that there were not a great many more of these mobs served in the same way.

It would occupy a book five times as large as this one to give the details of Mr. Lincoln's campaign against the Democratic newspapers of the North. Not less than *three or four hundred* were either denied the use of the mails, or mobbed. In Maryland, Kentucky and Missouri they were completely crushed out.

Mr. Lincoln, however, did not stop with suppressing the freedom of the press. He hated freedom of speech just as much. Mr. Seward seemed to relish the work of sending people to Bastiles without any charge being made against them. Up to December, 1861, a period of little over seven months from the time the war began, *three hundred and fifty-one* persons had been sent to the different military prisons by order of Mr. Seward alone, whose names were known and registered. Besides these there were *one hundred and fifty* more, known to have been arrested, whose names of those arrested should be *kept secret.*

The number of persons arrested in the East by Lincoln and Seward during three years of the war was estimated at *ten thousand!* Taking the whole North and the number could not have been less *than thirty thousand!*

A great number of females were among the prisoners. In

many cases there seems to have been no ground for the arrest but an anonymous letter, some private gossip or the gratification of some old personal or political grudge. Every Abolition politician seized the opportunity to persecute his Democratic neighbors. Thousands of letters were sent to Mr. Seward urging him to arrest individuals whom the writers accused of "disloyalty." One minister of the Gospel in Western New York wrote thirty letters to Seward in two months giving him in each letter lists of "traitors" to arrest.

All sorts of means were resorted to in order to intimidate people from expressing their opinions. In New York city the writer saw several copies of the following circular sent to ladies to frighten them into submission to Lincoln:

> Headquarters of the Union Vigilance Committee
> New York, April, 1861.
>
> Madam: As a person favoring traitors to the Union, you are notified that your name is recorded on the Secret List of this Association, your movements are being strictly watched, and unless you openly declare your adherence to the Union, you will be dealt with as a *traitor*.
> By Order,
> 33, *Secretary*.

At the same time the Abolition papers were filled with mysterious threats. It was stated that lists of prominent "traitors" in New York city, who opposed Mr. Lincoln's policy, had been made out, by a secret detective police which "the Government" had formed. These spies, pimps and informers dogged the footsteps of every man whom they suspected of bold and unqualified opposition to Mr. Lincoln and his party. The Abolition papers were joyous over these evidences of "vigor" as they called the illegal arrest and imprisonment of persons without any trial or charge being made against them. The New York *Tribune,* one of the loudest yelpers for (Negro) freedom, declared that "the system of detective police was bearing the happiest fruits."

All this time, while Democratic newspapers were denied the use of the mails or mobbed, and while thousands of Democrats were being thrown into loathsome dungeons for simply opposing the policy of Mr. Lincoln's Administration, the Boston *Liberator* continued to flaunt the motto, *"The Constitution is a league with death and a covenant with hell."* Mr. Lincoln not only did not object to that, but it transpired afterwards that he was at that very time a subscriber, reader, and supporter of this paper!

But I have not begun to tell as yet one-half of the outrages perpetrated during this "reign of terror" in America. I must give you a few samples of the multitude on record.

On the Sunday of February 9th, 1862, as the Rev. Mr. Stuart, of St. Paul's Episcopal Church, Alexandria, Virginia, was officiating at the altar, a brutal officer, with a file of soldiers, seized him, and, wrenching the prayer-book out of his hand, dragged him from the altar, and through the streets, in his robes of office. The charge against him was that he did not pray for Mr. Lincoln! It is believed that about one hundred clergymen in all were arrested. One, Rev. J.D. Benedict, of Western New York, was seized at night, and spirited away in a carriage, and finally confined in the Old Capitol Prison at Washington. His offence was preaching a discourse from Christ's Sermon on the Mount, "Blessed are the peacemakers."

Judges were arrested. In some instances dragged from their judicial seats to the dungeon, and kept for months in prison, and then discharged, no crime being alleged against them.

Ladies were seized and imprisoned, subjected to nameless insults, forbidden the visits of friends, and hurried from prison to prison by Mr. Lincoln's satraps. The case of a Mrs. Brinsmade may be mentioned. This lady came to New York from New Orleans, and went to Washington to visit some friends. While there she was arrested and brought on to New York city, and kept in a station-house for forty days, by order of John A. Kennedy, Superintendent of the New York Police.

I ought to have mentioned that the Police Department of New York had been the most serviceable tool of Mr. Seward's tyranny. Its superintendent, Kennedy, was a man of low and vulgar instincts, who seemed to rejoice when he had some one to persecute. He was a native of Baltimore, Maryland, and never seemed so well pleased as when making war on those whom he charged with "sympathizing with the South."

This is the man who had seized Mrs. Brinsmade, and he boasted that the police station was just "the place for her."

Kennedy had been appointed provost marshal, and no one could have been better fitted for the dirty work of tyrants. Among the appliances of torture which he kept for his victims was a place called "Cell No. 4." The Black Hole of Calcutta or the prison hulks of the Revolution could scarcely compete with it. It was only about three feet wide by six in depth. A pine board had been nailed across one end as a pillow, and there were neither bed-clothes, mattress, nor straw – nothing but the naked floor for a bed. The door was composed of iron bars tightly riveted together. It was the dirtiest, filthiest place possible to be conceived of. It swarmed with vermin, which ran riot over the unfortunate victims confined there, who could neither lie down nor sit down for very agony. In the hottest and most stifling weather, sometimes three persons were confined in this three by six cell at one time!

On one occasion a young man was arrested for refusing to give his name to an enrolling officer.

Kennedy. – "What is your name?"

Young Man. – "Well, I decline to give my name."

Kennedy. – "Oh, you do. Well, I think you will give it before being here a great while." (Rings his bell.) "Here, officer, take this man downstairs and give him No. 4."

The iron door swung upon its ponderous hinges, and in went the young man. In less than fifteen minutes his cries were heard, and going thither, he was found in profuse perspiration, the vermin crawling over him and tormenting him beyond expression! He was glad to give his name to escape Kennedy's torture.

I have now to relate what seems most astounding of all. Even boys and young children were arrested, and imprisoned for months and even years. In September, 1861, a poor newsboy, named George Hubbell, was arrested on the Naugatuck Railroad, and sent to Fort Lafayette, for selling Democratic newspapers! In December, 1862, a boy seventeen years of age was released from the same Bastile, whose only known cause of arrest was that his father was an ardent Democrat of Connecticut. In Kentucky, a school of boys was seized and required to take what was called "the iron-clad oath." Most of them, I am sorry to say, got frightened and submitted; but two brothers, named Woolsey, stoutly refused, and were sent to jail, where Lincoln kept them for over two years.

This showed the right spirit. We ought always to be willing to go to jail for our principles, and to yield our life even before we will give them up. If everybody who was arrested by Lincoln and Seward had followed the example of these noble boys, they would have been compelled to send so many to jail that their prisons would have been too small to hold them, and they would have seen such pluck exhibited that they might have got frightened, and given up their usurpations.

As I have said, Democratic editors were arrested and sent to these Bastiles. Mr. J. A. McMasters, editor of the New York *Freeman's Journal,* was not only thus arrested, but carried handcuffed through the streets to Fort Lafayette. Mr. F. D. Flanders, editor of the Malone *Gazette,* and his brother Judge J. R. Flanders, both prominent men opposed to Lincoln's policy in Franklin County, New York, were also arrested, and confined by order of Mr. Seward in Fort Lafayette. No doubt, he thought he would by this means stop the bold little paper which Mr. Flanders published.

But in this I am happy to say he was mistaken; for his wife, a brave and talented woman, seized the pen herself, and with great energy and determination kept the paper going while her husband was in prison for opinion's sake. The name of this lady, Louisa B. Flanders, ought to become as historic as that of the brave woman of the Revolution, who, at the battle of Monmouth, when her husband, who was a cannoneer, was shot down, seized the ramrod and loaded the gun herself. All through this war, it is the noble women, whether North or South, who seem to have grasped, as if by instinct, how horrible is the crime of trying to degrade and debauch our race to a level with Negroes.

The character of the prisons where Democrats were confined was entirely on a par with "Cell No. 4." In Fort Lafayette rats were at one time very numerous. One night a prisoner was awakened by finding several on his bed-clothes, and at another time felt one nibbling at his toes. At Camp Chase, Columbus, Ohio, there was also a political prison, where five or six hundred prisoners were sometimes confined at a time. The prison was awfully filthy, alive with lice and vermin. A man was found dead in the dead yard one morning, covered all over with vermin. Two men got into a scuffle one day, trying their strength, when the guards shot among the prisoners, killing an old man named Jones from West Virginia. These prisoners, it should be remembered, were convicted of no crime, did not even know why they were arrested, but were simply held to gratify some one's spite and malice.

Sometimes people were arrested for the most trivial causes. For instance, Mr. David C. Wattles, of North Branch, Michigan, was arrested, and sent all the way to Fort Lafayette. And for what? Why; his children had raised upon a pole an old shirt, which had been dyed red by straining blackberry juice through it. Some one on the strength of this reported that Mr. Wattles had raised a secession flag, and without a why or a wherefore, he was kept in Fort Lafayette *five months!* Dr. L. K Ross, of Illinois, was arrested and kept for months in the Old Capitol, at Washington, because he had been seen in the public street *to draw his finger under his nose.* It was reported to Seward that this was the private signal of a secret organization, but it was found afterward that no such organization existed!

Early in 1861, almost the entire Legislature of Maryland had been arrested. The Police Commissioner of Baltimore, Mr. Charles Howard, and his associates, had also been sent to Fort McHenry, by order of General Banks. Afterwards the editors of the Baltimore *Exchange,* subsequently the *Gazette,* together with many other prominent citizens of Maryland, were seized and immured in Bastiles, where some of them remained nearly two years.

So great had these outrages become, both on the press

and upon persons, that the fall elections of 1862 were generally carried by the Democrats. Horatio Seymour was nominated for Governor of the State of New York by the Democratic party. He was a gentleman of the highest social character and position, and deservedly popular. He was pledged to restore the freedom of the press in the State *at all hazards.* On this ground he received the united and earnest support of all Democrats, and was elected.

When Mr. Lincoln and Mr. Seward heard of this, they were a little cowed; and as they did not wish to provoke an issue with the great State of New York, they did just what they had done when John Bull demanded Messrs. Mason and Slidell – they backed down. Before the day of Mr. Seymour's inauguration, January 1st, 1863, they issued an order, allowing all papers to circulate in the mails as usual. Thus there had something been wrenched from the usurpers.

They also thought it prudent to relax a little in their system of arbitrary arrests. Mr. Seward, after boasting to Lord Lyons that "he could ring one bell on his right hand, and arrest a citizen in New York, and another bell on his left, and arrest a citizen in Ohio," turned the matter of arrests over to Stanton, of the War Department, who instituted a kind of mock trials before military commissions, by which they tried to give a semblance of legal form to their usurpations.

It must be confessed, however, that the stoppage of Democratic newspapers and the large number of arrests had produced the effect that Lincoln and Seward anticipated. It prevented a full and free development of public opinion, which would, no doubt, have put Mr. Lincoln and his party out of power. It operated on the timid, and thousands were roped in and made to serve the purposes of the Abolitionists by the cry of "supporting the Government."

Such was the real effect of Mr. Lincoln's campaign in the North.

CHAPTER THIRTY-FOUR
The Battle of Murfreesboro –
Doings in The West, Etc.

Leaving the Army of the Potomac for awhile, let us now return to Tennessee and see what has been passing there. The Confederate army, under General Bragg, to the number of about thirty thousand had been resting at Murfreesboro for more than a month.

There General Bragg was resting in happy, but not over useful, security, when, on Friday, the 26th of December, he was startled, as from a dream, with tidings that Rosecrans had broken up his camp at Nashville, and was marching rapidly upon him.

Bragg's pickets were driven in that very afternoon. The next day, December 27th, Rosecrans made a feint attack to feel the position of the Confederate army, but General Wheeler's cavalry gained his rear and captured a good many wagons and a number of prisoners. But the great battle did not really begin until the morning, the 31st of December, when General Bragg ordered an advance. It was an impetuous one, and the position of Rosecrans' line upon which the assault was made, wavered, and finally broke and fell back.

Before noon Bragg captured five thousand prisoners, thirty pieces of cannon, five thousand stand of arms, and a large number of ammunition wagons. The right wing of Rosecrans' army was driven back over five miles. Thus matters stood when darkness shut down upon the battle-field.

The next day neither party made any sign of renewing the

fight. Bragg telegraphed to Richmond that he had won a great victory. It was the 1st day of January, and he said, "God has granted us a happy New Year." The next day Rosecrans showed no sign of either retreating, or beginning the fight again. But he had made the best of the two days' rest which Bragg had given him, and to a naturally strong position he had hastily added strong defensive works.

At three o'clock of that day General Bragg opened an assault upon the Federal lines again. It was the beginning of another terrible battle, in which, after a desperate struggle, the Confederate forces were repulsed, and lost about all they had gained before. But night fell upon both armies occupying nearly the position they held in the morning.

The next day was a cold rain-storm, and neither army made any movement. But towards evening General Bragg heard that his enemy was receiving reinforcements; and that night he withdrew the Confederate army to a place called Tullahoma, twenty-two miles from Murfreesboro.

At the very time these battles were going on in Tennessee the Confederates gained some important victories in Texas, by which they retook the City of Galveston, which had for some time been in the hands of the Abolition army.

Alternate Confederate victories and reverses were transpiring throughout the West and South; but as yet no visible impression had been made upon what was called "the rebellion." Indeed, thus far, the general tide of victory had been almost everywhere in its favor.

The Abolitionists were discouraged. Many in the North who had given their influence to the cause began to waver, and the hearts of the most sanguine were despondent.

For a long time the siege of Vicksburg had been going on without any favorable results. Millions of dollars had been expended, and a great many lives lost, but no positive gain had been realized. Indeed, the Confederates had been generally winners on the Mississippi River and its approaches.

They had a stronghold at Port Hudson, three hundred miles below Vicksburg and sixteen miles above Baton Rouge, which had long proved itself too much for all the fleets of Abolition gun-boats. About this time the *Indianola* and the *Queen of the West* fell into the hands of the Confederates.

On the 15th of March, 1863, a desperate effort was made to take this place. An immense fleet of gun-boats, under the command of Admiral Farragut, was moved against it, and after a terrible fight, Port Hudson was still the Sebastopol of the Mississippi. The Federal fleet was forced back terribly shattered, torn and exploded.

A gloomy malice settled upon the faces of the Abolitionists. All things appeared to go wrong. Among the other things which they had looked for before this, was a general uprising of the Negroes to murder their masters and mistresses. But the Negroes had shown a decided leaning against the Abolitionists. The following specimen of darkey lingo is reported, and is a fair specimen of the general temper of the Negroes before the Abolitionists had corrupted them.

There was a very old gray-haired cook in an Alabama regiment, who would follow his young master to the war, and had the reputation of a saint among the Negro boys of the brigade; and as he could read the Bible, and was given to preaching, he invariably assembled the darkies on Sunday afternoon and held meetings in the woods. He used to lecture them unmercifully, but could not keep them from singing and dancing after "tattoo." Uncle Pompey, as he was called, was an excellent servant, and an admirable cook, and went on from day to day singing hymns among his pots round the camp-fire, until a battle opened. When the regiment moved up to the front and was engaged, Uncle Pompey, contrary to orders, persisted in going also.

One day he was met by another darkey, who asked: "Whar's *you* gwine, Uncle Pomp? You isn't gwine up dar to have all de har scorched off yer head, is you?"

Uncle Pompey still persisted in advancing, and, shouldering a rifle, soon overtook his regiment.

"De Lor' hab mercy on us all, boys! here dey comes agin! take car, massa, and hole your rifle square, as I showed you in the swamp! Dar it is," he exclaimed, as the Yankees fired an overshot, "just as I taught! can't shoot worth a bad five-cent piece."

"Now's de time, boys!" and as the Alabamians returned a withering volley and closed up with the enemy, charging them furiously, Uncle Pompey forgot all about his church, his ministry, and sanctity, and while firing and dodging, as best he could, was heard to shout out:

"Pitch in, White folks, Uncle Pomp's behind yer. Send all de Yankees to the 'ternal flames, whar dar's weeping and gnashing of – sail in Alabamy; stick 'em wid de bayonet, and send all do blue ornary cusses to de state ob eternal fire and brimstone! Push 'em hard, boys! – push 'em hard; and when dey's gone, may de Lor' hab marcy on de last one on 'em! don't spar' none on 'm, for de good Lo'd neber made such as dem, no how you kin fix it; for it am said in de two-eyed chapter of de one-eyed John, somewhar in Collusions, dat – Hurray, boys! dat's you, sure – now you've gob 'em; give 'em, goss! show 'em a taste of ole Alabamy!" etc.

The person who saw Uncle Pompey during this scene was wounded and sat behind a tree, but said, although his hurt was extremely painful, the eloquence, rage, and impetuosity of Pomp, as he loaded and fired rapidly, was so ludicrous, being an incoherent jumble of oaths, snatches of Scripture, and prayers, that the tears ran down his cheeks, and he burst out into a roar of laughter.

Such a state of feeling as this among the Negroes was certainly most discouraging to those who impatiently expected to see them cutting the throats of Southern women and children.

CHAPTER THIRTY-FIVE
General Hooker's Campaign

We now return to the Army of the Potomac. General Hooker had spent full three months in re-organizing and bringing that army out of the wretched chaos and demoralization in which it was left by General Burnside. It must be confessed that General Hooker put forth a great deal of energy, and evinced a great deal of executive ability in repairing that army. When he had concluded his labors in that direction, and was about to commence operations in the field, he pronounced it "the finest army on the planet." It numbered one hundred and thirty-two thousand men of all arms, with an artillery force of four hundred guns.

To meet this tremendous army Lee had not over fifty thousand men. Again Abolition faith ran high. The "On to Richmond" shout, for the fifth time, reverberated over the North. To doubt that Hooker would take Richmond in less than twenty days called down upon the sceptic the suspicion of "disloyalty." And many a man was mobbed for simply venturing to entertain a doubt of Abolition success that time.

General Hooker certainly began with a great promise of success. His army outnumbered Lee's almost three to one, and never was an army better equipped. In this respect, too, his advantages over Lee were quite as great as his very great excess of numbers. And all his plans for the decisive battle, up to the very hour of its first gun, prospered wonderfully. His army crossed the Rappahannock at several points, and concentrated at Chancellorsville, which place General Hooker himself reached on the night of Thursday, April 30th, 1863. He immediately issued an order to his troops, couched in language not much calculated to inspire the respect and confidence of men of good taste and good sense. He said: "The enemy must either ingloriously fly, or come out from behind his defences and give us battle on our own ground, where certain destruction awaits him." His conversation was of the same boastful style as his order. He said: "The rebel army is now the legitimate property of the Army of the Potomac. They may as well pack up their haversacks and make for Richmond; and I shall be after them." This talk is precisely like Hooker.

An intelligent writer remarks that, "Lee, with instant perception of the situation, now seized the masses of his force, and with the grasp of a Titan, swung them into position as a giant might fling a mighty stone from a sling."

Hooker's line of battle, formed on Friday evening, was five miles in extent, on ground of his own choosing. In this position he awaited an attack from Lee on Saturday morning, May 2d. But Lee simply showed very active signs of beginning an attack, while he, with great secrecy and despatch, sent Stonewall Jackson, with a force of twenty thousand men, to flank Hooker by assailing his right and rear. This plan was executed with such celerity and skill, that Hooker had no suspicion that he had not the whole of Lee's army before him until he heard Stonewall Jackson thundering and crashing into his rear. He fell upon Hooker like an avalanche, and drove this portion of his army before him in utter rout and confusion. The blow was dealt with such power that everything fell before it.

The Federal historian of the campaigns of the Army of the Potomac says:

> The open plain around Chancellorsville now presented such a spectacle as a simoon sweeping over the desert might make. Through the dusk of night-fall a rushing whirlwind of men and artillery and wagons swept down the road, and swept past head-quarters, and on towards the fords of the Rappahannock; and it was in vain that the staff opposed their persons and drawn sabres to the panic-stricken fugitives.

The Confederates had won a sudden and a great victory, but at a cost which was really a greater loss to them than twenty great battles, for Stonewall Jackson was mortally wounded while riding over the battle-field in the dark, by his own men, who mistook him for a stray Federal.

I shall not pause here to speak of the shock which the news of Stonewall Jackson's death gave, not only to Lee's army and the Confederate States, but to the whole world. For he had won a fame which will last as long as valorous deeds command the admiration of mankind.

Lee received the news of Jackson's fall before daylight on Sunday morning, and the messenger who brought the sad news said: "It was General Jackson's intent to press the enemy on Sunday." General Lee replied, with deep emotion: "These people shall be pressed to-day." General Stuart temporarily was entrusted with Jackson's command, and at daylight he opened the attack with the battle-cry, "Charge, and remember Jackson!"

The charge was impetuous, and threw the enemy back in great confusion. At the same time, Lee attacked Hooker's centre, and in a short time his whole line was forced precipitately back. By ten o'clock Hooker's defeat was complete, and the Confederates occupied the field at Chancellorsville.

General Hooker made two or three abortive strategic movements to regain his lost fortunes. His fate was sealed. The enemy whom he was sure to "bag," had whipped him unmercifully, and now it was even a serious question whether he would not himself be "bagged" by Lee's comparatively small army. But he succeeded in retreating across the river, and found safety only in flight. He had lost seventeen thousand two hundred and eighty-one men, nineteen thousand stand of arms, and a vast amount of ammunition. Lee's loss was less than ten thousand men. Hooker was obliged to leave his dead and wounded in the hands of the Confederates. He retreated until finally he brought up precisely where McDowell, Pope, and Burnside had before him, in the defences in front of Washington. He went out as proud and as boasting as Lucifer, and came back as badly fallen. All his division commanders despised his generalship, and there were none to do him reverence. His command was finally taken from him and given to General Meade, who had been a division commander under McClellan.

Military matters now remained in a quiet state until the first week in June, when General Lee began to move northward again. All doubt as to his real intention vanished when it was announced that his infantry had crossed the Potomac and that his cavalry was in Pennsylvania. The North was again aroused by frantic appeals for help from Washington. "The capital in danger" had again taken the place of the cry of "On to Richmond." Crowds of soldiers again rushed to Washington.

Lee marched with his veterans straight across Maryland into Pennsylvania, and occupied Chambersburg. No officer or soldier was allowed to commit any depredations, and the people, not used to seeing such soldiers, laughed at the "barefooted rebels," and the women jeered them from the sidewalks. On the morning of the 30th of June, when General Lee's army left Chambersburg in a northerly direction, a panic seized the whole surrounding country.

People ran away in droves from Harrisburg, Pittsburg, and even from Philadelphia money and valuables were sent on to New York. In Pittsburg five thousand men were set to work building forts to protect the city.

General Lee finally concentrated his forces near the town of Gettysburg, and here, on the 1st of July, 1863, commenced perhaps the most important battle of the war. On the 1st day, Major-General Reynolds, of the Abolition army, was killed, and the Confederates took some 600 prisoners and ten pieces of artillery.

The next day remained quiet until about four o'clock in the afternoon, when General Longstreet commenced the attack by a heavy cannonade. The day's work, on the whole, was favorable to the Confederates, but in the meantime the Federal army had been reinforced, and was concentrated in a strong position on Cemetery Hill, used as a burial place by the citizens of Gettysburg.

The real contest was to drive General Meade's troops from

this position. At one o'clock on the 3d of July, General Lee concentrated all his guns upon it. The cannonade was terrific. The shower of shot and shell went crashing and smashing through the graveyard with fearful effect. The slaughter among the Federal troops was fearful, but they held the ground manfully. About three o'clock the Confederates prepared for a grand charge upon the position. Never was there a braver or more gallant charge. Though hundreds of cannon mowed through their ranks a swath of death, these war-worn veterans heeded them not. They thought themselves invincible, and rushed into the very jaws of death, if thereby they could save their beloved land from the Abolition destroyer. But in vain. No mortal men could withstand this tempest of leaden and iron hail. Slowly they fell back, but without dismay or confusion.

The Federal army was too much shattered to follow; indeed, so far as the battle was concerned, it was a drawn game. It was only in its effects that it was disastrous to the Confederates. General Lee was short of ammunition. He had expected to capture it from his enemies. But failing in that, was forced to fall back for supplies.

It was slow work, for besides his prisoners, he had an immense train of wagons, horses, mules, and cattle, captured in Pennsylvania. Still he pursued his course without any serious attack from the Federals, and safely crossed the Potomac with his captures.

An amusing incident is related of this retreat, which serves to show the fidelity of the Negro character when uncorrupted. General Longstreet passing one day, observed a Negro dressed in a full Federal uniform, with a rifle at full cock, leading along a barefooted White man, with whom he had evidently changed clothes. General Long-street stopped the pair, and asked what it meant.

"Wall, massa, you see," said Sambo, "de two sojers in charge of dis here Yank got drunk, so for fear he might git away, I jis took car of him myself."

This was spoken in a most consequential manner. If any Abolitionist could have seen this Negro, so-called slave, thus leading a White Northern soldier, *alone and of his own accord,* he would no doubt have been greatly disgusted.

CHAPTER THIRTY-SIX
The Siege of Vicksburg

We must now return to the West. The cry of opening the Mississippi River had been second only to the demand of taking Richmond. The Confederates, after the loss of their fortifications further up the river, had fortified the city of Vicksburg in the most substantial manner. The town is built upon high bluffs, and is well adapted for defence. General William T. Sherman had attacked it in December, 1862, but had been so badly repulsed that he was glad to abandon the job.

As this General Sherman loomed up very largely afterwards, it may be proper to say that he was an officer of the old army in the Mexican war, and when this one broke out, was President of the Military Academy of Louisiana. He came. North, however, and joined Mr. Lincoln's army, and has made a name which will be forever associated with cruelty and barbarism.

After he was repulsed at Vicksburg, he took some vessels of Admiral Porter's fleet, and steaming up the Arkansas River, took a Confederate fort at Arkansas Post, and many guns and prisoners.

Gen. William T. Sherman

After General Sherman's failure to take Vicksburg, General Grant was placed in command of the forces for its reduction. To take it in front was impossible. So General Grant spent three months or more in making experiments to flank it. His first plan was to cut a canal on the west side of the river, to cut it off, but the waters came near drowning his own men, without harming the Confederates in the least. Then the Abolition papers came out with the terrible announcement that General Grant was going to cut a new channel for the Mississippi, from Lake Providence to the Gulf of Mexico! But General Grant also failed in this. He then tried to cut a canal from the Yazoo River to a point south of Vicksburg. But in all these efforts to change the face of nature General Grant was unsuccessful.

However, during this time Admiral Porter kept up the excitement by the operations of his fleet. Waiting for a night dark enough to suit his purposes, he took five iron-clads, the *Benton*, *Pittsburg*, *Carondelet*, *Lafayette*, and *Louisville*, and several transports, and resolved to run by the Confederate batteries. The whole fleet was so managed that it made not so much noise as a ripple of a single oar. Thus noiselessly, breathlessly, they dropped along down the river, until, when directly opposite the city, *bomb!* went the signal gun on the heights of Vicksburg, and in an instant all the batteries opened upon them. The scene was terrific. The blackness of the heavens was illuminated with the lurid flames vomited from the mouths of the cannon in the numerous batteries along the shore.

But the instant Admiral Porter saw that he was discovered, he gave command to put on the steam and run the gauntlet – a feat which was accomplished with the loss of the transport *Forest Queen*, and with more or less damage to the whole fleet.

After the guns of Vicksburg were passed, there were no other Confederate works on the Mississippi, until they reached Grand Gulf, twenty-five miles south of Vicksburg. There were no Confederate soldiers stationed in the space between Vicksburg and Grand Gulf at the time of Porter's running past Vicksburg, and yet, for two weeks, he amused himself by sailing up and down the river, and throwing shells into the houses which were occupied almost exclusively by women and children. This was not only a needless cruelty, but it was a violation of the laws of civilized warfare. It was simply the murder of women and children.

Grand Gulf was an important point, and Admiral Porter made up his mind to take it, if possible. One morning he gave an early order to move upon it, but was answered by the captains, that their men had not yet had breakfast. To which Porter replied: "O never mind about breakfast; we will take the place in half an hour, and breakfast afterwards."

The *Benton* led the attack, then followed the *Carondelet*, the *Pittsburg*, the *Louisville*, the *Tuscumbia*, and *Lafayette*. The line of battle was so formed as to pour a cross fire upon the Confederate works. For five hours the battle raged without a moment's cessation, and without producing the least visible impression upon the Confederate batteries. But the *Tuscumbia* was destroyed, the *Benton* terribly riddled, and indeed the whole fleet wore a most ragged and ruined aspect. The thing that Porter promised should only be half an hour's job before breakfast, proved to be not only an all day's job, but even an impossible task.

The passage of Admiral Porter's fleet of gunboats down the river in safety now emboldened General Grant to transfer his armies south of Vicksburg, and march to the attack of Vicksburg in the rear. On the 30th of April, his army, having gone down on the west side of the river, crossed and landed at Port Gibson, and commenced its march to Vicksburg. The Confederates were overpowered, and forced to fall back, and were defeated in several severe engagements. One Federal column took possession of Jackson, the capital of the State of Mississippi, and burned and pillaged the town in a most shameful manner. They gutted the stores, and destroyed what they could not carry off, burned the Roman Catholic Church, the principal hotel, and many other buildings.

Seeing the danger in which Vicksburg now stood, General Joseph E. Johnston tried to organize an army for its relief, but he was not successful. General Pemberton, the commander of the Confederate forces in Vicksburg, was now compelled to fall back to his defences, and await General Grant's siege. In the meantime, Grant drew his lines tighter and tighter around the fated city. He made an effort to carry it by storm, but was beaten back with terrible loss.

The condition of the city, however, was becoming every day more fearful. Food was becoming scarcer and scarcer. Women and children were compelled to live in caves to escape being killed by the bombshells that were continually bursting about them. This could not last always. General Johnston could not raise an army strong enough to attack General Grant in the rear, so that there was but one thing for General Pemberton to do. He must surrender. It was a terrible ordeal, but there was no escape. So on the 3d of July, General Pemberton proposed an armistice, and on the following day, surrendered his army as prisoners of war, to be allowed to go to their homes, but not to serve again, unless regularly exchanged. The officers were allowed to retain their side-arms and their servants.

This was a terrible blow to the Confederates. They lost over 20,000 prisoners, guns, military supplies, &c., besides the control of the Mississippi River. General Pemberton was greatly blamed for his alleged bad management.

There was, indeed, one place further South, Port Hudson, under General Frank Gardner, which still held out. In March, as I have stated, Admiral Farragut had attacked it, but was repulsed with the loss of the *Mississippi*, one of the largest vessels in the Federal Navy. General Banks, who now commanded at New Orleans in place of General Butler, had also attacked it twice; but as large portions of his troops were Negroes, the Confederates had easy work in whipping them. The Abolitionists tried to make the world believe that the Negro troops fought bravely at Port Hudson, but it is not so. They were forced into a bad position, where they were mowed down mercilessly.

Of course, after the fall of Vicksburg, General Gardner saw that all attempt to hold out longer would be fruitless. So he surrendered to General Banks.

The Mississippi River was now open from its source to its mouth. Its loss to the Confederates was mainly owing to the fact that it cut them off from Texas, whence they received many supplies, and opened a large extent of country to the vandalism and plundering of the Abolitionists.

These outrages upon private property are the great stigma upon the Northern army, or rather upon the Northern generals; for soldiers are not expected to understand the rules of war. A lady, writing of her treatment by Grant's army, says:

> They loaded themselves with our clothing, broke my dishes, stole my knives and forks, broke open my trunks, closets, and, finally, burned our gin-house and press, with one hundred and twenty-five bales of cotton, six hundred bushels of corn, six stacks of fodder, a fine spinning machine, and five hundred dollars worth of thread, &c., &c.

Such recitals really make the heart sick, and yet this is only one out of a thousand such instances.

I will give one more; for this is a case in which the parties were personally known to the writer.

A few miles back of Vicksburg lived a rich planter, whose accomplished wife was a daughter of one of the wealthiest and most respectable citizens of the State of Connecticut. This family had remained quiet upon the plantation during the war, and although naturally and justly sympathizing with the South in its wrongs, had taken no active part in the strife. The planter was a man of great wealth, and was very happy in the society of a refined and happy family.

A few days after the fall of Vicksburg, one of Grant's regiments, while on a plundering tour, came across this peaceful and unoffending planter and his family. The soldiers at once entered the house and commenced to steal every article of value which they could lay their hands upon. They tore the lady's watch from her bosom, and the rings from her fingers. There was not a work-box, nor a bureau drawer in the house that was not rifled. Every article of wardrobe belonging to the lady and her little girls was stolen. Even the shoes and stockings were taken *from her own and her children's feet.* Family miniatures were taken, for their gold settings. Not so much as a silver teaspoon escaped the vigilance of these Abolition thieves.

Every article of food, even to the last pound of pork in the house, was also stolen. In vain the lady entreated the wretches to leave her some food for her children. The only answer she received was the most brutal oaths, with threats that they would "bayonet the brats unless she held her tongue." After they had swept the house of every article of value, they went to the barn and stole several horses, and all the cows; and there being several hogs, which, as they could not drive them off, *they stuck their bayonets through, and left them dead in the yard!*

They drove off all the Negroes, except two old females who were too feeble to travel. So unwilling were some of these Negroes to leave the plantation that they had to tie them together, and threaten to bayonet them, and thus forced them away under kicks and blows. A short time after the pillage of this plantation the estimable lady died of a fever brought on by the fright and hardship to which she had been exposed; and in a few days more her youngest child, an infant, followed her to the grave. Her surviving daughters are now with their grand-parents in Connecticut. They will grow up to hate the name of an Abolitionist as they will that of a fiend. So, in hundreds of thousands of broken hearts all over the land, the name of Abolitionism will be coupled with thief, robber and murderer as long as time shall last.

Abolition officers driving Negroes from the plantations.

The driving off Negroes from the plantations was no uncommon occurrence throughout the South. The Negro is naturally very much attached to his home, and when the Abolition officers came among them and told them they were free to leave their masters and they did not do so, they often became very angry with them, and *compelled* them to enjoy what they called "the blessings of freedom." These "blessings," it has been proved, consisted mainly of "disease and death."

The Hon. Mr. Doolittle of Wisconsin, an Abolition Senator in Congress, has stated that good judges estimate that *one million* of Negroes have perished since the war began, and appalled by those facts, Mr. Doolittle, like an honorable and humane man, is disposed to pause and reflect before he endorses further inhumanity towards these innocent and suffering people.

CHAPTER THIRTY-SEVEN
The Naval Defeat Off Charleston – General Gillmore's Repulse

No place had been such an eyesore to the Abolitionists as the hated city of Charleston. They regarded it as "the cradle of the rebellion" and had vowed all sorts of vengeance upon it, even to blotting it out forever from the face of the earth. Several efforts had been made to reduce it. General Hunter had felt of it and came away satisfied. The truth was, that General Beauregard, who had planned its defences, was one of the ablest military engineers in the world, and it had been made well nigh impregnable. Strong forts had been built to guard all its approaches and the chief channel had been obstructed by rows of piles, among which were scattered numerous torpedoes.

Chagrined at their repeated defeats to take the city the Abolitionists finally conceived the barbarous idea of destroying the harbor of Charleston by sinking in the channel a large number of vessels laden with stones! The strong current of the water, however, made another channel just as good as the old one, so that this piece of Abolition malignity miscarried.

It would not do, however, to let this little city thus defy the power of the whole North. So Mr. Lincoln's Naval Department went to work and built a large number of iron-clad vessels, at the expense of many millions of dollars, for the reduction of Charleston. On the 7th day of April, 1863, they steamed up the harbor very gaily, under the command of Admiral Dupont, who, no doubt, thought the city would fall soon into his hands.

But in this he was mistaken, for the Confederates opened upon him from all their batteries and rained such a torrent of shot and shell upon his fleet that he was glad to beat a hasty retreat. So thick was this iron-hail that as many as one hundred and sixty shots were counted in a minute! The *Keokuk* was sunk and over half of the fleet were more or less disabled. The flag-ship, the *Ironsides*, was rendered helpless. No injury had been done to the Confederates whatever, so that all this vast preparation and expenditure of money had amounted to nothing.

The Abolition Government at Washington now resolved to try the effect of a formidable land-force, and General Quincy A. Gillmore was entrusted with the command. It was declared that Fort Sumter must be taken at all hazards. So in July General Gillmore with a large army began the siege of Charleston. He landed on Morris Island and tried to take Fort Wagner, a strong Confederate work on the north end of the island, but was terribly repulsed and glad to abandon the job.

Gillmore finding he could not succeed in this way fell back on siege operations. He got an immense cannon that would carry a ball five miles, and calling it the "Swamp Angel" set it to work, throwing shell right into the city of Charleston among the women and children and hospitals containing the sick. When General Beauregard protested against this violation of civilized warfare, Gillmore told him very insolently to remove his women and children and sick out of Charleston.

This pleased the Abolitionists of the North very much, for they never seemed so happy as when some one of their Generals was performing some act of brutality.

General Gillmore fired away for weeks and weeks, until finally the Confederates abandoned Fort Wagner and all of Morris Island. No effort had been spared to reduce Fort Sumter, and on the 24th of August General Gillmore telegraphed that it was a "shapeless and harmless mass of ruins." If this were so it only needed to be occupied, but "shapeless" as it was the Confederates, under Major Elliot, still held it.

However, Admiral Dahlgren, now naval commander in Charleston Harbor, made a demand on General Beauregard, on the 7th of September, for its surrender. The General, in his most polite French style, sent word to Mr. Dahlgren "to come and take it."

The Admiral determined to do so; and, accordingly, on the very next night, sent off an expedition of some twenty small boats and five hundred men to take it by surprise! Major Elliot, however, was not the man to be taken by surprise. He saw the approaching expedition, and reserving his fire until the enemy were within a few yards of the fort, he fired into them a devouring fire. Instantly the bay was lighted with signals, and all the Confederate batteries opened upon the barges. Some of the men gained the parapet of the fort; many fell in trying to scale the wall; some were drowned, and the balance were glad enough to get away.

The Confederates did not lose a man, but captured five boats, over a hundred prisoners, and five flags, one of them said to have been the identical flag that Major Anderson had lowered in 1861, and which Admiral Dahlgren felt so sure he was going to raise on this occasion.

The Abolition authorities pretended to continue the siege after this, but it was virtually abandoned. The Northern people got sick of hearing about Charleston. It had been taken so many times, and Fort Sumter had been captured so often, that it became a standing joke.

Unquestionably its defence had been one of the most gallant and noble on record.

CHAPTER THIRTY-EIGHT
General Morgan's Raid Into the West – The Battle of Chickamauga

We must now return to the West, and notice the closing events of the year 1863 in that section. General John H. Morgan, the bold cavalry man, whose exploits we have already mentioned, had gathered together a force of two thousand mounted men, and four pieces of artillery, and on the 4th of July started on an expedition into Indiana and Ohio.

He advanced very rapidly; and on the 8th of July, after throwing the cities of Louisville and Cincinnati into a great fright, he stood upon the soil of Indiana. He rode rapidly through the State, destroying railroads, government stores, &c., and struck the Ohio line at a place called Harrison. By this time thousands of armed men were in pursuit of him, and finding himself hotly pursued, he tried to cross the Ohio River near Belleville. Part of his command succeeded in doing so, but a good number were taken prisoners. Morgan himself, with a few trusty followers, succeeded in cutting their way out, but were pursued, and, finally, being surrounded near Wellsville, surrendered.

It was thought by the Abolitionists a terrible thing for the Confederates to invade the North, though all right for the North to invade the South. General Morgan and his command were denounced as "felons" and "murderers;" and, though I think that his expedition was a reckless and even foolhardy one, for he was going into a populous country, where the people for self-defence would be compelled to concentrate and cut him off, yet it was not so criminal as the Abolition raid upon the South, for it had the fact of retaliation to justify it.

Not so, however, thought the Abolitionists. It was *their* ox that was gored now, and in their rage they refused to regard General Morgan as a prisoner of war, and sent him and twenty-eight of his officers to the Ohio Penitentiary. Here they were subjected to every possible indignity. First they were stripped naked and washed by Negroes. Then their hair was cut off close to the scalp. After which they were put in solitary confinement.

General Morgan, however, was not idle in prison. On the 20th of November, he and six of his officers escaped. They had dug out of their cells with small knives, after weeks and weeks of patient toil. He left this motto behind for his Abolition tormentors, "Patience is bitter, but its fruit is sweet."

After the escape of General Morgan, the rest of the prisoners were treated with still greater rigor. Their food consisted of only three ounces of bread and a pint of water per day! When the physician remonstrated with their brutal jailer, the wretch replied, "They do not talk right yet." He went into the cell to taunt one of them, Major Webber.

"Sir," said the Major, "I defy you. You can kill me, but you can add nothing to the sufferings you have already inflicted."

The spirit of these men was unconquerable, even in their direst calamity.

It will be remembered that after the battle of Murfreesboro, between General Bragg and General Rosecrans, that the Confederate forces had fallen back to Tullahoma.

After the fall of Vicksburg, of course, troops could be spared to reinforce Rosecrans. It was soon ascertained that General Rosecrans with 70,000 men and General Burnside with 25,000 were concentrating against General Bragg. Burnside was covering General Rosecrans' rear by occupying Knoxville. In the meantime Cumberland Gap was surrendered by the Confederate commander without firing a shot.

General Rosecrans now had all his plans matured for a grand battle. So on the 19th of September he opened the great battle of Chickamauga. The first day was little more than heavy skirmishing, but on the 20th the battle opened with tremendous fury. Bragg had been reinforced with Longstreet's corps from General Lee's army, and never was a battle-field more hotly contested. At length, late in the evening, the Confederates made one of their sweeping charges and carried everything before them. Rosecrans was not only defeated but routed, and had it not been for the coolness of General Thomas his whole army would probably have been captured. As it was, it fled in dismay to Chattanooga where it had entrenchments. General Bragg took 8,000 prisoners, 54 cannon and 15,000 stand of small arms. It was one of the most decisive Confederate victories of the war.

Gen. Ulysses S. Grant

Poor General Rosecrans! The battle also ended his military career. The Abolitionists had now made it a rule to depose every general who lost a battle, and Rosecrans, who is believed to be a pretty good military man, was now sacrificed to their clamor.

General Grant was now appointed to the command of the Mississippi Department. He commenced at once his old plan of superior numbers. He brought two corps from the Army of the Potomac, and called General Sherman, with the Vicksburg army, from Memphis. General Bragg on the contrary did just the reverse of this. He sent General Longstreet off on an expedition to take Knoxville.

General Grant at once availed himself of this mistake and commenced his plans to defeat General Bragg. After a good deal of manœuvering on both sides the battle of Missionary Ridge was fought, on the 24th of November, in which General Bragg was defeated with the loss of 6,000 prisoners and 40 cannon.

In the meantime General Longstreet had had bad luck on

his Knoxville expedition. General Burnside was strongly fortified there, and though Longstreet made a gallant assault upon him he was not strong enough to take his forts. In the meantime, as soon as Grant had defeated Bragg, he sent reinforcements to Burnside, who then assumed the offensive, and Longstreet was compelled to retire towards the Virginia line.

This ended the principal military events of 1863.

There had been some skirmishing between Generals Lee and Meade in Virginia, and once General Meade started out with a great flourish of trumpets to capture Lee's army. But after marching a day or two and taking a look at it, he was glad to fall back.

At Sabine Pass, the dividing line between Louisiana and Texas, the Confederates had achieved a brilliant little naval victory. Five Federal gun-boats steamed up the Pass, and were opened upon by the Confederate batteries. Two of them were captured, and the others beat a hasty retreat.

Generals Marmaduke and Sterling Price had also made efforts to gain a foothold in Missouri, and engagements had taken place at Springfield, Missouri, and Helena, Arkansas, but the loss of life was of no avail. General Steele had been sent into Arkansas with a strong force and had taken Little Rock, the base of the Confederate supplies. This secured Missouri, for the time, against further invasion.

When Congress met in December, 1863, it made General Grant Lieutenant-General of the armies of the United States. His success at Vicksburg and Missionary Ridge had made him the hero of the hour.

CHAPTER THIRTY-NINE
The Confederate Navy and Privateers

One of the greatest difficulties the Confederates labored under from the beginning was their want of a Navy. Almost all the Abolition successes at the commencement of the war were owing to gunboats. The South had never been a mechanical or manufacturing people, but had yielded all these advantages to the North, content to pursue their course as planters and farmers. They saw now, when their social life was in danger, how important these vocations were to their defence.

Lincoln declared a blockade of all Southern ports and the North exerted every effort to make it effectual. President Davis tried to overcome somewhat of the inequality between his people and the North by issuing letters of marque – that is, he commissioned privateers, just as our fathers did in the wars of 1776 and 1812 against Great Britain. This has always been held to be legitimate warfare, and yet the Abolitionists styled the Confederate privateers pirates," and said they would not treat them as prisoners of war. When, however, they captured some they never dared to carry their threats into effect. If the Confederate cruisers were "pirates" then Paul Jones and thousands of the heroes of 1776 were pirates also. But such trash ought to deceive no one.

One of the most gallant and startling events of the war was the sudden attack of the iron-clad ship *Virginia* on the Federal fleet in Hampton Roads in 1862. This vessel was formerly the U. S. frigate *Merrimac*. She had been sunk by the Federals in 1861 at Norfolk when they abandoned the Navy Yard at that place. The Confederates raised her, changed her name to the *Virginia* and plated her over the top like an ark with railroad iron. It was the first iron-clad vessel the world had ever known.

On the 8th of March she steamed out of Norfolk Harbor. The United States had four vessels in Hampton Roads, the *Minnesota* and *Roanoke*, large steamers, and the *Cumberland* and *Congress*, sailing vessels.

On she came, that queer-looking black ark, taking no heed, to the right or the left. She steered directly for the *Cumberland*. The *Congress* fired a broadside into her, but the balls danced from her sloping sides like hail-stones. When she came within range of the *Cumberland*, that vessel opened her guns upon her. But in vain. Her iron armor was invulnerable. The *Virginia* did not fire a shot. But with her monster iron prow now plainly visible made direct for the *Cumberland*. Crash! went the timbers, and soon down, down went the *Cumberland* with all on board.

The *Virginia* then turned to the *Congress*. But the commander of that vessel, fearing the fate of the heroes of the *Cumberland,* ran her ashore. She then steamed for the *Minnesota*, but that vessel had got aground, and the *Virginia* could not approach her. She fired some shots into her without effect, and, as night was now coming on, she steamed back to Norfolk.

The fight between the *Monitor* and the *Virginia*.

The next day the *Virginia* came out and confronted the *Monitor*, a new species of war vessel invented by a Mr. John Ericsson. This vessel has been described as "an iron cheese box set on an iron raft, and the whole set on a light hull shaped like a bark canoe." The fight between these two strange vessels lasted several hours, without any material damage to either. At last the *Virginia* returned to Norfolk. She had twisted her prow in sinking the *Cumberland*, or else the little *Monitor* might not have got off so easily. The commander of the *Virginia*, Franklin Buchanan, was wounded, and afterwards she was placed under the command of the gallant and noble Commodore Tatnall.

Both of those vessels finally ended their career without further glory. The little *Monitor* went down in a gale off Hatteras, while the Confederates were compelled to blow up the *Virginia* when they evacuated Norfolk, as she drew too much water to take her up the James River.

Notwithstanding all the drawbacks under which the Confederate Secretary of the Navy, Mr. Mallory, labored, it must be confessed he had achieved great results. He had been chairman of the Naval Committee in the U.S. Senate for many years, and his experience there was invaluable to him.

In the short space of two years he had purchased and equipped forty-five war vessels; had built twelve wooden and fourteen iron-clad vessels, besides having in progress of construction twenty more.

Several privateers, too, had been fitted out, and had done great damage to Northern commerce. And yet, though Great Britain and France recognized the Confederate States as belligerents – that is, as a government *in fact* – they refused to allow their vessels to take prizes, that is, captured ships, into neutral ports. This was a serious drawback upon the Confederate cruisers, for it left them no course but to destroy the captured vessels. An immense number of Northern ships were thus destroyed.

One of the first vessels got afloat by the Confederates was the *Sumter*, under the command of Admiral Raphael Semmes. Then came the *Florida*, and afterwards the *Alabama* and *Geor-*

gia. The Abolitionists charged that all these vessels were fitted out with the knowledge and connivance of the English Government, for the purpose of driving all American ships from the sea.

It is impossible to say whether such was the fact or not. But certain it is it had that effect. No Northern man scarcely dared to send a ship to sea, for the *Sumter*, or the *Alabama*, or *Florida*, was pretty sure to pounce upon her and destroy her. Sometimes when one of these saucy Confederate cruisers would approach our coasts, whole squadrons of vessels would start out to catch her, but after a fruitless search would return home as wise as they went.

It would require a good deal of space to detail all the movements of these daring Confederate privateers. Sometimes they would be heard of in the Atlantic Ocean, and the next time they were heard from, they would be in the Indian Ocean, or the Cape of Good Hope, or in the China Seas, or the South Atlantic. They gave the North an infinite deal of trouble. Finally, the *Alabama*, while under the command of Admiral Semmes, engaged in a fight with the United States steamer *Kearsarge*, Captain Winslow. The *Kearsarge* was too much for her, and she was sunk. But Admiral Semmes escaped, and was picked up by an English vessel and taken to England. This escape of Semmes made the Abolitionists very mad, and to tell the truth, I think they have owed him a great grudge ever since.

The Confederates at last tried to build two large iron-clad rams in England, with which they expected to be able to break the blockade. But the earnest efforts made by Mr. Adams, the Abolition minister in England, induced Earl Russell to seize them, though it is said it was done on suspicion, and not from any valid evidence that they were destined for the Confederates.

This was after Lincoln had issued his so-called Emancipation Proclamation. Before that the British Government seemed disposed to favor the Confederates. But after Mr. Lincoln made the war distinctly for Negro equality, then the monarchists in England looked upon Mr. Lincoln as simply carrying out their policy on this continent, and were disposed to favor him. Indeed the Abolition papers openly stated that the United States Government could not receive the sympathy of the monarchical countries of Europe until they came out distinctly for Abolitionism.

This, no doubt, accounts for the change in the course of the British ministry. They ignored the Treaty of Paris, which requires that a blockade in order to be binding shall be effectual. But it was notorious that the Confederates always had more or less egress and ingress from their ports. At one time the steamers ran almost regularly from Charleston and Wilmington.

It has been well said that the South not only fought the North, but the whole world, leagued together in deadly warfare against the democratic and republican principles of liberty. The monarchists of Europe knew that to degrade Whites to a level with Negroes was the first step for the re-establishment of monarchical institutions in America. It was, in fact, the secret mine underneath the government of George Washington, which would blow it to atoms.

CHAPTER FORTY
Events in the North in 1863

I cannot dismiss the events of the year 1863 without referring to political affairs in the North, for it must be borne in mind all the time that Mr. Lincoln was carrying on two wars: one against the South and the other against everybody in the North who had the independence and courage to differ from him.

All who did not fall down and worship Mr. Lincoln were denounced as "traitors," "Copperheads" and "rebel sympathizers," and no punishment was thought too severe for them.

On the 1st of January, 1863, Mr. Lincoln issued his long announced "Emancipation Proclamation." In other words, he declared in the style of a dictator that all the Negroes in the South should be "free" to do as they pleased, to go where they pleased, and to be as lazy and useless as they pleased. And he declared that he would use the army and navy of the United States to protect them in these "rights." That was a part of the meaning of this Abolition Proclamation. But it was even more. It really meant the amalgamation of the races. It was the first step in the direction of degrading and destroying the masses of the people by poisoning them with Negro equality.

This "free" Negro edict was followed by various acts of Congress authorizing the use of Negroes as soldiers in the army. The Abolitionists had been clamorous for this from the beginning, and they were now having things entirely their own way. This use of Negroes to fight the South was the vilest, meanest and most barbarous act of all that Lincoln and Seward were guilty of, for it comprehended all crimes. Besides it was a confession that twenty-five millions of White men in the North could not whip eight millions in the South.

But the real object of the Abolitionists was to degrade the White soldiers to a level with Negroes, and familiarize the people with their amalgamation policy. They got up flags to present to these Negro regiments. Even women, calling themselves ladies, I am ashamed to say, were guilty of this disgusting business, and in New York they presented a flag to a Negro regiment as a memento, to use their own words, "of *love* and honor from the daughters of this metropolis." This revolting spectacle actually took place in Union Square, New York, and the women were "the fashionables," so called, of Fifth Avenue! Future ages will scarcely be able to believe that such madness could have existed among otherwise sane people.

Lincoln and Seward had now completely thrown off their masks, and openly falsified all their solemn pledges. It would seem as if they would have broken down the war by their bold Negro equality policy, but about this time the "greenback fever" began to be felt. Everybody was getting rich on paper money. Most cunningly had the finances of the country been conducted. Instead of taxing the people to carry on the war, the Abolition Secretary of the Treasury, Mr. Chase, had brought about a general suspension of specie payments, and issued paper-money, which was declared by Congress "a legal tender," right in the face of the Constitution, which stated that nothing but gold and silver should be a legal currency.

This paper money was issued in floods, and with it the North was corrupted. With it high bounties were paid for soldiers, as volunteering for an Abolition war was not even thought of. True, some of the more reckless of the Abolition journals said, that as soon as Mr. Lincoln issued his Emancipation Proclamation, the roads would swarm with volunteers. But no one saw them.

The effect of Mr. Lincoln's Negro edict in the army was very marked. In the winter of 1863, the soldiers in some instances were almost in a state of mutiny. Their letters home to their friends were very desponding. Desertions were numerous. A young soldier, writing to his mother, January 10th, 1863, from Camp Slocum, says:

> One of the sweetest comforts of my life, while lying on the cold, damp ground here, is to hear from you. Mother, I tell you I am sorry that I ever enlisted. Not that I am afraid to fight for my country; no, no, I am willing to fight for the Stars and Stripes, but not for the nigger. If I was home again, I would never leave you until forced to do so, by seeing the rebels before our chestnut trees.

This letter is only a sample of scores and scores that I might quote, if my space allowed. It is sufficient to show, however, that the private soldiers knew how they had been swindled by Lincoln and Seward. But it was too late then to remedy the mistake they had made. Their officers, generally, kept a strict watch upon them; and some were shot for mutiny, because they said they did not "want to fight to free Negroes."

The effect of the Lincoln proclamation was very great all over the North, and produced a decided reaction against his Administration and the war. But again Mr. Lincoln resorted to every effort to control public opinion, and to try to make it appear that it endorsed him.

In April, an election for Governor came off in the State of Connecticut. The Democrats had nominated as Governor, Thomas H. Seymour. Now Mr. Lincoln and his party hated Gov. Seymour with all their might, for he had denounced their war from the beginning. No man was so beloved by the Democracy of Connecticut. When the Mexican war broke out, he volunteered to fight the enemies of his country; and he it was, who, at the final charge on Chapultepec, cut down the Mexican flag with his sword, and raised the Stars and Stripes in its place.

When Mr. Lincoln commenced his war upon the South, some Abolitionists in Hartford used Gov. Seymour's name without his consent at a war meeting; but he came out at once in a bold letter and told them they had no business to do it. They thought he would not *dare* to speak out. But they mistook their man. They then talked of mobbing him; but they knew there was too much fight in him, and so the cowards kept away.

The Democrats did a good thing in nominating him, and right nobly too did they labor to elect him. They were sure of success; but Mr. Lincoln thought it would be a death-blow to him to allow it, so he sent home some two or three thousand soldiers from his army to defeat him. As it turned out, it was these soldiers' votes that defeated Mr. Seymour.

Early in the year, General Burnside had been appointed to the command of "the Department of the Ohio," which included the States of Ohio, Kentucky, Illinois, and Indiana. As there were elections for Governor to come off in the first two of these States, one in October and the other in August, it does not require a good guesser to tell what he was sent there for.

He commenced his despotic course by arresting, on the 5th of May, the Hon. Clement L. Vallandigham. Mr. Vallandigham had been a member of Congress since 1861; and no one did the Abolitionists hate more cordially than he, and for no other reason than because he opposed the policy of Mr. Lincoln's Administration. They knew that the Democrats intended to nominate him as their candidate for Governor in October. Hence they wanted to break him down. So they trumped up charges that Mr. Vallandigham had "talked treason" in some of his speeches, and they tried him before "a military commission," which sentenced him to imprisonment. But Mr. Lincoln did no exactly dare to put him in prison, for it is doubtful whether it would not have been torn down, and Mr. Vallandigham released, so great was the indignation of the people. So Mr. Lincoln thought it was a "smart joke," no doubt, and sent Mr. Vallandigham across the lines into the Confederate States.

Hon. Clement L. Vallandigham

Mr. Vallandigham quietly pursued his way to a seaport,

and sailed for Canada, where he remained some time. He was defeated in October for Governor, though the Democrats made a gallant effort to elect him. Mr. Lincoln's "men and money" were too much for them. After awhile Mr. Vallandigham returned of his own accord to Ohio, despite of Mr. Lincoln's order of exile. They at first talked of arresting him again, but did not venture to do it.

In Kentucky, General Burnside's "political campaign" was equally serviceable. In that State the Democrats had nominated the venerable Hon. Chas. A. Wickliffe, a name known and honored throughout the whole country. On the 30th of July, just three days before the election, General Burnside declared martial law in the State. Several Democrats, who were running for Congress, were arrested and Burnside ordered that no "disloyal men" should be allowed to vote; but as all Democrats were called "disloyal," he might as well have ordered that no Democrats be allowed to vote. In some counties no one was permitted to cast a vote for Wickliffe. The result was a defeat, or rather there was no election held. Never was there a more complete overthrow of the ballot-box. Shameful as it was, the Abolitionists gloried over the result.

But this does not begin to exhaust the chapter of General Burnside's tyranny. All over the West there existed a complete "reign of terror." No Democrat's life or property was safe if he dared boldly to doubt the wisdom of Mr. Lincoln. In 1862, after the mails had been reopened to Democratic papers, a new process had been resorted to, to injure their circulation and break them down. It was held that any commander of a Department, or provost marshal, could prohibit the circulation of any paper in his district which he regarded as detrimental. This, of course, was an invitation to every petty provost marshal to turn upon the Democratic newspapers. Its effect was also to stimulate mobs, and Democratic editors all over the West were insulted and outraged, and their offices often destroyed.

Some were killed for the defence of the right of free speech. At Dayton, Ohio, the home of Mr. Vallandigham, Mr. Bollmeyer, the editor of the Dayton *Empire,* was deliberately shot dead by an Abolitionist, and a jury of his own county actually cleared the assassin!

General Burnside also turned his attention to suppressing newspapers. On the 1st of June, he issued an order suppressing the publication of the Chicago *Times,* a leading Democratic paper in the West, and also one suppressing the circulation of the New York *World,* in his Department. In this movement, General Burnside made the same mistake he did at Fredericksburg; he got whipped. The Democrats of Chicago were determined to be fooled no longer by Mr. Lincoln's satraps. So the editor of the *Times,* Mr. Story, called a meeting of citizens in front of his office to see how the Democrats felt about it.

The upshot of the whole affair was, that they sent word to Mr. Lincoln that if he did not rescind the order of his man Burnside, and allow the Chicago *Times* to be published, then there should no Republican or Abolition paper be allowed to be published in that city. And the Democrats went to work quietly and determinedly to carry out their threat. Mr. Lincoln, however, backed down, when he saw the pluck displayed, and so Mr. Burnside had all this splurge for nothing.

The interference of the little provost marshals, however, continued, and for a long time all Democratic papers were denied circulation in Missouri and Kentucky. Mr. Lincoln never yielded his warfare on the freedom of the press, only when compelled to do so. He seemed to feel by instinct that he stood no chance if free discussion was allowed.

So greatly had the Democrats of the West suffered from the minions of arbitrary power, that they organized a society called the "Sons of Liberty" for self-protection. But even this was used against them; for it was denounced by the Abolitionists as "a secret organization to overthrow the Government," and many of its leaders were arrested and cruelly imprisoned. Three of those, Messrs. Bowles, Horsey, and Milliken, were sentenced to death by a "military commission," and only escaped death through the clemency of President Johnson, after his accession to office.

I must now turn to some remarkable events which occurred in the city of New York, in July. Mr. Lincoln was in great want of soldiers at this time. Men would not volunteer to fight to put themselves on an equality with Negroes. So Congress passed a rigorous conscription act, which would compel men to go whether they wanted to or not. The Abolitionists had hesitated to put it in force, knowing how unpopular it was. Finally, after deceiving the people several times by false alarms, they suddenly, one Saturday afternoon, set the fatal wheel in motion.

Many citizens of New York woke up on Sunday morning to find their names on Lincoln's army list, for every man was declared a soldier from the moment his name was drawn, and liable to be shot as a deserter if he got out of the way.

The pent-up wrath of the people now broke out. The war had always been unpopular in New York city, and when the first announcement was made, that the people were resisting the draft, the greatest excitement occurred. The Abolitionists were terribly frightened. A good many ran away from the city. Others hid themselves. The drafted men first destroyed the enrolling offices, burning them to the ground, and came very near killing Kennedy, the police superintendent.

Like all popular outbreaks of this kind, it ran into every form of riot and outrage. The popular feeling seemed to regard with peculiar hatred the Negro, as if he were the cause of the war and all the trouble resulting from it, while in fact it was the Abolitionists and not the Negro who were responsible.

The rioters burnt down the Negro Orphan Asylum, hung Negroes to the lamp posts, and sometimes threw them into the docks. Boys particularly seemed to be engaged in the rioting. The writer of this was all through the city at all times of the day and night, during the continuance of the trouble. On one occasion he saw a crowd, and asked a little boy what it meant. "Oh, it is nothing but a dead nigger," was the reply. This shows how callous to human suffering even children may become in times of war and bloodshed.

These riots continued for four or five days, and it was fully a week before complete order was restored. All the stages and cars stopped running, and the stores and shops were closed.

Men and women peeped cautiously out of their doors and windows, for fear bullets might hit them. Fires were burning almost constantly, and together with the ringing of the bells and the tramp of soldiers, New York city seemed like a military camp.

If the matter had been taken hold of properly at the start it might have been soon disposed of. But the mayor of the city, an Abolitionist by the name of Opdyke, was afraid to go in the street. Governor Seymour hurried to the city as fast as he could, and by calm words and a firm policy soon brought order out of chaos. The Abolitionists, however, tried to thwart his endeavors, and with some troops under Colonel Harvey Brown, from the forts in the harbor, shot down a good many innocent people.

The whole story of the riots can be easily summed up. They did not originate in a desire to harm any one, but simply to inform Mr. Lincoln that New Yorkers would not be dragged into the army to fight to free Negroes. After they got under way, bad men used the confusion to rob, plunder, and steal.

One thing, however, these riots did do. They settled the draft in New York city. For though Mr. Lincoln sent on a large force, and threatened great things, yet no man, I believe, was ever taken out of New York city for the war without his consent. The Common Council was forced to offer large bounties, and to get by buying what they could not secure by force.

During this year, too, the Abolitionists did all they could to stimulate the war feeling in the North by alleged cruelties on the Federal prisoners in the South, and particularly at Andersonville, Georgia. I have not space to go into a detail of this matter here, but it is certain that if Northern soldiers were suffering in the South, the Abolition authorities could have got them out of it any day by exchanging prisoners, which the Confederates were anxious to do. The truth was, however, that the Abolition Government at Washington purposely refused to do so. They said the thirty or forty thousand Confederates the North had would go to recruit the Southern army, while in the case of the Federal prisoners their terms were mostly out and they would not probably re-enlist.

No doubt a good deal of hardship was experienced, but

I saw soldiers who were in Andersonville nine months, who came out as healthy and as rugged as when they went in. Persons who were filthy and did not take care of their health, of course, suffered and died.

Southern officers confined at Chicago, Illinois, and Elmira, New York, however, declare that they were more cruelly treated than the Federal prisoners in the South. I will not stop here to more than say that I believe from all I know that General Winder was a humane man and did all that his limited means would allow for the Federal prisoners at the South, and I am fully satisfied that the Abolitionists intentionally got up their horrible stories in order to inflame the Northern mind and keep it up to the work of abolishing "slavery." In fact this atrocious design was boldly avowed in a printed pamphlet, gotten up with horrible cuts, for Northern circulation.

CHAPTER FORTY-ONE
The Opening Events of 1864

Another year had now rolled around, and yet the South was not whipped. The year 1863 had closed with gloom to the Confederates. But still their spirits seemed as firm as ever. The year 1864 opened more auspiciously. General Rosser's raid into Western Virginia in January, and Pickett's expedition against Newbern, North Carolina, in February, had both been successful, and materially assisted in dispelling the despondency.

But greater operations than these were soon to transpire favorably to the Confederates. General Sherman, with thirty-five thousand men, started early in February on an expedition from Vicksburg, marching eastwardly. He was supported by the cavalry of Generals Smith and Grierson, and it is supposed his design was the capture of Mobile; but he failed utterly. General Forrest fell upon the Federal cavalry and cut it to pieces, and General Sherman, having advanced as far as Meridian, Mississippi, and finding himself without support, retraced his steps.

Finding he could not conquer, he fell to marauding and pillaging. While at Meridian he sent out detachments and burnt or desolated Enterprise, Quitman, Hillsboro, Canton, Decatur, Lauderdale Springs, and other towns in Mississippi, destroying the provisions of the inhabitants and robbing them of their valuables. It is said he drove off not less than 10,000 Negroes from the plantations, many of whom were taken to Vicksburg and forced into the army.

The next unlucky expedition the Federals attempted was

that commanded by a rampant Abolition officer, one General Truman Seymour. He tried to penetrate the interior of Florida, but having marched as far as Olustee, he was there met by General Finnegan, with a small Confederate force, who whipped the Negro-loving general so severely that he ran almost back to Jacksonville before he stopped.

I have now to relate a still more remarkable defeat. This time it is General Banks, whom Stonewall Jackson so soundly whipped in Virginia. Mr. Lincoln had sent General Banks to New Orleans, in place of Butler. In March, he concocted, in connection with Admiral Porter's fleet, an expedition up the Red River against Shreveport. The real object of this movement was "to steal cotton," but General Banks called it a military expedition. When General Banks arrived at a place called Mansfield, he found something in his path. It proved to be Generals Kirby Smith and Dick Taylor with an army. A battle took place, in which General Banks was literally "whipped out of his boots." He fell back to a place called Pleasant Hill, and there he got whipped again the next day. At night he ran away, and did not stop until he got under the shelter of Admiral Porter's fleet at Grand Encore. From thence he fell back to Alexandria, and was in a great hurry to get back to New Orleans.

Admiral Porter, too, came very near being caught with all his fleet. The Red River fell very suddenly, and he could not get his boats over the rapids at Alexandria. So he was forced to dam up the waters of Red River, which he did as speedily as possible, and thus he got his boats away.

Thus ended General Banks' military exploits, for he soon after returned to Massachusetts, where they elected him to Congress.

Besides these marked successes of the Confederates, they had been very active with their cavalry. General Forrest, after defeating Smith and Grierson, had moved into Kentucky, going even into Paducah and Columbus. Mosby was almost every day surprising the Federal outposts in the vicinity of Washington.

Colonel John S. Mosby was one of the most daring partisan chiefs in the Confederate service. He was here, there, and everywhere. Intimately acquainted with all the country about Washington, he scarcely allowed the Abolition crowd there a chance to sleep. Time and again they had tried to catch him by all sorts of devices, but he was too much for them every time.

I have now to relate one of the most remarkable episodes of the war. On the 28th of February, General Kilpatrick, with 5,000 *picked men,* started on a raid to Richmond. When he set out vague hints were given in the Abolition papers that the country would soon be startled by great events. This man, Kilpatrick, was a low, brutal fellow, and well adapted to any vile work, as we shall see before we get through with what we are relating.

After he reached Beaver Dam, near Richmond, he divided his force into two parts, which took different directions. One portion he commanded himself. The other was placed in charge of Colonel Ulric Dahlgren, a giddy, foolish, impulsive young man, who probably did not even realize what a criminal errand he was on.

Kilpatrick reached the outer defences of Richmond, and though there was scarcely any force to resist him, he seems to have got frightened, and, satisfied with boasting that he had seen Richmond, galloped off towards the Peninsula.

Dahlgren, more impulsive and fool-hardy, resolved to fight, and though there was nothing but a regiment of boys, mostly clerks in Richmond, to oppose him, yet he was badly whipped and tried to retreat. His command broke up into squads. Riding along, he saw a few Confederates, and supposing they were skulkers, he shouted, "Surrender!"

"Fire," cried Lieutenant Pollard, who commanded the young men, and the next moment poor Dahlgren was dead.

And now comes the remarkable part of this story. From papers found on young Dahlgren's body, it was discovered that the object of the expedition was to release the Federal prisoners confined in Richmond, to destroy and burn the city *and kill Jefferson Davis and his Cabinet!*

It is not necessary to give these papers in full here, but the above is their purport. The Abolition papers denied the authenticity of these documents, and declared that they were forged by the

Confederates. It certainly seems almost impossible to believe that such a horrible crime as the cool and deliberate murder of Davis and his cabinet could have been contemplated, and yet, if the alleged papers are authentic, there is no room to doubt it.

Upon this point I will quote the authority of Mr. E. A. Pollard, the Southern historian. He says:

> Yankee newspapers, with consistent hardihood, disputed the authenticity of these papers. The writer, whose relative was engaged in the affair, and who himself was familiar with all the incidents relating to these papers, may assert most positively that there is not a shadow of ground to question their authenticity. He saw the originals. In half an hour after they were found, they were placed in the hands of General Fitzhugh Lee; and the soiled folds of the paper were then plainly visible. The words referring to the murder of the President and his Cabinet were not interlined, but were in the regular context of the manuscript. The proof of the authenticity of the papers is clinched by the circumstance that there was also found on Dahlgren's body a private notebook, which contained a rough draft of the address to his soldiers, and repetitions of some of memoranda in the papers. The writer has carefully examined this note-book – a common memorandum pocket-book, such as might be bought in New York for fifty cents – in which are various notes, some in ink and some in pencil; the sketch of the address is in pencil, very imperfectly written, as one who labored in composition, crossed and re-crossed. It does not differ materially in context or language from the more precise composition, except that the injunction to murder the Confederate leaders is in the rough draft made with this additional emphasis, *"kill on the spot."*

Right here the terrible thought comes up, if this be true, these men would never have dared to attempt the deed referred to, if it had not received the open or secret sanction of *higher authority!* People may doubt whether Lincoln and Seward could have been guilty of even such a thought; but when we remember into what monsters fanaticism has transferred men in all ages of the world, we are prepared to believe anything possible. How many thousands of people have been killed in cold blood by men, while lifting up their hands to heaven, and claiming they were doing God service.

And this Abolition fanaticism or delusion is no exception to the general rule. How many otherwise good people have been led to sanction war, and all sorts of cruelty, to crush out what they believe, or think they believe, is a sin? This whole war shows how Abolitionism brutifies mankind, and crushes out all the generous traits of humanity from those who have come thoroughly under its influence.

CHAPTER FORTY-TWO
General Grant's "On to Richmond"

General Grant, who was now Lieutenant-General, had formed his plans for a grand advance of all his armies during the first week in May, 1864. He had concentrated nearly all his troops into two grand armies. One under his own command to march on Richmond, and the other under General Sherman to advance to the capture of Atlanta.

His first move was to send off various supporting expeditions. One, under General Sigel, was sent down the Shenandoah Valley against Lynchburg, and another, under General Butler, was sent by way of Fortress Monroe, to take Petersburg. If these expeditions had been successful, General Grant might have had an easy time of it. But we shall see they were not. His forces numbered nearly two hundred thousand men of all arms; General Lee's army numbered about fifty-two thousand.

On the 3d of May, General Grant set his tremendous army in motion. A train of 4,000 wagons was a proof of the vast host on the march. Grant's intention was to cross the Rapidan River, and march his army directly to Gordonsville, which, if once accomplished, would place his army between the army of Lee and Richmond. The fact that General Lee offered no objection to his passage of the river, impressed General Grant with the idea that the Confederate commander would at once retreat with his whole army to Richmond.

When, therefore, on Thursday morning, the 5th of May, Grant found a Confederate force in his front, at a place known as the Wilderness, he imagined it to be a movement of the retreat of Lee's army. It was not, however, long before he found his fatal mistake. In Lee's initial movement, before the real battle commenced, Grant lost 3,000 men. And when the darkness of the night put a stop to the fierce conflict that raged for hours, Lee's forces occupied the same ground they did at the beginning. Grant had been manfully repulsed at every point; and his men slept on their arms that night to be ready to renew the engagement in the morning. Lee was also waiting to open the battle in the morning. Both generals were, therefore, determined to open the fiery ball the next day. But Lee was ahead of his antagonist; and while Grant was preparing to strike, he dealt the first terrible blow. Then followed one of the most deadly and terrible battles which occurred during the whole war. General Lee here inflicted a terrible chastisement upon General Grant. Grant lost 15,000 men, and Lee about 7,000. It was a great victory for so small an army to win over one so vastly its superior in numbers.

The historian of the Army of the Potomac speaking of the battle, says, that General Grant "avowedly despised manœuvering. His reliance was exclusively on the application of brute masses, in rapid and remorseless blows, or as he himself phrased it, 'in hammering continuously.'" But in this instance the hammer itself was broken by Lee's superior generalship.

After this fatal experiment of "hammering" in the Wilderness, where he had hammered so many thousand of his own men to death, General Grant withdrew as secretly as possible with a view of reaching Spottsylvania Court House, where he would be between Lee's army and Richmond – that is, provided Lee would remain where he then was, in order to accommodate him. But to General Grant's very great surprise and discomfiture, when he arrived in the neighborhood of Spottsylvania, he found Lee was there before him. So without any attempt at manœuvering, he here set to work again to hammer his way through Lee's lines. But everywhere was he thrown back with fearful slaughter. And thus he hammered away for twelve days and nights without making the least impression upon Lee's lines, and only getting his own men killed. The ground was literally covered and heaped up with the dead.

The result of this hammering on the two battlefields of the Wilderness and Spottsylvania was a loss of forty thousand men, who were ignominiously slaughtered by incompetent generalship. General Meade's official report admits a loss of thirty-nine thousand seven hundred and thirty-one; and his report does not include the losses of Burnside's corps.

The soldiers of the Army of the Potomac were not very secret in their denunciations of General Grant. They called him a "butcher," and but for the popularity of several of the division commanders there would have been very great difficulty in persuading the army to fight under Grant. So terribly had his army been cut to pieces in these battles of the Wilderness and Spottsylvania that he was obliged to send for reinforcements before attempting a further march towards Richmond.

On the night of the 20th of May, General Grant set his army on the march again towards Richmond. The next day brought him to the banks of the North Anna River, where he found a portion of Lee's army in his front. But Lee made just opposition enough at this point to impress Grant with an idea of his weakness, and then retreated to the South Anna. To this point General Grant marched with the fullest confidence that he would meet with no serious check. But he was doomed to a very sad disappointment; for he soon discovered that Lee had so manœuvred as to place the very centre of his army between the two wings of Grant's army, thereby cutting the Abolition army in two in the middle.

Out of this trap into which he had so proudly marched, Grant beat a very hasty retreat. He was forced to re-cross the North Anna River, and take a circuitous and tedious route in another direction. The only thing he had accomplished in six days of painful marching was to get a great many of his men killed.

General Grant withdrew as secretly as possible from the North Anna, on the night of the 26th of May. His direction was south-east towards the Chickahominy River. It was on the banks of this river that the next great battle was fought, at a point called Cold Harbor. This place proved to be another of Grant's slaughter-pens, where he hammered his own gallant men to sure destruction without making the least visible impression upon the enemy. In a single assault of Lee's lines, he lost thirteen thousand men, while Lee did not lose as many hundreds. And when General Grant gave the order for another assault, the whole army, as one man, refused to obey his order.

The historian of *The Campaigns of the Army of the Potomac*, who was a spectator of the events he describes, says of the order for another assault: "The order was issued through these officers to their subordinate commanders, and from them descended through the wonted channels; but no man stirred, and the immobile lines pronounced a verdict, silent yet emphatic, against further slaughter."

It is, perhaps, the only instance on record where a whole army of such vast numbers refused to obey orders. But the soldiers knew that by obeying the order they simply devoted themselves to destruction. They had ceased to feel any respect for General Grant, and although they were brave and gallant men, they positively refused to be further slaughtered by what they believed to be incompetent generalship.

In this short march from the Rapidan to the Chickahominy, Grant had lost between sixty and seventy thousand men. It is safe to say that a skillful general would have accomplished the same march with one-fifth of that loss. In these battles Grant lost twenty thousand more men than Lee's whole army numbered. The reinforcements he received between the Rapidan and the Chickahominy amounted to more than Lee's whole army.

The history of these battles affords a very striking illustration of the very great difference between good and bad generalship. Grant's theory was that he could afford to slaughter three of his men to kill one Confederate. But in these battles the proportion of his slaughtered was greater than that. It was more than three to one. And all he had gained was a position in front of Richmond, which, after a few days, he was obliged to abandon for the precise spot adopted by McClellan two years before.

On the night of the 12th of June, Grant began to withdraw from the region of Cold Harbor, in front of Richmond, and com-

General Grant's "On to Richmond" 275

menced his march across the Peninsula to the James River. The distance was fifty-five miles, which brought him to the James a little below Harrison's Landing, the scene of General McClellan's operations. This march was completed, without opposition on the part of Lee, in two days. On the 18th of the month Grant's whole army was on the south side of the James, and prepared to take the same steps for the capture of Richmond which McClellan had fixed upon at the time he was ordered from Washington to withdraw his army from the Peninsula.

In an effort to take Richmond from this point, the first thing to be done was to take the city of Petersburg, which is twenty-two miles south of Richmond, and was the outer line of the defences of Richmond. The Lynchburg Railroad, James River Canal, and Danville Railroad connected this place with the west and south-west sections of the country from which Richmond largely drew its supplies.

Grant felt sure that he would be able to seize this city before Lee's army would be there to defend it. In this calculation he was doomed to another bitter disappointment, for no sooner did he begin his "hammering" process than he found the same invincible anvil of Lee's army was there to throw back his blows. After "pegging away" two days, during which time he lost six or seven thousand of his men, on the morning of the 18th of June he ordered a general assault of Lee's lines, which resulted in his complete repulse everywhere, with a terrible loss of life. The failure was such a disastrous one that even Grant gave up, for the time, his favorite "hammering" process, and fell to entrenching his army before the city of Petersburg, and began to attempt something like manœuvering.

The first effort, however, made after completing his entrenchments, proved a very disastrous one; as Lee, by a bold dash, swept down through a portion of his lines and captured several entire regiments and one of his most powerful batteries. General Grant exhausted two weeks in fruitless raids and assaults, in every one of which he was indeed greatly the loser. In this way he lost between 15,000 and 20,000 men, without inflicting any considerable damage upon Lee. Indeed he had literally worn his own army out again. Swinton says: "Indeed the Union army, terribly shaken as well in spirit as in material substance, by the repeated attacks on entrenched positions it had been called on to make, was in a very unfit moral condition to undertake any new enterprise of that character."

Grant was at last convinced that it was impossible for him to carry the city by assault. So there was no resource left him but to give up again his "hammering" system and to go to digging. So he kept busy for five or six weeks in constructing and arming defensive works. Among other things an extensive mine was dug under a portion of Lee's works, which was to be exploded, as it was thought, with the most disastrous consequences to the Confederates.

Grant fixed upon the morning of the 30th of July, for the exploding of this mine, and for a general assault upon Lee's lines through the opening which the exploded mine was to make. The explosion of the mine took place at half-past four in the morning. The shock was terrible, and vast masses of earth were thrown more than two hundred feet into the air. The only damage done was to surprise the Confederates for a few minutes, when they made the best possible use of what turned out to be a great folly on the part of General Grant.

The explosion produced a huge crater one hundred and fifty feet long, sixty feet wide, and thirty feet deep. Through this opening in Lee's works Grant undertook to push his assaulting column. In this assaulting column was a brigade of Negroes under Burnside, which led the van, and which, on meeting a fierce fire from Lee's works, fled wildly back, and doubled up upon the White troops behind them in such a manner as to produce a scene of fright and confusion that would have been laughable if it had not been so terrible. An army correspondent, who witnessed the whole affair, said:

> Blacks and Whites tumbled pell-mell into the hollow of exploded earthworks – a slaughter-pen, in which shells and bombs rained from the enemy's lines, and did frightful havoc. Failing to advance, it soon proved almost equally difficult to retreat, though parties of tens and twelves, crawling out, ran back

as best they could. Above four thousand were killed or captured.

Such was General Grant's first attempt at strategy against Lee. With herculean labor, he produced an immense hole in the earth, which served no other purpose than a frightful slaughter-pen for his own men. In September, he made an attack with a portion of his army on the defences of Richmond north of the James River. But here he met with another decided repulse. This ended General Grant's offensive movements for some months.

It will be remembered I stated, that when General Grant started for Richmond, in May, he sent off General Sigel to take Lynchburg, and General Butler to take Petersburg. Both of these expeditions signally failed. General Sigel got severely whipped by General Breckinridge, and General Beauregard, who had come up from Charleston, soon disposed of Butler. Butler, as usual, made himself the laughing-stock of all sensible people. At one time he telegraphed that "he held the key of Richmond." But no one ever saw "the key," except Butler, and he only in imagination.

Grant, however, did not give up his design of capturing Lynchburg. So he sent General David Hunter to take it; but Hunter not only got badly whipped, but seems to have become awfully frightened. He not only ran away, but did not stop until he got into Western Virginia, where he arrested two editors for speaking disrespectfully of his campaign. He found time, however, in his flight, to burn the Virginia Military Institute, with its library, &c., Governor Letcher's dwelling-house, and to commit several other outrageous and fiendish acts.

The defeat of Hunter opened the Shenandoah Valley again; and General Jubal Early, who now commanded on Stonewall Jackson's old battle fields, came rushing down the valley, capturing Winchester, Martinsburg, Harper's Ferry, and, crossing the Potomac, started another panic in the North. Some people thought General Lee was coming again with his whole army.

General Lew. Wallace, a bitter Abolition general, who commanded at Baltimore, went out to whip Early, and met the Confederates at a place called Monocacy, but was so badly beaten that he did not stop running until he got safely back to

Baltimore, where he barricaded the city.

The troops under Generals Early and Breckinridge now scoured over Maryland, capturing railroad trains, the cavalry, under the daring Harry Gilmore, coming almost to the Pennsylvania line. For a few days General Early threatened Washington, some of his troops actually firing shots into the city. He burned the houses of Governor Bradford and Montgomery Blair of Maryland, in retaliation of Hunter's devastations in the valley, and then started off with his stores across the Potomac.

General Grant now resolved upon savage measures, the like of which had never been known in civilized warfare. He entrenched his army before Petersburg, and then detaching two corps, sent them, with a heavy force of cavalry, all under General Philip Sheridan, to the Shenandoah Valley. These troops, with the remains of Hunter's army, made a force that it was impossible for General Early to contend against. He was driven out of the valley with heavy losses of guns and men.

And now General Sheridan, with the instincts of savage warfare, determined to utterly devastate this beautiful valley. He therefore set his troops at work, and all the way from Staunton to Winchester was soon one scene of desolation. He burned every house, every barn, every mill, all the corn cribs, hay-stacks, and the entire food crops of all kinds for the year. Not only this, but he seized all the ploughs, harrows, spades, and every description of farm implement, and putting them into piles, made his soldiers burn them. He then drove off all the cows, horses, oxen, cattle, sheep, pigs, and every living animal for the use of man in all that wide valley. In fact, nothing that devilish ingenuity could invent was left undone to transform the loveliest and most fertile valley in the world into a desolate and howling wilderness.

General Grant himself stated that he had burned *two thousand barns;* but the half is not yet told, for not less than *ten thousand* innocent women and children were by this savagery reduced to starvation, and thrown, in the fall of the year, out of comfortable homes, to perish in tents and caves by the cold of the winter. General Early and his troops incensed by the brutal devastation of the valley, made superhuman efforts to chastise Sheridan, and in one engagement severely defeated him. But they could not hold their ground. Sheridan's greatly outnumbered them, and falling upon them again, drove them to Staunton. This, I believe, closes the chapter of military movements in the sadly stricken and impoverished Shenandoah Valley.

CHAPTER FORTY-THREE
Sherman's "On to Atlanta"

I have now to relate General Sherman's part of the campaign which General Grant had planned. His headquarters were at Ringgold, in the northeastern part of Georgia, and he had not less than 100,000 men in three grand divisions, under the command respectively of Generals Thomas, Schofield and McPherson.

The Confederate army was under the command of General Joseph E. Johnston, and did not number more than half of General Sherman's force. It was strongly entrenched at Dalton.

General Sherman began his march for Atlanta about the same time that Grant started for Richmond. When he got to Dalton, he took a good look at General Johnston's position, and as he did not like the appearance of it, he determined not to attack it. So he moved his army in a roundabout way to Resaca. Johnston, seeing the movement, was too quick for him, and when Sherman's army arrived there, they found the Confederate commander ready for them.

General Sherman now tried an assault upon General Johnston's works, and considerable battles took place on the 14th and 15th of May. General Sherman was badly repulsed, and General Johnston took up his retreat in a leisurely manner in the direction of the Etowah River. Again General Johnston assumed such a strong position that General Sherman did not dare to attack him, but tried the flanking process again. Compelled to fall back once more, General Johnston now took a strong position on the Kenesaw Mountain.

Here he held his ground for a month. General Sherman tried in vain to dislodge him, and on the 27th of June made a general assault of his whole force upon Johnston's lines. He was everywhere repulsed, with great loss, the Confederates, in some instances, rolling stones down the mountain sides upon the Federal troops.

Finding it impossible to carry Johnston's position, Sherman again resorted to his flanking movements. He marched his army around the mountain, and Johnston was now compelled to fall back across the Chattahoochee River. It was now the 4th of July.

It was about this time that time Confederate General Bishop Leonidas Polk was killed by a shell while taking a survey of General Sherman's position. At the opening of the war, he took off the robes of his ministerial office and went heart and soul into the contest to save his country from the pollution of Abolitionism. He remarked only a short time before his death, "I feel like a man who has dropped his business when his house is on fire, to put it out, for as soon as the war is over I shall return again to my sacred calling." He was a brave, good man, and beloved by all who knew him.

The Southern people were very much chagrined at the loss of territory. All northern Georgia was now in the possession of Sherman's army, who devastated it without mercy. Some of the finest wheat growing districts of the South, and these almost ripe for harvest, had fallen into the enemy's hands. Besides these, iron rolling mills and Government works of great value, on the Etowah River, had been abandoned.

General Sherman now crossed the Chattahoochee River, and General Johnston was compelled to fall back to the defences of Atlanta. This city was a very important position for the Confederates. Here they manufactured a great many of their army stores. It was well fortified, and if properly defended, ought to have held out for a long time.

There were now general murmurs of dissatisfaction against General Johnston for retreating before Sherman. People

Sherman's "On to Atlanta" 283

in the South said he ought to fight, and not be forever falling back. I do not pretend to decide this question, but a great many persons now think that if he had been let alone, he would have whipped General Sherman. However, President Davis thought he was not doing exactly right, and so he removed him from command, and appointed General John B. Hood in his place.

General Hood was comparatively a young man from the State of Texas, but was renowned as a great fighter. He it was who, at the head of the Texas brigade, stormed McClellan's position at Gaines' Mills, and turned the tide of battle in that day's fight. He had lost one leg in the service, and was very popular in the army.

As soon as he was appointed to the command, he determined to fight General Sherman. He attacked him on the 20th and 22d and 28th of July, and in each engagement punished him severely, capturing guns, colors, and prisoners. He then fell back to the defences of Atlanta, where General Sherman did not dare to molest him. There is no doubt that Sherman's army was now in a critical position. It could not take Atlanta, nor could it retreat. Just at this time General Hood sent all his cavalry off to operate on Sherman's rear, and break up his line of communication.

When General Sherman heard of this, he conceived the bold idea of throwing his army south of Atlanta, and cutting off General Hood's communications. The absence of the cavalry rendered this movement now possible, and before General Hood could recall them, he found himself compelled to evacuate Atlanta. He was forced to blow up the Confederate foundries and factories and destroy immense quantities of army stores of all kinds. If was a sad day for the people of Atlanta, for they knew they were to fall into the hands of a remorseless military chieftain. It was the 1st of September when Atlanta was evacuated by Hood, and thus in four months, with a vastly inferior force to General Grant, General Sherman had achieved the object he aimed to accomplish.

General Sherman did not despise "manœuvering," and though a cruel warrior, he had displayed military genius of a very high order.

His march from Ringgold to Atlanta was a scene of desolation. Houses were fired, churches pillaged, towns sacked, and hundreds of men, women and children were compelled to seek shelter in the mountains. It pains me to write of such vandalism. But Sherman told the people that this year he would only take their property. But next year, if the war continued, he would take their lives.

At one place he captured some four hundred factory girls, and forcing them to get into army wagons, transported them north of the Ohio River, far from home and friends, there to remain during the war. What became of these poor girls I cannot tell, but when they arrived at Louisville, Kentucky, they were in a most destitute condition. It is cruel enough to exile men, but when hundreds of young women are thus torn from their home and friends, the act is worse than inhuman – it is barbarous.

The Abolitionists of the North, however, were so crazy with joy over the capture of Atlanta that they did not stop to rebuke the wrongs inflicted upon innocent people.

General Sherman signalized his capture of Atlanta by further displays of his cruelty. He at once ordered that all the White inhabitants should leave the city – should be driven from their homes, men, women, and children, without any regard to age or sex. None were spared. Those who would take the Lincoln oath were sent North. Those who would not must go South. Then commenced an exodus such as the world had never before known. For ten days a steady stream of men, women, and children – tottering age and prattling infancy – poured out of the desolated city. They could take only a few articles of clothing, some of the simplest implements of cooking, and just enough food to support nature. All the rest of their worldly effects they were forced to leave to the tender mercies of General Sherman's soldiers.

General Hood protested against this as "a crime against God and humanity." But Sherman heeded it not. The Mayor of the city denounced it as "wanton cruelty." General Sherman's brutal retort was, "war *is* cruelty;" and thus these poor people were driven forth to suffer and to starve. How many little children died from exposure I cannot say. But, no doubt, scores of darling babes perished. Some, it is said, died by the roadside; and many a feeble old grandfather cried his very last breath away as he turned his back forever upon his lost home.

General Hood finding himself out of Atlanta, now started upon one of the most remarkable military movements of the war. It was bold in conception; and if it had been successful, would have been the most brilliant affair of the war. Marching past Atlanta, he struck for Chattanooga. General Sherman sent General Thomas back with a strong force to check him, and so stubbornly did the Federal forces defend some of the mountain passes that General Hood did not succeed in reaching his destination.

He then crossed the mountains into Northern Alabama, and started for Nashville. General Thomas, seeing the danger that menaced him, hastened to its defence. He collected a large army, and adding to the already formidable defences of the city, awaited Hood's attack.

Hood's advance was at first a splendid success. On the 30th of November, he whipped General Schofield in a severe battle at Franklin, and then marched directly for Nashville.

Thomas was not only strongly fortified, but his forces far outnumbered Hood's. The Confederates fought several brilliant engagements, in which it is acknowledged they performed prodigies of valor. In one of these engagements, General Pat Cleburne, the commander of the Irish Brigade in the Confederate Army, was killed. His loss was a severe one, for he was not only the idol of the army, but was always in the thickest of the fight.

It was now the middle of December. The weather was unusually cold and rainy, combined with snow and sleet. General Hood's men suffered fearfully. On the 16th, he was compelled to fall back. In his retreat he lost very heavily; and had it not been for some blunder on the part of Thomas in forwarding pontoons to cross the Tennessee River, his reverses might have been much greater. Thus ended the year 1864 in the West.

CHAPTER FORTY-FOUR
The Presidential Election and Other Events of 1864

Four years had now rolled around since the Presidential Election of 1860: and oh! what a four years of blood and sorrow they had been to our country! The great conspiracy against our democratic and republican system of government had now been fairly successful. You will recollect what I showed to you in the first chapters of this book had ever been the design of the monarchical or anti-republican party in America. They wished to make the States mere dependencies or provinces, and to erect a great centralized government at Washington, which should be, in all but the name, a despotism. The few nabobs of New England wanted to rule the whole country, and place everybody under tribute to the cotton lords of that locality.

Such had come to be nearly the case. The vast patronage which Mr. Lincoln now wielded was greater than that of any king on the earth. He had an army of over a million of men to do his bidding. He had thousands of officials scattered all over the country in the persons of postmasters, assessors, tax-collectors, revenue officers, provost marshals, detectives, spies, informers, and every species of vermin known to the worst ages of despotism. If he needed more, he had only to manufacture more paper money to purchase them. The four years of his Administration had been a period of the most shameless extravagance and corruption. Vice reared its head everywhere. Millions and millions of money had been squandered upon government favorites through contracts for the army and navy.

There seemed to be a general mania for stealing, for defalcations, and robberies. Mr. Dawes, an Abolition Congressman, from Massachusetts, declared that "the public treasury had been plundered in a *single year* as much as the *entire current yearly expenses* of Mr. Buchanan's Administration." Even women, and those too relatives of Mr. Lincoln's family, were found to have interests in contracts! Members of Congress, professed ministers of religion, broken down gamblers, nasal-twanged Abolitionists, all classes and conditions, were mixed up in these shameless robberies.

So fearful had these corruptions become that Congress was fairly shamed into investigating and denouncing them. A committee was appointed, and their report made a volume of over *one thousand pages.* I will quote what an Abolition paper said of this report:

> It is a *monstrous book* – monstrous in its hugeness, monstrous in the ugliness of its revelations, monstrous in the devilishness of its contents. The truths therein shown, by *sworn and legal testimony,* are infinitely stranger than fiction. This monstrous book is the Record of Infamy! It will stand attesting to the nation and the world the blighting, scorching, scathing ignominy which the nation and the world can heap upon those who would lie, cheat, and steal from their country!

When we remember that all this was done by a party that claimed to be the representative of "great moral ideas," that was engaged in crushing out "a great sin," we can easily see how hollow were the professions of its leaders. They were using the delusion about Negroes not only to overthrow the Government, but to rob and plunder the people, and rivet upon the masses the chains and slavery of a huge public debt. Mr. Lincoln's great banker, who made, it is said, over a million of dollars in selling government bonds, issued a pamphlet declaring "that a national debt was a national blessing." And at this very time, and while he was building a mansion to live in, rivaling the palaces of the kings of Europe, the poor women of New York, whose husbands had died in the war, were starving to death for want of food!

But "greenbacks," as Mr. Lincoln's paper money was called, ruled the hour; and when the Abolition convention, to nominate a candidate for the Presidency, met in Baltimore, in June, no one was mentioned except Mr. Lincoln. Some of his party wanted another candidate, but the machinery was too perfect. For Vice-President, they put on Andrew Johnson, of Tennessee, in order to show to the people, as they said, that their party was not sectional, but national. Mr. Johnson had been very strongly opposed to secession, and had refused to go with his State. They also insisted on calling themselves "the Union Party," and under this deception got thousands of votes.

The Democratic Convention met at Chicago, on the 29th of August, and nominated for President, General George B. McClellan, of New Jersey, and for Vice-President, George H. Pendleton, of Ohio. Neither the nominations nor the platform were such as pleased the entire Democratic party. General McClellan was admired as a gentleman and a Christian soldier, who had refused to turn the war into one of plunder and arson. But he announced himself for the prosecution of the war, while a great many Democrats wanted peace. They were willing to trust their Southern brethren in settling the future of our Government on a basis of a perfect equality of the States. They did not believe that one State had the right to lord it over another. But that as our Government was formed by a convention, wherein each State acted without coercion, so only could it be perpetuated.

However, all these differences were thrown aside in view of the great importance of getting the Abolition party out of power. Democrats forgot that they differed, and went to work with heart and soul to defeat Mr. Lincoln, believing that if they could elect General McClellan, they would yet save their country from the perils of consolidation and Abolitionism.

It was soon discovered, however, that no fair election was to be allowed. No sooner had a paper in Baltimore raised McClellan's name for President than it was suppressed by Mr. Lincoln. Most of the States had passed laws to allow the soldiers to vote in the army. Nearly all of these votes were controlled by the Abolition officers. In New York, however, an effort was made to secure a fair return of the soldiers' votes; but Mr. Lincoln caused the agent of New York State, Colonel North, to be arrested, and kept him in prison until after election. Thousands of soldiers who wanted to vote for McClellan were deprived of doing so.

But the queerest movement I have yet to state. Three days previous to the election, General Butler, the famous "hero of New Orleans," was sent to New York to take command of troops there, and large reinforcements were sent with him. When he arrived, he put on the same pompous swagger that had made him so ridiculous in the Crescent City. He took a large hotel for his headquarters; had telegraphic wires carried to his room, and stationed his orderlies around his hotel as if he was in camp.

He then commenced his "campaign" by sending for a gentleman whom he had heard had spoken against him. The next day, when the Democratic papers got hold of it, they made all manner of fun of Butler. I think, on the whole, he did not like the atmosphere of New York; for right off after the election, he slunk away between two days, I believe, and was not heard of much for some time afterwards.

It has always been somewhat of a mystery why Butler was sent to New York. The Abolitionists pretended that they feared a riot on election day; but as there was not the slightest danger of that, it has been suspected that if the election went against them, they intended to seize power at once, and prevent the inauguration of General McClellan. In fact, this was actually threatened by some of the more ultra of the Abolition papers.

The result, however, was all that Mr. Lincoln could have desired. General McClellan carried Kentucky, Delaware, and New Jersey. All of the rest of the States voted for Mr. Lincoln, and so the Abolition party had another four years' lease of life.

For a long time it had been intended to make an attack on Mobile. So in July, Admiral Farragut and General Granger began to make preparations to that effect. The battle opened on the 5th of August. There were two forts guarding the entrance to the harbor, Forts Gaines and Morgan. Farragut's guns were too much for them, for he passed them in spite of their brave fighting,

The Presidential Election and Other Events of 1864

and cut them off from the city, so that they were compelled to surrender.

Farragut, however, was not through with the fight yet. The Confederates had an iron-clad ram called the *Tennessee*, and with this they gave battle to Farragut's whole fleet. It was one of the fiercest fights of the war. But the odds were too great for the *Tennessee*, and after a terrible conflict, she surrendered. Her commander was Franklin Buchanan, who commanded the *Virginia* in her fight with the *Monitor* in Hampton Roads. Farragut lost many men, and the monitor *Tecumseh*, which was blown up by a torpedo.

Wilmington, too, had long been an eyesore of the Federals; for despite all their efforts to blockade it, they had never succeeded, and vessels ran in and out almost daily. The only way to shut up Wilmington was to take Fort Fisher, a strong work on the east mouth of the Cape Fear River. So the famous General Butler was sent with a land force along with Admiral Porter with a fleet to take it.

General Butler now conceived the grandest idea of the age. He thought he would blow Fort Fisher into little bits of pieces by exploding a ship filled with three hundred tons of powder as near to it as he could float it. So the experiment was tried, and, lo! "nobody was hurt." There was a great dull sound like that of a dying earthquake, and that was all. Porter now bombarded the fort with his fleet, and declared that he had silenced all the guns. General Butler then sent his troops ashore to assault the fort from the land side, but did not dare so much as to set foot on shore himself. His troops marched up to the fort, and, it is said, killed one old horse, and returned, stating that the fort could not be taken. Butler then re-embarked all hands, and sailed for Fortress Monroe. He was now laughed at more than ever, and called the "hero of Fort Fisher."

CHAPTER FORTY-FIVE
General Sherman's March to Savannah and Goldsburg

    We left General Sherman with his army at Atlanta. He now conceived the bold idea of marching it directly for the seacoast at Savannah or Charleston. He had left, even after sending off General Thomas, not less than fifty-five or sixty thousand men, and the Confederates had no forces to contend with him except the local militia of Georgia and a few troops on the seacoast.

    On the 12th of November General Sherman evacuated Atlanta for his grand march. He supplied his army with sixty days' rations of hard bread and took along several thousand beef cattle; for all else he told his soldiers they must live off of the country, that is, by stealing and plundering. Before leaving Atlanta he completed the work of destroying the city by fire, and had it not been for the influence of a devoted Roman Catholic priest, who went among his soldiers and restrained them, there would probably have been scarcely a single house left standing. Rome was also burnt.

    General Sherman began his march by throwing out his cavalry in all directions and threatening several places at the same time; and this deception he kept up during his entire march. The main body of his troops really never deviated far from the shortest route to Port Royal or Savannah. After reaching Milledgeville, the capital of Georgia, he threw out strong detachments, threatening both Macon, on the south, and Augusta, on the north, while his main column moved directly for the coast. General Wheeler, with some Confederate cavalry, had several skirmishes with Kilpatrick of Sherman's army, but beyond this there was little or no fighting.

It seems to have been Sherman's intention at first to go to Port Royal, where reinforcements under General Foster, and supplies for his army awaited him; but in order to do this he had to cross the Savannah River. General Kilpatrick, however, in trying to do this, was badly repulsed, and so General Sherman lost no time in moving further south.

General Foster now tried to open communications with Sherman, and moving out a force towards the Savannah River, was met by General Gustavus W. Smith, with a few Georgia militia, who fought so gallantly that Foster was obliged to give up his design, and allow Sherman to work out his own deliverance.

Sherman now moved quickly to the south of Savannah, and on the 13th of December assaulted and captured Fort McAllister, one of the outer defences of the city, and thus opened his way to Ossabaw Sound, where the Federal fleet was awaiting him.

This march of Sherman's had been marked with more than his usual destruction. Dead horses, cows, sheep, hogs, chickens, turkeys, together with corn, wheat, cotton, books, paper, broken crockery, and fragments of every species of property, strewed the roads in the path of his army. He had stolen thousands of Negroes, mules, and horses, and destroyed over two hundred miles of railroad.

In a few days he determined to attack Savannah. It was held by General Hardee, with about 15,000 troops, altogether too small a number to contend with the great army opposed to it. So General Hardee one night quietly evacuated the place, blowing up the Confederate vessels and destroying such stores as he could. Sherman was very angry when he saw how nicely the Confederates had slipped out of his hands, for he thought certainly that he had them secure.

He now remained in Savannah about a month, recruiting and preparing his army for another march. This time he intended to move northward towards Columbia, the capital of South Carolina, and strike the coast at or near Goldsboro or Wilmington, in North Carolina.

For many miles he had a severe march through the swamps and thickets which cover the low lands of the Carolinas. The Confederate forces, once more placed under the command of General Joseph E. Johnston, were also being organized to oppose him. Still, by the middle of February, he reached Columbia, with but little opposition.

And here a scene occurred which the pen of history almost refuses to record. Ever since General Sherman had entered South Carolina, he had "shut his eyes," if he had not given express orders for the commission of the acts of savage atrocity with which his path was now marked. It had been supposed that he was cruel enough, heretofore, but now there seemed to be no restraint whatever upon his soldiers.

Columbia was one of the most beautiful cities of America. It was the residence of the wealthiest and most refined people of South Carolina. They were justly proud of their city, and took every pains to preserve it from destruction. When General Sherman's army was known to be near, General Wade Hampton, who commanded the cavalry for its defence, at once evacuated the city, so as to give Sherman no excuse for bombarding it. The mayor of the city went out to meet his advance forces, and formally surrendered it to Colonel Stone, of the Fifteenth Corps, who assured him that the city should not be harmed *while he had command.* And it was not. This was about nine o'clock A.M. of the 17th of February. About eleven o'clock the head of Sherman's main column reached the city, and then the work of destruction commenced.

Gen. Wade Hampton

Woe unto men who wore gold watches, or had on good

coats, boots, or shoes. They were stripped off instantly. Stores and houses were broken open and pillaged, and no one interfered with the riotous soldiers. About one o'clock P.M., to add to the horrors of the scene, the inhabitants were startled by the cry of "fire." The citizens rallied and subdued it. Soon there was another fire. Again they rallied and put it out. During all this time Sherman and his officers were in the streets, but did nothing to check the lawlessness of the soldiers, who now destroyed the fire engines, and chopped the hose into pieces with their swords or pricked it with their bayonets, so as to render it useless.

Night now added to the horrors of the scene. As many as twenty fires were burning at a time, and the lurid flames lit up the sky for miles and miles. The soldiers carried from house to house vessels containing some liquid, like spirits of turpentine, saturated with which they made balls of fire, and with these sent the devouring flame from dwelling to dwelling.

A writer describing this fearful scene says:

> Old men and women and children were to be seen often, while the flames were rolling and raging around them, while walls were crackling and rafters tottering and trembling, in the endeavor to save their clothing and some of their more valuable effects. They were driven out headlong, pistols clapped to their heads, violent hands laid on their throats and collars, and the ruffians seemed to make little distinction in their treatment of men or women. Ladies were hustled from their chambers with the strong arm, or with the menacing pistol at their hearts. A lady undergoing the pains of labor had to be borne on a mattress out into the open air to escape the fire. It was in vain that her situation was described to the incendiaries as they applied the torch to her house. They beheld the situation of the sufferer and laughed to scorn the prayer for her safety. Another lady was recently confined. Her life hung upon a hair. The demons were apprised of the facts of the ease. They burst into her chamber, *took her rings from her fingers, plucked the watch from beneath her pillow, shrieked offensive language in her ears, and so overwhelmed her with terror that she lived but a day or two.*

At one time the people sought the churches for safety; but

the Abolition fiends drove them from these refuges, and they were forced to seek the open park of the city. Even here they were not allowed to rest, for these devils incarnate amused themselves by throwing firebrands among the weeping women and children that crowded and crouched in the enclosure. At a single blow thousands of people were homeless; and the morning of the 18th of February dawned upon a city of blackened and smouldering ruins.

Sherman had this time done his work thoroughly. All the business portion of the city, the main streets, the old capitol, &c., were only a pile of rubbish and brick. The long chimneys looked like grim sentinels of the ravages of uncivilized warfare. The stately trees that lined the streets were blasted and withered, and broken furniture, rich paintings, works of art, all that a refined taste and elegant culture could have wished, laid scattered over the streets. On every side were despairing, weeping, and helpless women and children, in groups, reduced at once from plenty and luxury, so that they had neither food to eat nor a place to lay their heads.

But I will draw the veil over this horrible scene, and pass on. It is proper here to say, however, that General Sherman afterwards, apparently shocked by the excesses of his soldiers, denied that he ordered the burning of Columbia, but alleged that it took fire from burning cotton, which had been ordered to be set on fire by General Wade Hampton. Of course General Hampton was not the man to rest under such an imputation; and he accordingly wrote a letter giving an account of the burning of Columbia substantially as I have written it, in which he says, "I assert what can be proved by thousands, that not one bale of cotton was on fire when he [Sherman] took possession of the city. His assertion to the contrary is false, and he knows it to be so."

To this letter General Sherman has never made any reply; but General Hampton, seeing some other assertions to the same effect, wrote a letter to a member of Congress, asking for a committee to investigate the matter; but the Abolition Congress did not dare to face the music. So they said General Hampton was "a rebel," and under cover of this mere subterfuge, keep on repeating the falsehood in their histories that General Hampton caused Columbia to be burned.

But this will not succeed. General Hampton is well known to be incapable of a falsehood, the soul of honor and chivalry. He comes from the best liberty-loving stock of our Revolution. His grandfather, General Wade Hampton, was a gallant officer in the war of 1776. His father, Colonel Wade Hampton, was aid-de-camp to General Jackson at the battle of New Orleans; and General Hampton himself, when he found that the Abolitionists had determined to invade the South, raised a legion, and marched at once to Virginia. Though a man of great wealth, he left his splendid home of luxury and art, and campaigned it all through the war like a common soldier.

From Columbia, General Sherman's army marched northward toward Charlotte. All along his army had been preceded by a gang of men called "bummers," who robbed, plundered, and murdered with impunity. A more graceless set of scamps never went unhung. Some of these General Sherman said had been killed after capture; and he wrote to General Hampton a very impudent letter, stating that he would hang man for man. General Hampton wrote back that he knew nothing of the killing of any of his "foragers," as he called them; but he gave him fair notice, that if he hung a single Confederate soldier, he would hang two Federals; furthermore, he told General Sherman that he had directed his men to shoot down any Abolition soldier found burning houses, and that he should continue to do this as long as he (Sherman) disgraced the profession of arms by destroying private dwellings. "Your line of march," said General Hampton, "can be traced by the lurid light of burning houses; and in more than one household there is an *agony far more bitter than death* – a crime too black to be mentioned."

This bold talk convinced General Sherman that he had a man to deal with, who would stand none of his barbarity, and who would do what he said he would. He never dared to hang any Confederate as he threatened, and soon afterwards made his army behave rather better. He pursued his way towards Fayetteville, North Carolina, and finally came up with General Johnston's forces, who attacked him near Averysboro, on the 16th of March, and drove back his advance. On the 19th, another fight took place at Bentonsville, Johnston falling back with his forces towards Raleigh. Sherman now marched into Goldsboro, where he met the Federal fleet and army transports, and rested his men, after the vilest plundering tour on record.

    He had mowed a swath of fire right through the country. Besides burning Columbia, he had wholly or partially destroyed in South Carolina the villages of Barnwell, Blackville, Graham, Bamberg, Buford's Bridge, Orangeburg, Lexington, Alston, Pomana, Winnsboro, Blackstacks, Society Hill, Camden, and Cheraw. Along the line of his march, there was scarcely a house left standing from the Savannah River to the Pedee!

CHAPTER FORTY-SIX
Events of 1865 – General Lee's Surrender

Events in the opening of 1865 flew along thick and fast. It was evident now that nothing short of remarkable good fortune could save the Confederates from defeat. Still they stoutly held out. They believed so sincerely in the justice of their cause, and had such undoubting faith in their generals, that they refused to look defeat in the face or even to think it possible.

General Grant, after Butler's failure at Fort Fisher, sent General A.H. Terry, with a large force and Admiral Porter's fleet, early in January, to reduce it. Porter bombarded it fiercer than ever, and then General Terry assaulted it with a strong force. The Confederates fought with the most determined bravery, but were overpowered and forced to surrender.

Wilmington, of course, soon followed, and now the last remaining port through which there was any chance of running the blockade was gone.

Charleston had been evacuated when Sherman took Columbia. The gallant city had after all never been taken, but fell only as the result of a flank movement.

About this time various efforts were made towards effecting a peace. Mr. F.P. Blair, Senior, went to Richmond to see the Confederate President, and through his exertions Mr. Davis appointed three commissioners, Messrs. R. M. T. Hunter, A. H. Stephens, and J. A. Campbell, to confer with the United States authorities. Mr. Lincoln would not allow these commissioners to come to Washington. So on the 3d of February, he and Mr.

Seward met them in a steamer off Fortress Monroe.

Congress had just at this time passed a so-called amendment to the Constitution, which was intended to legalize Mr. Lincoln's free Negro edict. Mr. Lincoln and Mr. Seward would offer no terms of peace except upon their accepting this Negro equality overthrow of the Government. Of course they could do no worse if the war continued, and while there was life there was hope. The South, therefore, rejected Mr. Lincoln's insulting proposal to get down voluntarily to a level with their Negroes. If forced by the fortunes of war into that position, they at least determined not to go there willingly.

This so-called amendment to the Constitution was in fact no amendment at all, but the introduction of *new matter* into the Constitution. The power to control the Negro population in the different States had never been given to the Federal Government, hence it could not be amended. Besides it was a usurpation to change the Constitution when eleven States had no voice in the matter, and afterwards compel them to submit to it at the point of the bayonet. This consolidation of power at Washington, however, was just what the monarchical Abolition party desired. This "amendment," fully carried into effect, changed the whole character of our system of government, and made the States simple provinces ruled over by a central power. The desire of Alexander Hamilton, who wished to blot out the States, was really accomplished. So we see how exactly this so-called Republican party corresponded with the Tory, Monarchical, Federal party against which Mr. Jefferson so earnestly warned the country.

All hopes of peace having now been banished from men's minds, the tug of war was soon again to commence. Grant's army around Richmond had been for a long time inactive, with the exception of severe and heavy skirmishes, sometimes on one end of the line and sometimes on the other. It was evident now that the Confederates were suffering severely from the want of supplies. General Sherman's terrible march of plunder and fire through Georgia and the Carolinas, and General Sheridan's destruction of the Virginia Canal, had cut off the sources of General Lee's supplies. During the whole of the winter of 1864-65, the daily rations of Lee's soldiers were only a pound of flour and a quarter of a pound of meat. Nothing but a miracle could keep an army together under such circumstances.

The spring of 1865 therefore opened gloomily enough. The Abolitionists had a million of men in arms against the South; while the South had really less than one quarter of that number, and these for the most part reduced to half rations.

It was therefore evident that the South, after one of the most gallant and glorious struggles ever made by any people on the face of the earth, must soon yield to the overwhelming physical force which the Abolitionists had combined against her.

Had General Lee a well-provisioned army, one half as large as General Grant's, the results would have been different.

In the month of March, however, he saw plainly that there was no way open to save his little army but to get his half-starved men out of the trenches in front of Richmond, and leave that city to be occupied by the Abolition army. But how was he to get out? Every point was occupied by an immense army, entrenched in works which Grant had been almost a whole year in building.

On the morning of the 25th of March, General Lee made his first attempt to break through the Federal lines, at a point known as Fort Steadman. The fort was surprised and taken, and for a short time the Confederates swept everything before their furious assault. Their victory was of a short duration, for they were soon forced to retire before the overwhelming numbers and the impregnable works which confronted them. Lee's loss in this attempt was about twenty-five hundred men, and Grant's about the same. But while that number was a great loss to Lee's little army, it was of no importance whatever to Grant. In his vast army twenty-five hundred men would not be missed. He could have slaughtered as many thousands and yet remained vastly the superior of his antagonist in point of numbers.

On Sunday morning, April 2d, General Lee sent a despatch to President Davis that he should that night evacuate the defences of Richmond. This news reached Mr. Davis while he was at worship in St. Paul's Church. It is said that as he walked out of church his face bore the too evident marks of the unwelcome nature of the despatch.

As soon as the darkness of night shut down, Lee commenced the withdrawal of his entire army. It was effected with so much secrecy and skill that Grant had no idea of what was going on until the Confederate army, numbering about twenty thousand men, was sixteen miles away on the road towards Danville.

Indeed Grant had no idea of Lee's movement until the next morning the sky was illumined and the earth shook with the blowing up of the ironclad vessels in the James River, and the burning of the Confederate warehouses in Richmond. So at last the Abolition army occupied Richmond without capturing it.

General Grant, however, bestowed little attention upon Richmond; all his energies were directed to the pursuit of Lee.

Before General Lee abandoned Richmond, he gave orders that large supplies for his army should be sent forward from Danville to Amelia Court House, and there await his arrival. These supplies reached their destination on Sunday afternoon; but the officer in charge received a dispatch from President Davis in Richmond to bring the train immediately to that place, as the cars were to be used to transport the personal property of the Confederate Government. The officer stupidly supposing that the order called for the contents of the train at Richmond, pushed on with the loaded cars; and so when Lee went to Amelia Court House, he found himself entirely in want of supplies for his army.

All hopes of escape were now dashed in an instant to the ground. He was compelled to remain the best part of two days at this point to provide his army with the means of preserving life. This pause was fatal; for on the afternoon of the 4th of April, Sheridan's cavalry, eighteen thousand strong, overtook his rear, at a place seven miles distant from Amelia Court House. Directly behind Sheridan was coming an overwhelming force of the Abolition army; and Lee's troops were literally in a condition of starvation. They had commenced the retreat on one ration a day, and now they were reduced to less than half a single ration a day. An eye-witness of these harrowing scenes says: "Towards evening of the 5th, and all day long upon the 6th, hundreds of men dropped from exhaustion, and thousands let fall their muskets from inability to carry them any further."

On the evening of the 7th of April, General Lee received a letter from General Grant, asking for the surrender of the Army of Northern Virginia. General Lee replied, asking what terms General Grant had to offer. To which he returned the answer, that he should require the following terms:

> All officers to give their individual paroles not to take up arms against the United States, until properly exchanged; and each company or regimental commander to sign a like parol for the men of their commands. The arms, artillery, and public properly to be stacked and packed, and turned over to the officers appointed to receive them. This will not embrace the side-arms of the officers, nor their private horses or baggage. This done, each officer and man will be allowed to return to his home, *not to be disturbed by the United States authorities so long as they observe their paroles, and the laws in force where they may reside.*

General Lee at once accepted these terms; and on the 9th of April, 1865, Grant and Lee met at a farm-house, and completed the arrangements of surrender. It was a sad and touching sight. Stalwart men who had faced death in a score of battle-fields wept like children. Others broke their muskets in very rage. Thousands crowded around their noble chief, to take him once more by the hand. Words could not express his feelings. With tears pouring down both cheeks, General Lee commanded voice enough to say, in the simplest language of the heart, "Men, we have fought through this war together. I have done the best I could for you."

There is but little more to be written of the war. When President Davis received General Lee's dispatch, that Richmond must be evacuated, he had with all convenient speed moved the archives of the Confederate Government to Danville. Here he awaited news from Lee, and was of course overwhelmed with grief when he heard the fatal story of his surrender.

In the meantime General Sherman had been pushing General Johnston. He had forced him from Raleigh, from whence he had fallen back towards Hillsboro. When Johnston heard of Lee's surrender, he knew that all further resistance was useless. He and General Sherman arranged terms of surrender, which recognized the rights of the States, and which in effect restored the old Union – just what the Abolitionists declared in 1861 they were going to fight for. No sooner, however, did they hear of it, than they raised a hue and cry in the North perfectly deafening. Sherman was every where denounced in the most bitter language, and the authorities at Washington rejected the terms he had made with Johnston.

Soon after this, Mobile capitulated, and the last week in May, General Kirby Smith, commanding the Confederate troops west of the Mississippi River, also surrendered all his forces to General Canby.

The last fight of the war occurred on the 13th of May, at Brazos, in Western Texas, between a Federal regiment and a band of Confederates. The Confederates won the day; so in the first and last battles they were victorious!

CHAPTER FORTY-SEVEN
The Assassination of Mr. Lincoln

The war had ended. Four weary years of bloodshed and misery had passed away. The Abolitionists had subdued "the rebellion," as they nicknamed the resistance of the South to their revolutionary projects; and now Mr. Lincoln was brought face to face with an issue which he could no longer dodge, or upon which he could no longer prevaricate.

Would he consent to allow the Southern States to resume their old places in the Union, or would he use the power now in his hands to compel them to relinquish their State laws and institutions? He had told the world in the commencement of the war that "the condition of each State and each person would remain the same, whether the war succeeded or failed." But would he stand by his word? No one except those blinded by an insane admiration of the man expected it.

His falsehoods and broken pledges would make a monument of infamy before which any honorable man would have hid his head for shame. On the 4th of March, 1861, he declared "that he had no lawful right to interfere with slavery, nor any inclination to do so." In July, 1861, he endorsed the resolution that "the war was waged to preserve the rights and equality of the States unimpaired." On the day before the extra session of Congress adjourned in 1861, and when he was trying to get troops, he told Mr. Mallory, of Kentucky, that "the war was carried on by him on the idea that there was a Union sentiment at the South, which, set free from the control of the Confederate Government, would replace the States in the Union. If there were not," then, he said; "the war is not only a wrong, but a *crime.*"

In his Inaugural Address he declared that the *"endurance* of our political fabric depended upon the right of each State to control its domestic institutions." Yet January 1st, 1863, he issued a proclamation declaring that he would use the army and navy to prevent this *"endurance* of our political system." On the 12th of December, 1862, he wrote to Fernando Wood of New York, that "if the people of the Southern States would cease resistance and submit to the Constitution of the United States, then the war should cease on the part of the United States." But July 18th, 1864, he published "To whom it may concern," in which he declared that he would listen to no terms of peace from the South which did not agree to the abandonment of their rights under the Constitution!

Mr. Lincoln had played his part well. With a cunning that passes human comprehension he had gone just fast enough and not too fast for the safe accomplishment of his purposes. As war had increased the hate of the people, Mr. Lincoln found he could take a step or two further, and so he had gone on from one thing to another, until his record, as we have shown above, was that of a trickster, a falsifier, and an oath-breaker.

Such, after the false and lying flattery of the hour passes away, must be the candid judgment of history on Abraham Lincoln. I do not give this view of his character and acts as any justification for what I am about to relate occurred to him, for private individuals have never, in organized society, the right to take the punishment of crimes in their own hands. That belongs to the law. I feel it a duty, however, in writing this history, and particularly for the sake of the young, to show them what sort of a man Mr. Lincoln really was. Thousands of pages have been written to extol his virtues and praise his name, simply because he was the representative of the Abolition delusion, but it is the record of history which time can never blot out that his career – as President was a shameless four years of deceptions, falsehoods, and crimes against liberty.

No sooner was Richmond evacuated than Mr. Lincoln

paid it a visit. He was received in gloomy silence by its citizens, and after gratifying his curiosity by staying a few hours in the deserted residence of Jefferson Davis, he returned to Washington. While in Richmond he had a conference with Judge John A. Campbell, in relation to the restoration of Virginia to the Union. The details of this conference are as yet unknown, for but one of Mr. Lincoln's letters bearing upon it has ever been published. All patriotic men who desired to see our country restored were in hopes that Mr. Lincoln would allow the Virginia Legislature to meet and make arrangements for that purpose.

In his interview with Judge Campbell he agree to do so, and gave orders to General Weitzel, then in command there, to allow the members to come to Richmond, upon the terms that they would restore the State to the Union. When Mr. Lincoln, however, returned to Washington, he again deliberately broke his promise, and while the whole country was congratulating itself upon the adoption of a policy which would heal the wounds the war had made, it was startled on the afternoon of the 12th of April with the news that Mr. Lincoln had refused to allow the Virginia Legislature to meet – in fact, had given General Weitzel positive orders to prevent it. Thus had Virginia, the grand old State of Washington and Jefferson, been completely stricken down as a commonwealth. The fact of driving the Confederate Government from Richmond did not affect the dignity and sovereignty of Virginia, but this last act blotted out the State and reduced her to the condition of a province of the Federal Government.

It was, however, the last order that Mr. Lincoln lived to promulgate. That very night he visited Ford's Theatre in Washington, and was killed by a pistol shot fired by one John Wilkes Booth. Booth had entered the theatre unobserved, and making his way to the President's box, took deliberate aim and fired, then dropping his pistol and drawing a knife, jumped from the box to the stage of the theatre, and, brandishing his weapon, cried, *"Sic semper tyrannis.*[1] Virginia is avenged." And, in a moment, before the people could recover from their fright, he dashed across the

---

1. So always with tyrants.

stage, out of the back door of the theatre, and jumping upon a fleet horse that he had awaiting him, was soon lost in the darkness of the night.

At about the same hour of the night a man had applied at the residence of Mr. Seward, Secretary of State, and desired to see him, but was refused, as Mr. Seward was ill from the effects of an injury he had received a few days previously by being thrown from his carriage. The man, however, refused to take no for an answer, and knocking down the servant who opened the door, pushed his way upstairs to Mr. Seward's room. Here he was met by one of Mr. Seward's sons and an attendant. He stabbed both so severely as to disable them, then rushed upon Mr. Seward and cut him so badly about the face and neck that his life was for several days despaired of, but he finally fully recovered. Mr. Lincoln lingered but a few hours.

John Wilkes Booth

As the news of these deeds spread, the country was fairly wild. The excitement of the war had been nothing to the fierce gust of passion that now swept over the land. The imagination of every Abolitionist formed a thousand conspiracies. For over two weeks the real actors in this tragedy were veiled in profound mystery.

Mr. Lincoln's friends and adherents made the most of the circumstances. All sober-minded people felt deeply pained that the soil of America should be stained with an assassination, but they could not help thinking that the Holy Bible had taught us, "Be not deceived. God is not mocked. That which a man soweth, that shall he also reap." Many of the Abolition clergy, however, declared that Providence had raised up Booth to remove Lincoln, as it was evident that he was going to be "too lenient with the rebels."

The funeral of Mr. Lincoln was gotten up in the most magnificent proportions. No monarch was ever buried with such pomp and expense. No one then even dared to protest against the ridiculous display. His body was borne on a funeral car costing some twenty thousand dollars, and exhibited to the people in all the principal cities from Washington to Springfield, Illinois, where he was buried. The foolish Abolitionists seemed to think that they were going to cheat history out of telling the truth about their hero, by the grand display they made.

I will now return to Booth and his fate. John Wilkes Booth, who had shot Mr. Lincoln, was a young man of no ordinary character. He was the son of Junius Brutus Booth, the celebrated actor, and was born in Maryland. He was noted for his generous, manly deportment, and was dearly beloved by all his associates. He had a faculty of winning people to him. His personal appearance is described as remarkably beautiful. "His chest was full and broad, his shoulders gently sloping, and his arms as white as alabaster, but hard as marble. His dark eyes, lofty, square forehead, crowned with a weight of curling jetty hair, gave him a countenance at once striking and haughty."

When he left the theatre, after firing the fatal shot, he was accompanied by but one attendant – a simple-minded young fellow named Harold, who seemed always to do his bidding. In jumping from the box to the stage, he had broken a bone of one of his ankles, and this retarded his flight. As it was, he had succeeded in making his way through Lower Maryland, and across the Potomac, and was quietly resting at night in a barn near Bowling Green, in Virginia, when a force of twenty-five men, which had been sent from Washington, under Lieutenant-Colonel Conger and Lieutenant Baker, to search for him, surrounded the barn and demanded his surrender.

Booth replied with defiance. They then threatened to fire the barn. Harold got frightened and wished to surrender. Booth generously let him out of the barn; but so afraid were these twenty-five soldiers of one unarmed boy, that they insisted he should put his arms out of the barn first, and have them shackled! Booth was now alone, and determined to sell his life as dearly as possible.

Again the demand was made upon him to surrender. Again he refused. "Draw off your men," he shouted to Colonel Conger, "and I will fight them singly. I could have killed you six times to-night, but I would not murder you."

And no doubt, protected by the barn, he could have done as he said. The barn was now fired, and while it was burning, a man named Boston Corbett, one of Conger's men, took deliberate aim, and shot him. He lingered a short time and died. His last words were, "Tell mother I died for my country. I thought I did for the best."

His body was taken to Washington, and the savage Abolitionists gloated over it with cannibal ferocity. As I have said, this vile delusion transforms men into brutes. They not only refused to turn the body over to his weeping mother, but they tore out its entrails, and threw them to the hogs. His skull was placed in some museum, his heart preserved in spirits, his spinal column given to some medical college, while the balance of his remains were deposited no one knows where![2] Such is Abolition Christianity!

When John Brown was tried and executed, his remains were placed in a decent coffin and handed over to his friends. Yet "slavery" is said to have made the South semi-savage.

Whatever history may say of the crime of John Wilkes Booth, he was surely no common murderer. It was from no thirst for blood, no mean personal revenge, no expectation of gain or reward, that he took the life of Abraham Lincoln. Indeed he sacrificed all that a young man might hold dear. Behind him he left a letter, in which he showed the marks of a mind that comprehended fully the political situation of the country. He referred to the wrongs the Abolitionists would inflict upon the Negro by their insane course, and concluding it, said:

> Right or wrong, God judge me, not man. I love peace

---

2. These statements were made by Hon. B.G. Harris, of Maryland, without contradiction in a speech on the floor of Congress, June 16th, 1865.

more than life. Have loved the Union beyond expression. For four years have I waited, hoped, and prayed for the dark clouds to break, and for a restoration of our former sunshine. To wait longer would be a crime. All hope for peace is dead. My prayers have proved as idle as my hopes. God's will be done. *I go to see and share the bitter end.*

The investigations of the War Department seemed to reveal a plot or conspiracy, in which Booth, as the master spirit, had involved several persons. The individual who had stabbed Mr. Seward proved to be one Louis Payne, and besides him Harold, a man named Atzerott, Mrs. Surratt, Dr. Mudd, and one or two others, were tried by a Military Commission, and the first four were condemned and hanged. The others were sent to the Dry Tortugas.

This body was an illegal court, and had no more right to try the prisoners before it than the people of Washington had to lynch them. Their execution was in law murder. But the Abolitionists were so raving crazy at the time that nothing else would satisfy them. They were all executed in the most indecent haste, being allowed but twenty-four hours after their conviction to prepare for death.

One singular fact in connection with all these remarkable scenes, such as, I trust America will never again be called upon to witness, remains to be mentioned. There was no coroner's inquest held on Mr. Lincoln's body; no *legal evidence* taken as to the manner of his death, nor was a single person accused of connection with it ever brought into *a court of law, nor is there to this day any legal testimony whatever as to the manner of his death, the cause of it, or who killed him.*

All we know of it is such evidence as was furnished the public by a military tribunal, which was managed in such a one-sided, arbitrary and insulting manner, that the Hon. Reverdy Johnson, the counsel of one of the prisoners, left "the Court" in disgust, his self-respect not allowing him to remain where all just rules of evidence were set at defiance, and where respectable lawyers were continually subjected to the insults of ignorant and brutal military officers.

CHAPTER FORTY-EIGHT
The Capture of Jefferson Davis

When Mr; Davis heard of General Lee's surrender at Danville, he immediately started for North Carolina, where he met and had a consultation with General Johnston. He then left for Charlotte, where he remained until after the news arrived from Washington of the rejection of General Sherman's terms of surrender. He then crossed the State of South Carolina, and reached Washington, Georgia, attended by a few friends and a small escort of cavalry who had belonged to General Morgan's brigade.

Here Mr. Davis heard for the first time of his wife and family, who had left Richmond more than a month previous to his own departure. They were intending to go to the coast of Florida, and sail for Cuba. Mr. Davis himself intended to work his way across the Mississippi River, and to make such further resistance as he could, "in hopes," as he said, "to get some better terms for the South than surrender at discretion."

At Washington, however, Mr. Davis heard fearful rumors of the robberies and outrages which gangs of disbanded soldiers were perpetrating upon defenceless people, and being pretty well convinced that Mrs. Davis was in danger, he resolved to go to her succor.

He rode seventy miles in a single day, in order to reach his family, and believing that they were in real danger, resolved to travel with them for a few days, until they got out of the region that was infested with deserters and robbers.

In the early morning of the 10th of May, a month after the evacuation of Richmond, Colonel Pritchard, of the Michigan cavalry, surrounded the little camp of Mr. Davis and his family, near Irwinsville, Georgia, and made them all prisoners. Some one started the falsehood that Mr. Davis tried to escape in his wife's clothes, and this ridiculous story was telegraphed all over the North for the especial delight of the Abolitionists. Colonel Pritchard's official report, however, did not confirm the story, so this Abolition falsehood fell to the ground.

Mr. Davis and his family were taken to Macon, Georgia, and thence to Savannah, where they were placed on board a vessel, which at once sailed for Fortress Monroe. Here he was separated from his family, and placed in a casemate of the fort, under a strong guard, his wife and family being sent back to Savannah.

For a long time Mr. Davis was shut out entirely from public view. He was placed in solitary confinement, allowed to see no one, to have no books except the Bible and prayer-book, and fed for some time upon the poorest rations of a common soldier. His wife, too, was denied all access to him, and prevented from even writing to him. Two soldiers were ordered to pace his cell day and night; and as this treatment had not reached the sublimity of cruelty, another torture was invented. An order came from Washington that Jefferson Davis *must be shackled!*

When the officer, with the blacksmith and his assistant, came in with the shackles dangling in his hands, Mr. Davis exclaimed: "My God, you cannot have been sent to iron me."

"Such are my orders," replied the officer. "Do your duty, blacksmith," he continued.

In a moment the weak and emaciated form of Mr. Davis seemed to be transformed into that of a giant's strength, and with that superhuman power which only frenzy can impart, he seized the blacksmith and hurled him across the room; then with scorn and indignation on his pale, quivering lip, he fiercely said: "I am a prisoner of war. I have been a soldier in the armies of America, and I know how to die. Only kill me, and my last breath shall be a blessing on your head. But while I have life and strength to resist, for myself and my people, this thing shall not be done."

A file of soldiers were now brought in, and seizing Mr. Davis, of course the struggle was soon over, and this last act of Abolition infamy and barbarity was consummated.

In a few days it was discovered that Mr. Davis would not survive under this treatment, and as he was rapidly sinking, an order came for the removal of the shackles. Since then he has been in prison, denied his liberty, and refused a fair and speedy trial, such as even the vilest criminal is entitled to.

It is extremely doubtful whether the Abolitionists will ever dare to bring him before a fair tribunal; for in that case they would themselves be proved the traitors and rebels which they accuse him of being. After awhile he will probably, under some pretext, be allowed his liberty, and thus will end the last act in the four years' tragedy of sorrow and bloodshed, which Abolitionism, by its mad and sinful crusade, has inflicted upon our beloved country.

Whether the Union of our fathers, the Government *as it was formed,* can ever again be restored, remains to be seen! Yet that ought to be the supreme object to which every American, old and young, should now devote his life. Let every young man, then, register a solemn vow in Heaven, that, if God spares his life, he will devote it to the sacred duty of rolling back this Abolition monarchical revolution – to spreading the truth in relation to it, and thus educating a generation to hate it.

If every person, who loves the simple and Christian principles of republican government will thus do his duty, that Almighty Power which "chastens only to heal," will not forsake our country, nor give it over forever into the hands of those who "fear not God, nor regard man."

www.ingramcontent.com/pod-product-compliance
Lightning Source LLC
Chambersburg PA
CBHW050552170426
43201CB00011B/1662